UNIVERSITY OF NORTH CAROLINA
STUDIES IN THE ROMANCE LANGUAGES AND LITERATURES
Number 56

MEDIAEVAL STUDIES IN HONOR OF URBAN TIGNER HOLMES, JR.

MEDIAEVAL STUDIES IN HONOR OF
URBAN TIGNER HOLMES, JR.

EDITED BY

JOHN MAHONEY AND JOHN ESTEN KELLER

CHAPEL HILL

THE UNIVERSITY OF NORTH CAROLINA PRESS

DEPÓSITO LEGAL: V. 2.363-1965

PRINTED IN SPAIN

ARTES GRÁFICAS SOLER, S. A. — VALENCIA, 1965

TABLE OF CONTENTS

Page

EDITORS' FOREWORD ... 9

BIOGRAPHY AND BIBLIOGRAPHY ... 11

TWO ROMANCE ETYMA BASED ON OLD ENGLISH
BY PAUL W. BROSMAN, JR. ... 23

TWO OLD SPANISH VERSIONS OF THE *EPISTLE TO THE ROMANS*
BY SPURGEON W. BALDWIN, JR. ... 29

THE VOICES OF PLANTS AND FLOWERS AND THE CHANGING CRY OF THE MANDRAKE
BY ALFRED G. ENGSTROM ... 43

SOME OBSERVATIONS ON SYNTAX AND MORPHOLOGY IN THE *SOTTIE DES RAPPORTEURS* AND THE *SOTTIE DES SOTS FOURRÉS DE MALICE*
BY ROSALYN GARDNER ... 53

THE DEPRECIATORY COMPARISON: A LITERARY DEVICE OF THE MEDIEVAL FRENCH EPIC
BY A. ROBERT HARDEN ... 63

ON THE INFLUENCE IN ENGLAND OF HENRI ESTIENNE AND BONAVENTURE DES PERIERS: THE SOURCES OF SCOGGINS *JESTES* (1613)
BY J. WOODROW HASSELL, JR. ... 79

SOME ASPECTS OF THE TROUBADOUR CONTRIBUTION TO THE *DOLCE STIL NUOVO*
BY ELLIOTT D. HEALY ... 89

THE CHARACTER 'FIGURA' IN *LE MYSTERE D'ADAM*
BY ROBERT E. KASKE ... 103

FRENCH PRINTED VERSIONS OF THE TALE OF APOLLONIUS OF TYRE
BY FLORENCE MCCULLOCH ... 111

Page

ADVENTURES OF A CELTICIST IN THE WEST KERRY
GAELTACHT
BY ROBERT T. MEYER   129

FREDERICK II'S TRUE NOBLE FALCON
BY JAN A. NELSON   143

THE GENESIS OF THE *ROMAN DE THÈBES*: INDIVIDUAL
AND COLLECTIVE LITERARY CREATION
BY DANA PHELPS RIPLEY   157

THE HISTORICAL SETTING OF CHAUCER'S *BOOK OF THE
DUCHESS*
BY D. W. ROBERTSON, JR.   169

SOME DOCUMENTS ON ENGLISH PARDONERS, 1350-1400
BY ARNOLD WILLIAMS   197

THE *AUBE* IN *AUCASSIN ET NICOLETTE*
BY WILLIAM S. WOODS   209

TABULA GRATULATORIA   217

EDITORS' FOREWORD

Few tasks in the life of a teacher and scholar please him more than the opportunity to pay tribute to one of his own professors. And when the one to whom the tribute is being paid is a scholar whose influence has extended as widely as has that of Urban Tigner Holmes, Jr., the task becomes an uncommon delight.

The range of Professor Holmes' interests and knowledge is reflected in his list of published works. But the impact of these interests is felt at its best when one reviews the number and learned accomplishments of those who have been his students.

So the decision was made to compose this *Festschrift* of studies and essays by former students, a small enough tributary observance of Professor Holmes' sixty-fifth year. The roster of such former students mounts to an almost unbelievable number, and certainly those whose work appears herein must be regardad as representative of all the many who studied with him in the various fields of Romance Languages and Literatures, Comparative Literature and Comparative Linguistics, and English and Celtic studies, even though these essays all deal with medieval matters or matters closely associated with the Middle Ages.

We feel that the range, scope and scholarly approach presented in this volume displays graphically the breadth and achievement of Professor Holmes' teaching and influence. We hope that all who read will agree.

John Mahoney
Detroit, Michigan

John E. Keller
Chapel Hill, N. C.

URBAN TIGNER HOLMES, JR.

Urban Tigner Holmes, Jr. was born in Washington, D. C. on July 13, 1900. His father was a naval officer who specialized in steam engineering. He was attached to the Navy Department in Washington for most of the time until 1915, which meant that young Urban Tigner had his early schooling in Washington: Adams School, Force School, and Western High School. For one year (1911-12) the boy attended the Danville School for boys situated in Danville, Va. During this year he happened to read *The Alhambra* of Washington Irving and this spurred him on to buy a copy of Edgren's *Spanish Grammar*. This was the beginning of his passion for languages. Young Holmes was introspective beyond what is considered proper. He was not a very good student in school, but spent much time buying language books at Brentano's in Washington, and practicing the piano. His parents had long intended to send him to the Naval Academy. After a year at Schadmann's Army and Navy Prep School he entered the Academy in August of 1916. He could not be sworn in till after his sixteenth birthday, and his admission was delayed by an ear condition which had slightly affected his hearing. At that he was the youngest member of his class of 1920. This too was not a very happy year. Holmes gave the appearance of being older than he was, and his associates did not interpret correctly the meaning of his shyness and immaturity.

The ear condition did not get better and Holmes was obliged to resign from the Academy in the summer of 1917. His family had now removed to Philadelphia and he entered the University of Pennsylvania that fall, with some advance credits from the Academy. At the outset he was designated as a pre-ministerial student, and was registered as a postulant in the Episcopal

Diocese of Washington, D. C. Gradually as his interest increased in the direction of languages, this ecclesiastical vocation was forgotten, although he has always remained a staunch communicant of the Episcopal Church. In the University, from which he was graduated with honors in 1920, the scholars who made the strongest imprint upon him were Walter Woodburn Hyde of the Greek Department and J. P. W. Crawford of the Romance Department. Having once satisfied the requirements for the A. B. degree, Holmes studied many additional subjects, often without credit. Those were the days when the authorities did not frown upon an eager student who wished to go faster and farther than the average. Holmes studied some Semitic languages, Sanskrit, and three years of Russian. He took Old French in his senior year from J. P. W. Crawford and it was then that he decided mediaeval France would be his first subject matter. He has a vague memory that admiration for the Bayeux Tapestry helped this along in some way. Two other interests became very important for him; these were dramatics and bass singing. Without exaggeration it can be said that Holmes could have become an outstanding opera singer, or an actor, if he had been obliged to concentrate on one of these. They are interests that have been vital to him throughout his career, and he still has some reputation as a singer even at the rather advanced age which is attested by this present volume.

After graduation from Pennsylvania, there was a tuition scholarship at Harvard University, where he entered the graduate school in autumn of 1920. That summer he had his first experience before a class when he taught in the summer school at the University of Western Ontario in London, Canada. This position was owed to Professor Hyde. It was there that young Holmes met the lovely Margaret Gemmell whom he married on June 22, 1922, and who has meant so much to him throughout the years that followed. At Harvard he was tremendously busy. His principal teachers were J. D. M. Ford and Charles H. Grandgent. He finished the M. A. in 1921, and completed the Ph. D. by the spring of 1922, even though he was teaching three sections in that second year. He was awarded a Sheldon Travelling Fellowship and he and his young wife spent the years 1922-23 "in an attic in Paris". The teachers there were Mario Roques, Joseph Bédier, Antoine Meillet, and briefly, Edmond Faral and Vendryes. Holmes was not too popular with his masters. They recognized his ability, but still he had the awkwardness and brashness which were due to his being outside his proper age group.

That year, after returning to the United States, he formally received the Ph. D. degree (1923), taught again in the summer school at Western Ontario, and in the autumn became an Assistant Professor of French at the University of Missouri. A little daughter, Molly, was born in September 1923. The two years in Columbia, Missouri, were somewhat turbulent. The young Holmes became an intimate friend of A. H. Schutz, and the two planned and dreamed at a wonderful rate. The Department was tolerant of their fervor, and the experience that the two gained was invaluable in later years. Holmes first taught Old French in 1923-24 and he developed a special way of presentation which has been one of his greatest talents. Since he was a fine actor, as we have stated, Holmes has been able to translate dramatically from the original before a class, commenting with enthusiasm on the manners and customs of those mediaeval French people in a way that has astounded and fascinated many listeners across forty years.

In 1925 there came a call from the University of North Carolina to an Associate Professorship. This was accepted, and with profound regrets the two friends, Holmes and Schutz, separated — physically but not in spirit. From 1925 till the date of this *Festschrift* Urban Holmes has remained busy at his post at Chapel Hill. In 1927 came his principal promotion. He was made a full professor at the age of twenty-seven. This provoked much adverse comment from his colleagues, and again there were some years of difficult adjustment as the young man found himself still more out of his age group. A daughter, Anne, was born in 1925 and a son, Urban Tigner in 1930. On the suggestion of Professor George C. Taylor of the Department of English Holmes embarked on the long task of editing the *Works of Du Bartas,* with assistance from others. The first volume appeared in 1935, the second in 1937, and the third in 1940. While at Missouri the *History of Old French Literature* was begun. When this was completed by 1934, Holmes could not find a publisher. Finally it was printed locally. It obtained a following almost at once and was then bought by Crofts and Company. The *History of the French Language,* written in collaboration with A. H. Schutz, which has proved quite popular in later years, also had difficulty in seeing the light. The 1930's were not a good decade for a young Romance Philologist, with some original ideas. In 1935 there was a trip to Europe with the entire family, visiting in Scotland, England, Germany, Italy, Spain, and France. This provided much of the material for the book that was to come on mediaeval daily life, but the most fruitful result was the fine friendship which has become even warmer through the years with Helmut and Herta Hatzfeld. This began at Heidelberg. When World War II was declared Holmes was most eager to enter the service. He tried both Army and Navy, but he finally entered the OSS in Washington where he was appointed a liaison officer between the OSS and the Department of State (1942-44).

During the War years he lived with his family on Spring Road, N. W., just off Sixteenth St., and his work was largely inside the old War, State, and Navy building next to the White House. These were trying times, and it was with much relief that the family moved back to Chapel Hill, after the German surrender, but before the Japanese defeat. Molly had married while in Washington; Anne continued in school at the University of North Carolina. At this time the Holmes family became much larger, for the mother-in-law, Mrs John Gemmell, who had lost her husband, went to live with them, and Molly and her husband built a small cottage next door. This stress and — above all — the drowning of the first grandchild, a little boy of two named Victor Léon, produced a strain on Holmes which was almost too much to bear. But there were honors, too: Kenan professorship of Romance Philology (1945), Fellow of the Mediaeval Academy of America (1945) a Litt. D. degree from Washington and Lee University (1948), and the Chevalier of the Legion of Honor (1950). Then, in a burst of energy he produced what he considers his best book: *Daily Living in the Twelfth century* (1952, 53, 62, 64). The years from 1948 until about 1957 were hard, however. There was the fearful controversy over the meaning of the Grail theme in Chrétien's *Perceval,* and Holmes' theory, which was not really very revolutionary, and not carelessly thought out, nevertheless aroused a storm of criticism. [1]

---

[1] The reply to such criticism is made most convincingly by Edward B. Ham in his *Perceval Marginalia* (California State College), Hayward, California, 1964.

It was at this time that Holmes followed more and more his interests in mediaeval civilization, as differentiated from literature and philology. He became an active collector of mediaeval coins: French, English, Spanish, Italian, and German, with emphasis on the first two. Since 1957 he has cemented friendship in England which made it feasible for him to continue his great interest in twelfth and thirteenth century houses. He visited England and France 1957, 1959, 1960, 1961, 1963, 1964, and much of the time was spent driving about the shires and the Departments, visiting "his early houses". He owed much, very much to the affectionate friendship of Mr and Mrs Kaines-Thomas of Newbury (Berks). She is one of the foremost authorities on the mediaeval English house. Beginning in 1963 his interest in the excavations of the mediaeval town in Winchester, England, has been active and fruitful.

In 1940 Holmes had conceived the idea of a departmental Series which would publish theses and other monographs. This was started on a very modest basis, making use of a trade school's printing facilities. The Series grew slowly, but today, with the help of others in the Department of Romance Languages, it has become a worthy venture. In 1959 Holmes and his colleague Alfred Engstrom spoke of launching a new Journal — a small one, to appear twice a year. This journal, *Romance Notes,* also has been successful. Holmes and Schutz had wanted to do this very thing as far back as 1923.

In 1950 Holmes was a visiting Professor at Louisiana State University, and in 1959 (autumn), a Distinguished Visiting Professor at Michigan State University. In 1960, accompanied by his wife, he spent two terms at the University of Melbourne, Australia, as a Fulbright Lecturer.

Like every man in his mid-sixties, with the moment of full retirement not very far away, Urban Tigner Holmes, Jr. has spent much time seeking an appraisal of what his career has meant to himself and others. Probably his greatest achievement has been the magnificent body of students who have gone out from the University of North Carolina with a deep love for the French Middle Ages — particularly the Twelfth century — "his" century. His books are still standard throughout the land, although, as he keeps repeating, they are no longer fresh and new. The truths that one tries to "prove" in mediaeval research are always very elusive, because the evidence is not positive and because much depends upon one's point of view. He has written interestingly on the Grail, Marie de France, and the epics and the romances; but for a long time the image which will be most vivid in the minds of those who have known him will be that of the tall, portly man, with laughing eyes, beautiful bass voice, who has loved his teaching — and who has always been very kind.

He received another Lit. D. degree in 1965 at Western Michigan University.

Anon.

BIBLIOGRAPHY OF URBAN TIGNER HOLMES, JR.

Holmes, Urban T. "Some Provençal Etymologies," *Modern Philology,* XX (1922-23), 95-97.

"*Die betonten Objektpronomina mit unpersönlichen* Verben," *Zeitschrift, für romanische Philologie,* XLIV (1924), 337-39.

"Remarks on the Chronology of Chrétien de Troyes' Works," *Romanic Review,* XVI (1925), 43-53.

"Old French *prendre a 'to begin',*" *Modern Language Notes,* XL (1925), 377-78.

"Old French *De ne,*" *Language,* II (1926), 191-92.

"A Possible Source for Branch I of the *Roman de Renart,*" *Romanic Review,* XVII (1926), 143-48.

"Villon's *Testament,* line 1194," *Modern Language Notes,* XLI (1926), 116-18.

A French Composition. Columbia, Missouri: Lucas Brothers, 1926.

"The Phonology of an English-Speaking Child," *American Speech,* II (1927), 219-25.

"Renaut de Beaujeu," *Romanic Review,* XVIII (1927), 334-38.

"Books of Travel," *University of North Carolina Extension Bulletin,* V (1927), No. 7.

"Can Old French *caroler* Be of Celtic Origin?" *Language,* IV (1928), 200-03.

"The Vulgar Latin Question and the Origin of the Romance Tongues: Notes for a Chapter of the History of Romance Philology Prior to 1849," *Studies in Philology,* XXV (1928), 51-61.

"Old French *Carole,*" *Language,* IV (1928), 28-30.

"The Saracen Oath in the Chanson de Geste," *Modern Language Notes,* XLIII (1928), 84-87.

"Reply to Max Foerster on *Carole,*" *Language,* IV (1928), 201-03.

"Books of Travel," *University of North Carolina Extension Bulletin,* VIII (1929), No. 12.

"Notes on Child Speech," *American Speech,* IV (1929), 390-94.

Holmes, Urban T., and M. L. Radoff. "Claude Fauchet and his Library," *PMLA,* XLIV (1929), 229-42.

"Old French Camelot," *Romanic Review,* XX (1929), 231-36.

"A Study in Negro Onomastics," *American Speech,* V (1929-30), 463-67.

"The French Novel in English Translation," *University of North Carolina Extension Bulletin,* IX (1930), No. 7.

Holmes, Urban T., and Hugo Giduz. *Sept contes de la vielle France.* Boston: D. C. Heath and Company, 1930.

"Old French Yonec," *Modern Philology,* XXIX (1931), 194-99.

"French *gnaf.* Scottish *nyaff,*" *Studies in Philology,* XXVIII (1931), 569-73.
"Germanic Influence on Old French Syntax," *Language,* VII (1931), 194-99.
"New Thoughts on Marie de France," *Studies in Philology,* XXIX (1932), 1-10.
"Old French *fauterne,* Provençal *falterna,*" *Romanic Review,* XXIV (1933), 133-35.
"French Words of Chinese Origin," *Language,* X (1934), 28-85.
"Medieval Gem Stones," *Speculum,* IX (1934), 195-204.
"The Waldensian Dialects in North Carolina," *Zeitschrift für romanische Philologie,* LIV (1934), 500-13.
The Life and Works of Du Bartas. Vol. I. Chapel Hill: University of North Carolina, 1935.
"Villon's *Testament, lines* 1610-1611," *Modern Language Notes,* LI (1936), 33-34.
"French Words with *e* for *o* in Unaccented Syllables," *Language,* XI (1937), 231-37.
"Gerald the Naturalist," *Speculum,* XI (1937), 110-21.
"Preface" to *Aucassin and Nicolette,* trans. Moyer and Eldridge. Chapel Hill: Robert Linker, 1937.
"Portuguese Americans," in *Our Racial and National Minorities,* F. J. Brown and J. S. Roucek. New York: Prentice Hall, 1937. Pp. 394-405.
"Chaucer's *Tydif,* A small bird," *Philological Quarterly,* XVI (1937), 65-77.
Holmes, Urban T., and George C. S. Adams, and Clement M. Woodard. *A Census of French and Provençal Dialect Dictionaries in American Libraries.* Lancaster, Pennsylvania: Linguistic Society of America, 1937.
Holmes, Urban T., and W. M. McLeod. "Source Problems of the *Chetifs,* a Crusade *Chanson de Geste,*" *Romanic Review,* XXVIII (1937), 99-108.
A History of Old French Literature from the Origins to 1300. New York: Appleton-Century-Crofts, 1937, 1938, 1948, 1962.
"Provençal 'huelh de veire' and 'sec ... son agre'," *Modern Language Notes,* LII (1937), 264-65.
Holmes, Urban T., and A. H. Schutz. *A History of the French Language.* New York: Farrar and Rinehart, 1938.
Holmes, Urban T., and Hugo Giduz. *Les Contes des sept sages.* New York: Farrar and Rinehart, 1938.
"Old French Esterminals, a Gem Stone," *Speculum,* XII (1938), 78-79.
"Old French *Mangon,* Anglo-Saxon *Mancus,* Late Latin *Mancussus, Mancosus, Mancessus,* etc.," *PMLA,* LIII (1938), 34-37.
"The Position of the North Star in the 13th Century," *Isis,* XXI (1939-40), 166.
Holmes, Urban T., and A. H. Schutz. *Source Book for the History of the French Language.* Columbus, Ohio: H. L. Hedrick, 1940.
"Jean de Noyon in *Pathelin,* line 1519," *Modern Language Notes,* LV (1940), 106-08.
"Foreword" to *Incunabula in the Hanes Collection,* O. V. Cook. Chapel Hill: University of North Carolina, 1940. Pp. xiii-xvi.
"Chernubles de Munigre," *Speculum,* XVI (1941), 244-45.
"Preface" to *La Chanson de Roland,* eds. Gardner, Woods, and Hilton. Boston: Ginn and Company, 1942. Pp. i-ii.
"Gerald the Naturalist and his Welsh Journeys," *Modern Language Forum,* XXVII (1942), 101-10.
"*Ludos scenicos* in Giraldus," *Modern Languages Notes,* LVII (1942), 188-89.

"A Welsh Motif in Marie de France's *Guigemar*," *Studies in Philology*, XXXIX (1942), 11-14.

At the Crossroads on the Hill. Chapel Hill: Chapel of the Cross, 1942.

"Comparative Literature: Past and Future, American Colleges and Universities," *Studies in Philology*, XLII (1945), 440-51.

"Old French *Grifaigne* and *Grifon*," *Studies in Philology*, XLIII (1946), 586-94.

Holmes, Urban T., and D. C. Cabeen, eds. *A Critical Bibliography of French Literature*. Vol. I. Syracuse, New York: Syracuse University Press, 1946, 1952.

"The Background and Sources of Remy Belleau's *Pierres Precieuses*," *PMLA*, LXI (1946), 624-35.

"William of Malmesbury and the *Pelerinage de Charlemagne*," *Symposium*, I (1946).

Adenet, Le Roi. *Berte aus grans pies*, ed. Urban T. Holmes. Chapel Hill: University of North Carolina Studies in the Romance Languages and Literatures, No. 6, 1946.

Rice, Carlton Cosmo. *Romance Etymologies and Other Studies*, ed. Urban T. Holmes. Chapel Hill: University of North Carolina Studies in the Romance Languages and Literatures, No. 7, 1946.

"A New Interpretation of Chretien's *Conte del Graal*," *Studies in Philology*, XLIV (1947), 453-76. Reprinted in University of North Carolina Studies in the Romance Languages and Literatures, No. 8, 1948.

"The Suffix *-erna* in Latin and Romance," *Romance Philology*, I (1947), 105-11.

Holmes, Urban T., and A. J. Denomy, eds. *Mediaeval Studies in Honor of Jeremiah Denis Mathias Ford, Smith Professor of French and Spanish Literature, Emeritus*. Cambridge, Massachusetts: Harvard University Press, 1948.

The Voice of Prayer. Durham: Department of Religious Education, Diocese of North Carolina, 1949.

"Further on Marie de France," *Symposium*, III (1949), 335-39.

"The Arthurian Tradition in Lambert d'Arderes," *Speculum*, XXV (1950), 100-13.

"Les noms de saints invoqués dans la Farce de Pathelin," in *Mélanges d'histoire de théâtre offerts à Gustave Cohen*, Paris: Librairie Nizet, 1950. Pp. 125-29.

Holmes, Urban T., and others, eds. *Romance Studies for William Morton Dey*. Romance Languages and Literatures, No. 12, 1950.

Holmes, Urban T., Willi Apel, and R. W. Linker. *French Secular Music of the Late Fourteenth Century*. Cambridge. Massachusetts: Mediaeval Academy of America, 1950.

"The Dominican Rite and the Judaeo-Christian Theory of the Grail," in *Romance Studies Presented to William Morton Dey*, 1950. Pp. 95-98.

"The Idea of a Twelfth-Century Renaissance," *Speculum*, XXVI (October, 1951), 643-51.

"The Beast Epic of Reynard the Fox," *University of North Carolina Extension Bulletin*, XXXI (January, 1952), 43-59.

Daily Living in the Twelfth Century Based on the Observations of Alexander Neckam in London and Paris. Madison, Wisconsin: University of Wisconsin, 1952, 1953, 1962, 1964.

"Richard Jente, 1888-1952," *Studies in Philology*," XLIX (1952), 551-52.

The Septicentennial Celebration of the Founding of the Sorbonne College: Proceedings and Papers, ed. Urban T. Holmes. Chapel Hill: University of North Carolina Press, 1953.

"The Post-Bédier Theories on the Origins of the *Chansons de Geste,*" *Speculum,* XXX (1955), 72-81.

"Coins of Old French Literature," *Speculum,* XXI (1956), 316-20.

"Coins of Little Value in Old French Literature," *Medieval Studies,* XIX (1957), 123-28.

"Un trésor du onzieme siècle contenant des pièces immobilisées des Contes de Bordeaux," *Schweitzer Munzblätter,* XXVI (July, 1957), pp. 213-20.

The Fair Humanities. Chapel Hill: University of North Carolina Press, 1958.

"Helmut Anthony Hatzfeld," in *Yearbook of Comparative and General Literature,* No. 7. Chapel Hill: University of North Carolina Press, 1958. Pp. 1-3.

"The Houses of the Bayeux Tapestry," *Speculum,* XXXIV (April, 1959), 179-183.

Holmes, Urban T., and Sister M. Amelia Klenke. *Chrétien, Troyes, and the Grail.* Chapel Hill: University of North Carolina, 1959.

"Notes on the French Fabliaux," in *Middle Ages Reformation Volkskunde, Festschrift,* John G. Kunstmann. Chapel Hill: University of North Carolina, 1959. Pp. 39-44.

"Transitions in European Education," in *Twelfth-Century Europe and the Foundations of Modern Society,* Marshall Clagett, Gaines Post, and Robert Reynolds. Madison: Wisconsin University Press, 1961. Pp. 15-38.

"Three Notes on the *Flamenca,*" in *Classical, Mediaeval, and Renaissance Studies in Honor of B. L. Ullman,* Charles Henderson, Jr. Rome, 1964. Pp. 85-92.

"The Adventures of Fouke Fitz Warin," *Medium Aevum Romanicum, Festschrift für Hans Rheinfelder.* Munich: Max Hueber, 1963. Pp. 179-85.

Holmes, Urban T., and F. R. Weedon. "Peter of Blois as a Physician," *Speculum,* XXXVII (1962), 252-56.

"The Anglo-Norman Rhymed Chronicle," in *Studies in Honor of Helmut Hatzfeld,* Alessandro S. Crisafulli. Washington: Catholic University Press, 1964.

Holmes, Urban T., and Kenneth R. Scholberg, eds. *French and Provençal Lexicography: Essays Presented to Honor Alexander Herman Schutz.* Columbus: Ohio State University Press, 1964.

In addition to these separately published articles, Urban T. Holmes has written articles on the Basque Language, François Villon, French Literature, and Guillaume du Bartas for *Collier's Encyclopedia*; articles on Provençal, Guiraut Riquier, Bernart de Ventadorn, Bertran de Born for Joseph T. Shipley's *Encyclopedia of Literature*; and articles on aphorism, argot, axiom, cant, chançon, chrestomathy, colloquialism, creation epic, descort, jeu parti, lai, mal mariée, manner, mannerism, method, Old French and Provençal forms, pattern, platitude, sense, slang, sonnet, stereotyped, structure, thesaurus, vernacular in Joseph T. Shipley's *Dictionary of World Literature.* For the Princeton *Encyclopedia of Poetry and Poetics* he wrote articles on Beast Epic, Conte dévot, Dit, Lais, Laisse, Poetic Contests, Reverdie and virolai.

BOOK REVIEWS

Books Abroad
Holmes was a constant contributor from 1937-1942.

Comparative Literature
VI (Spring, 1945).

French Review
scattered reviews.

French Studies
scattered reviews.

Hispania
scattered reviews.

Journal of European History
I (September, 1929); XIV (March-December, 1942).

Language
XVI (1940); XVII (1941); XVIII (1942); XXIII (1947); XXVI (1950); XXXIV (1958); XXXVIII (1962); XXIX (1963).

Modern Language Notes
XXXIX (1924); XLI (1926); XLII (1927); XLIII (1928).

Modern Language Review (England).
XLV (1950).

Modern Philology
XXIII (1925); XXIV (1926); XXIV (1927); XXVII (1929); XXVIII (1930).

Romance Philology
II (1948); III (1949-1950); V (1951-1952).

Romanic Review
XXV (April-June, 1934); XXVIII (December, 1937); XXIX (October, 1938); XXXI (April, 1940); XXXII (December, 1941); XXXIV (October, 1943); XXXIV (December, 1943).

Speculum

VI (July, 1931); VII (July, 1932); VII (October, 1932); XII (October, 1937); XIII (January, 1938); XV (October, 1940); XVI (January, 1941); XVI (October, 1941); XVII (April, 1942); XVII (October, 1942); XVIII (July, 1943); IX (October, 1944); XX (January, 1945); XXI (January, 1946); XXII (April, 1947); XXII (July, 1947); XXII (October, 1947); XXIII (July, 1948); XXIV (January, 1949); XXIV (April, 1949); XXIX (July, 1949); XXIV (October, 1949); XXV (April, 1950); XXVI (July, 1951); XXVI (October, 1951); XXVII (January, 1952); XXVII (April, 1952); XXVII (July, 1952); XXVII (October, 1952); XXVIII (January, 1953); XXVIII (July, 1953); XXVIII (October, 1953); XXIX (January, 1954); XXIX (April, 1954); XXIX (April, 1954); XXIX (July, 1954); XXX (January, 1955); (April, 1955); XXX (October, 1955); XXXI (January, 1956); XXXI (July, 1956); XXXII (April, 1957); XXXIII (April, 1958); XXXIII (October, 1958); XXXIV (January, 1959); XXXV (October, 1960); XXXVI (July, 1961); XXXVI (July, 1961); XXXVI (October, 1961); XXXVIII (January, 1963); XXXVIII (April, 1963); XXXIX (April, 1964); XXXIX (July, 1964).

Word

II (April, 1946).

TWO ROMANCE ETYMA BASED ON OLD ENGLISH

PAUL BROSMAN, JR.
Tulane University

Not long ago I discussed the use which has been made of Old English evidence in the investigation of the origin of Romance verbs. [1] In so doing, I pointed out that it has been surprisingly slight when one considers that Old English, as a relatively well attested older Germanic dialect coordinate with those frequently employed by Romance scholars, should be potentially as valuable as most others in determining or substantiating the form of reconstructed Germanic etyma. A further statement was that unfamiliarity with Old English has greatly restricted the valid results of even this limited use because of a misconception concerning weak verbs which has caused the few reconstructions based on that dialect to be to a large extent incorrect. In Old English the infinitive of the second-class weak verbs corresponding to the *ôn*-verbs of Gothic, Old High German and Low Franconian ended in *-ian,* while that of the first-class weak or *jan-* verbs usually contained neither *j* nor *i.* Instances were cited in which virtually every major compiler of Romance etymology was shown to have reconstructed or accepted Germanic *jan-* verbs based at least in part on Old English verbs of the second class. [2] The conclusion drawn was that Old English offers a virtually unexploited source of evidence which should prove of considerable value in the

---

[1] Paul W. Brosman, Jr., *Romance Notes,* IV (1962), 1-6.

[2] Evidence that unfamiliarity with Old English extends beyond the question of the endings of the weak verbs is contained in a second note in the same journal (*Romance Notes,* V (1964), 1-3).

study of the origin of Romance verbs and, indeed, of Romance forms in general. If this conclusion is correct, we should be able rather readily to find Old English forms which establish the existence in other Germanic dialects of etyma capable of serving Romance words hitherto not satisfactorily explained. In particular, we should find Old English weak verbs capable of clearing up morphological uncertainties involving verbs in Romance. The purpose of the present note is to point to two possible instances of such verbs, neither entirely certain, but both obviously overlooked. The etyma involved are those given as *bram(m)ôn and *trippôn.

*bram(m)ôn 'bellow' has been reconstructed on the basis of MLG brammen, supported by OHG brëman, MHG brimmen 'buzz, growl, roar, bellow' and MHG brummen 'buzz, growl'.[3] That it existed and was borrowed by Romance from one or more Germanic dialects appears to be universally agreed. The works of Meyer-Lübke, Gamillscheg, Bloch and Wartburg, Corominas, and Battista and Alessio all concur on this point. To it have been ascribed the following verbs, all of which show the first-conjugation endings usual in the borrowing of a Germanic ôn- verb: Fr. bramer 'bellow' Prov. bramar 'bellow, covet', Cat., Sp., Port. bramar 'bellow', It. bramare, Engad. bramer 'covet', Calab. vramare 'bellow', Lothr. bramé 'desire', Vaud. bramá 'insult, scold', Piem. bramè 'bellow (from hunger)' and Surselvan bramar 'covet'.[4] The apparently related It. bramire 'roar, bellow' also occurs. Of the scholars mentioned above, only Gamillscheg, Corominas, and Battista and Alessio attempt to treat it, attributing it without explanation or comment to the same *bram(m)ôn,[5] though ôn-

---

[3] Alois Walde and Julius Pokorny, Vergleichendes Wörterbuch der indogermanischen Sprachen (Berlin and Leipzig, 1927-30), II, 202.

[4] Wilhelm Meyer-Lübke, Romanisches etymologisches Wörterbuch, 3rd ed. (Heidelberg, 1935), p. 113; Ernst Gamillscheg, Etymologisches Wörterbuch der französichen Sprache (EWFS) (Heidelberg, 1928), p. 139; Gamillscheg, Romania Germanica (RG) (Berlin and Leipzig, 1934-6), I, 366-7; II, 276; Oscar Bloch and Walther von Wartburg, Dictionnaire étymologique de la langue française, 2nd ed. (Paris, 1950), p. 83; Juan Corominas, Diccionario crítico etimológico de la lengua castellana (Bern, 1954), I, 508; Carlo Battista and Giovanni Alessio, Dizionario etimologico italiano (Florence, 1950-7), I, 588.

[5] RG I, 366; Corominas, loc. cit., Battista and Alessio, loc. cit. Battista and Alessio refer also to OF bramir, attestation of which I have not been able to verify.

verbs are generally thought not to have entered the Romance fourth conjugation. It is possible that *bramire* results from the influence upon **bram(m)ôn* of a verb such as Lat. *rūgīre* 'roar, bellow'. In support of this possibility it may be pointed out that the Latin and Germanic verbs appear to have been blended elsewhere in Trient. *bružir*. [7] However, it is pertinent that OE *bremman* 'rage, roar' points to a Gmc. **bramjan* which could have produced *bramire* directly through borrowing. [7] The fourth-conjugation termination would apparently be proper in a verb taken from Old High German before the period of the umlaut of *a>e*. [8] As far as can be told, it would be possible in a borrowing from Lombardic which, as Bruckner pointed out, held much of its vocabulary in common with Old English, but would probably be inappropriate in a short-stemmed *jan-* verb received from Gothic. [9] Whichever of the suggestions made here one prefers, it should be noted that while either the influence of *rūgīre* or borrowing of **bramjan* would be capable by itself of wholly explaining *bramire,* the two possibilities need not be considered mutually exclusive. A plausible account, only slightly idealized, of what transpired might hold that **bramjan* was responsible for the original occurrence of a second Italian form, retention of which was by development of a pair of distinct meanings through semantic influences shared for geographic reasons with Provençal, and that association with *rūgīre* caused assignment of the literal meaning to the verb of the fourth conjugation. [10]

That **trippôn* was borrowed from Germanic is less certain and somewhat less widely accepted. Citing MDutch *trippen* and Swed.,

[6] Meyer-Lübke, p. 613.

[7] Joseph Bosworth and T. Northcote Toller, *An Anglo-Saxon Dictionary* (Oxford, 1882), p. 123.

[8] Brosman, *Studies in Philology,* LIX (1962) 595-602.

[9] Ibid.; Wilhelm Bruckner, *Die Sprache der Langobarden* (Strassburg, 1895), pp. 24-32, 56-62; RG II, 215-6.

[10] If OF *bramir* (see fn. 5) actually existed, borrowing from Old High German would definitely appear the most likely explanation. Germanic borrowing alone would seem more likely than Germanic borrowing plus intra-Romance borrowing or the independent repetition of the blending of **bram(m)ôn* and *rūgīre* with identical results. For geographic reasons the most plausible source of such borrowing would be Old High German, from which the verb could have entered French via Rhine Franconian and Italian via Upper German.

Norw. *trippa* 'hop, jump', Meyer-Lübke, Bloch and Wartburg, Gamillscheg, and Battista and Alessio hold that it is the source of numerous Romance forms, including the verbs OF *treper, triper,* Prov. *trepar* 'skip, dance', It. *treppare,* Romagn. *tripè* 'hop', Venet. *trepar,* Gen. *trepá* 'jest', Grödn. *tripé* 'play', Wall. *tripé* 'stamp', Norm. *trepé,* Bearn. *trepá* 'walk on soft ground', Cat., Sp. Port. *trepar* 'clamber, climb'.[11] Corominas does not entirely rule out the possibility of borrowing, but believes it more likely that the Romance and Germanic forms are of common onomatopoetic origin.[12] Without reference to Romance, Kluge explains the Germanic root in the same manner.[13] Several signs indicate that the Germanic forms are not a normal Indo-European inheritance: their generally late appearance in Germanic, the scarcity and restricted distribution of possible Indo-European connections and their possession of $p(p)$ which, because of the rarity of PIE b > PGmc. p, is alone enough to make inheritance doubtful.[14] It is still possible that the root, though arising in Germanic through onomatopeia, entered Romance later through borrowing of **trippôn*. Although the frequency with which e of the Romance verbs correponds to i of the Germanic might be considered to support such an explanation, it is difficult to see how one can confidently accept this possibility as a definite solution of the Romance problem. If one does wish to accept it, however, one will be in agreement with the majority of Romance scholars who have treated the question and will, like them, be faced with the problem of accounting for Prov. *trepir* 'step, tread' which Meyer-Lübke mentions but does not attempt to explain.[15] Corominas, who cites the fourth-conjugation form as an indication that borrowing from Germanic did not take place, is alone among the remaining scholars to refer to *trepir*.[16] OE *treppan* 'step, tread' establishes the existence of PGmc. **trapjan* or, perhaps apart from

---

[11] Meyer-Lübke, p. 741; Bloch and Wartburg, p. 618; EWFS p. 862; RG I, 219; Battista and Alessio, V, 3885.

[12] Corominas, IV, 565-7.

[13] Friedrich Kluge, *Etymologisches Wörterbuch der deutschen Sprache,* 18th ed. (Berlin, 1960), pp. 792, 789, 786.

[14] Kluge, loc. cit.; Walde and Pokorny, I, 769-7.

[15] Meyer-Lübke, p. 741.

[16] Corominas, IV, 566.

the West Germanic consonant gemination, *trappjan*, with a degree of verity at least equal to that of *trippôn*.[17] From *trap(p)jan* would have resulted LFrk. *treppjan* and OHG *treppen*, *treppfen*. For a Low Franconian *jan-* verb to have entered the fourth conjugation after the umlaut of $a > e$ is apparently in keeping with the development to be expected.[18] It would therefore be more satisfactory morphologically as well as semantically to assign *trepir* to LFrk. *treppjan* rather than to *trippôn*.

---

[17] Bosworth and Toller, p. 1015; Walde and Pokorny, I, 796.
[18] *Studies in Philology*, loc. cit.

TWO OLD SPANISH VERSIONS OF THE EPISTLE TO THE ROMANS (ESCORIAL MANUSCRIPTS I-I-2 AND I-I-6): COMPARISON AND NOTES ON SOURCES

Spurgeon W. Baldwin, Jr.

University of Illinois

Saludat me a Urban,
nuestro ayudador por Christo.
Rom. 16,9

Thirteenth century Castilian versions of the New Testament translated from the Vulgate, survive in two manuscripts only. Publication of them has been fragmentary: for I-I-2, only the Epistle to the Romans [1] and the First Epistle to the Corinthians [2] have appeared; for I-I-6, only the Gospel of St. Matthew. [3] (This statement applies to the New Testament of I-I-6 only; of the Old Testament, Machabees, Daniel and the Song of Songs have been published.)

The author of the present study has entered into a collaboration with Professor Montgomery in the preparation of an edition

---

[1] M. Morreale, "La Epístola de San Pablo a los Romanos según el manuscrito escurialense I-j-2," *Revista de Archivos, Bibliotecas y Museos,* LXIII (1957), 423-451.

[2] ———, "La Primera Epístola de San Pablo a los corintos según el manuscrito escurialense I-j-2," *Analecta Sacra Tarraconensia,* XXIX (1956), 273-312.

[3] Thomas A. Montgomery, ed., *El Evangelio de San Mateo según el manuscrito escurialense I.16,* Anejos del Boletín de la Real Academia española, VII (Madrid, 1962).

and study of the entire New Testament of I-I-6.[4] The text has already been transcribed from photographs of the manuscript, and all references to I-I-6 in this study are based on this typed transcription. (References to I-I-2 are, of course, based on Professor Morreale's edition.)

Montgomery and Morreale[5] accept the statements of P. José Llamas concerning the relationship between I-I-2 and I-I-6, a relationship which all three regard as immediately obvious. Llamas, in the introduction to his edition of the medieval Spanish Bible (based on Hebrew sources), states: "Entre los libros del Nuevo Testamento contenidos en el Ms. I-I-2 (todos, excepto los Hechos de los Apóstoles y Apocalipsis) de la *Grande e General Estoria* Alfonsina y los mismos que constan en el I-I-6 es la coincidencia materialmente tan exacta que o el uno es copia fiel del otro, o ambos proceden por igual de un ejemplar tercero." A few pages later, he reiterates: "No hay opción a duda, con sólo juzgar por las muestras aducidas, de que ambos manuscritos son mutua y materialmente dependientes entre sí, o por vía directa, siendo copia el uno del otro, o por medio de un tercero del que copiasen los dos."[6]

Llamas' conclusions are based on a collation of two short passages from the Gospels of St. Luke and St. John. These passages contain sufficient linguistic data[7] to prove his main point, that I-I-2 is later than I-I-6 (and, therefore, that I-I-6 cannot come from I-I-2), but they do not contain adequate evidence to indicate either that I-I-2 comes from I-I-6, or that both stem from a common source. The first objective of this study will be to examine in more detail the relationship between the two manuscripts.

The two texts are certainly related;[8] Llamas could hardly be mistaken in his observation that his two passages are identical,

---

[4] We have undertaken a transcription of the text, a systematic presentation of the lexicon, a detailed linguistic study, a collation of selected books with the Vulgate, and a preliminary investigation into textual history, and sources of the prefatory material and glosses.

[5] Montgomery, *San Mateo*, p. 8; Morreale, "Romanos", p. 425.

[6] José Llamas, O. S. A., *Biblia medieval romanceada judío-cristiana* (Madrid, CSIC, I [1950]), xxxvi and 1.

[7] Montgomery's appraisal of the linguistic evidence is more thorough: *San Mateo*, pp. 8-9.

[8] The similarity is immediately evident in the introductory material; I-I-6 has a long prologue, while I-I-2 has both a prologue and an "argu-

reflecting only linguistic and not textual variations; he reasons that the two texts are too similar to be independent translations from the Vulgate. While this is undoubtedly true, the argument can be strengthened by comparing the two Castilian texts first with each other, and then with the Vulgate, pointing out the cases in which the Castilian texts coincide in a divergence from the Latin. There are at least fifteen such cases. (These errors must be distinguished from the common additions and omissions, of which there is a larger number, to be considered later in the discussion.) Some of these errors could represent textual variations in the Vulgate itself; hence we cannot eliminate the possibility that the Castilian versions exhibit correct translations of some unknown Vulgate text. Other cases are very likely error in the Castilian translation:

1) 10,6-7 V: *Ne dixeris in corde tuo: quis ascendit in cae-*
        lum? id est, Christum deducere: (7) Aut quis
        descendit in abyssum? hoc est, Christum ex
        mortuis reuocare.

    I-I-2: *Non digas en tu coraçon, ¿Quien subra al cielo?*
        esto es, Christo non subra ella; (7) o ¿Quien
        descendio al abismo? esto es, Christo non
        resuscito.

---

mento". It can be seen in Morreale's photographic reproduction of part of this introductory material that the prologue of I-I-2 is identical with that of I-I-6, reflecting only linguistic variations of the kinds to be expected between two such related manuscripts. Morreale identifies the prologue with a quote from the manuscript: "Prologo de Sant Iheronimo en la Epistola a los romanos," p. 432. This prologue is, in fact, a very close translation of the "Argumentum Pelagii in epistolam ad Romanos," as recorded in the Wordsworth and White edition of the Vulgate: Iohannes Wordsworth and Henricus Iulianus White, *Nouum Testamentum Domini nostri Iesu Christi, Pars Secunda: epistolae,* (Oxonii, 1913-1940). (Referred to henceforth as "Wordsworth and White" or "W-W.") This prologue is included as part of the established text, since it is found in the manuscripts of most of the Vulgates used in the collation, including *Codex Toletanus,* to which many references will be made in the present study. The Castilian versions translate the Pelagian prologue closely, with a common addition of several lines of commentary at the end. The addition amounts to a gloss on the prologue, and this prefatory material could help establish the sources of such prefatory material in general.

I-I-6: *Non digas en to coraçon, ¿Quien subra al cielo?*
esto es, Christo no subio alla; (7) o ¿Quien
descendio al abismo? esto es, Christo no
resucito.

Aside from the reading errors of I-I-2, the two Castilian texts coincide, ingeniously covering up their misunderstanding of the verbs *deducere* and *reuocare*.

2) 2,26-27 V: *Si igitur praeputium iustitias legis custodiat*
nonne praeputium illius in circumcisionem
reputabitur? (27) Et iudicabit quod ex na-
tura est praeputium legem consummans te
qui per litteram et circumcisionem prae-
varicator legis es.

I-I-2 and I-I-6: *El que guarda los derechos de la ley,*
aquel la tien; la cortadura (I-I-2: *cordura*)
daquel sera tenuda por circumcision. (27)
La circumcision que es de natura iudgara
a ti, que eres traspassador de la ley por
letra e por circumcidamiento.

The difficulties of the Castilian translation center around the word *praeputium,* which is translated here *cortadura,* and alsewhere *taiadura* (2,25 V: *Circumcisio tua praeputium facta est;* I-I-2 and I-I-6: *tu circumcision no es sino taiadura*); in 3,30, *praeputium is* transliterated and accompanied by the gloss *que es la taiadura por fe*; (afterwards, the transliterated form stands alone: 4,9; 4,10). Ths uniformity in error of the two Castilian texts provides the most conclusive evidence that they are related. [9]

---

[9] In addition, many examples can be cited in which I-I-2 and I-I-6 agree in an idiosyncratic rendition of the Latin; strong evidence, also, for the affiliation between the two manuscripts:

1,13 V: *nolo autem uos ignorare;* Cast: *quiero que sepades;*
3,9 V: *causati enim sumus Iudaeos et Graecos;* Cast: *non ponemos sin achaque a los iudios e a los griegos;*
8,30 V: *glorificauit;* Cast: *fizo grandes;*
10,11 V: *non confundetur;* Cast: *saluo sera;*
15,5 V: *sapere;* Cast: *sentir;*
16,25 V: *secundum revelationem mysterii;* Cast: *segund el descobrimiento de la incarnacion;*

Evidence can be adduced from the collation to indicate that I-I-2 cannot have been derived directly from I-I-6; in these cases I-I-2 is correct and I-I-6 is mistaken:

3,19   V: *ut omne os obstruatur;* I-I-2: *por que toda boca sea guardada;* I-I-6: *por que toda boca sea guarnida*

9,21   V: *ex eodem massa;* I-I-2: *de una massa misma;* I-I-6: *de una masma misma*

10,8   V: *Testimonium enim perhibeo;* I-I-2: *Testimonio do;* I-I-6: *Testimonio de*

10,18   V: *exiit sonus eorum;* I-I-2: *sallio el son dellos;* I-I-6: *salio en son dellos*

11,20   V: *sed time;* I-I-2: *temiente;* I-I-6: *tenient*

13,7   V: *timorem;* I-I-2: *temor;* I-I-6: *temer*

14,6   V: *qui non manducat Domino, non manducat* I-I-2: *qui non come, non come por Dios* I-I-6: *qui come, non come por Dios*

16,17   V: *offendicula;* I-I-2: *corroços;* I-I-6: *corrotos*

One might argue that the scribe of I-I-2 could be correcting the erroneous readings of I-I-6 in these cases. In 9,21, this could be done even without recourse to the Vulgate, since the error is so obvious, but in other cases, while I-I-6 makes little sense, it seems unlikely that I-I-2 could in every case supply the correction without reference to the Vulgate (how would he know where to correct?); this is especially true of 3,19. If we postulate that I-I-2, with the aid of a Vulgate, has corrected the mistakes of I-I-6, how can we explain the presence of at least sixty other textual errors [10]

---

[10] Examples of errors from I-I-2:

2,12   V: *peccauerunt;* I-I-2: *peccaren;* I-I-6: *pecaron*
3,13   V: *agebant;* I-I-2: *traen;* I-I-6: *trayen*
3,28   V: *hominem;* I-I-2: *nombre;* I-I-6 *ombre*
4,1   V: *inuenisse;* I-I-2: *hablo;* I-I-6: *fallo*
(etc.)

These sixty errors are in addition to those noted by Morreale, who corrects where she deems necessary; since my collation is based on the edited text of I-I-2, the total number of such errors in the manuscript itself is considerably greater than sixty.

Many corrections can be made in the edited version of I-I-2 on the basis of I-I-6:

in I-I-2? These are errors of the same kind that the scribe is supposed to have taken the pains to remove from I-I-6; in each case I-I-6 is unmistakable, and agrees with the Vulgate. It is unlikely that the copyist should have been meticulous enough to correct ten of the mistakes of I-I-6, while his own text has at least sixty other errors; one must conclude that I-I-2 cannot derive directly from I-I-6.

The proper names in chapter 16 furnish further proof of the two preceding arguments. The two Castilian manuscripts agree, for the most part, giving reasonable Castilian forms for the Latin names in the Vulgate. However, there are the following exceptions: 1) the two manuscripts display errors in treating four names;

16,11 V: *Herodionem;* Cast: *Bondion*
 15 V: *Philologum;* Cast: *Philiogolo*
 21 V: *Lucius;* Cast: *Luchas*
 14 V: *Asyncritum;* I-I-2: *Ansiecrito;* I-I-6; *Ansietoso*

4,2 V: *si enim;* I-I-2: *casi;* I-I-6: *ca si*
8,32 V: *tradidit illum;* I-I-2: *dio la muerte;* I-I-6: *diol a muerte*
9,26 V: *dei uiui;* I-I-2: *Dios vino;* I-I-6: *Dios uiuo*
10,1 V: *Frates;* I-I-2: *Mas, hermanos;* I-I-6: *Mios hermanos*
12,20 V: *congeres;* I-I-2: *ayuntaron* (editor's correction of original *ayuntadas*); I-I-6: *ayuntaras*
7,13 V: *appareat;* I-I-2: *perezca;* I-I-6: *parezca*

In two cases, Professor Morreale's corrections seem inaccurate:

1) 7,10 V: *Et inuentum est mihi mandatum, quod erat ad uitam, hoc esse ad mortem;*
 I-I-2: *Es agora para la muerte;* (editor's correction of original *essa hora*)
 I-I-6: *esse era pora la muert;*
2) 7,15 V: *...sed quod odi illud facio;* I-I-2: *...mas fago lo ques mal;* (editor's correction of original *lo que ques mal*) I-I-6: *...mas fago lo que quis mal.*

In this case, Professor Morreale has changed radically what seems to be a nearly accurate reading: *...mas fago lo que ques mal* is far more likely to be a scribal error changing one letter of a correct Castilian original: *...mas fago lo que quis mal.* *Quis mal* is a normal translation of *odi;* in 12,9, Vulgate *odientes* is translated *aborreciendo* in both Castilian texts; this seems likewise to be a good synonym for *querer mal;* elsewhere, *querer mal* renders *odio esse, odio habere,* etc. (Luke 1,71; 6,22; 19,14; frequently in Matthew.)

2) I-I-2 agrees with the Vulgate, while I-I-6 is wrong, three times:

16,1 V: *Cenchris;* I-I-2: *Cencris* (original: *Cencencris*);
   I-I-6: *Centris*
   7 V: *Iuniam;* I-I-2: *Iunia;* I-I-6: *Iulia*
   21 V: *Iason;* I-I-2: *Jason;* I-I-6: *Nason*

3) The reverse is true, four times:

16,8 V: *Ampliatum;* I-I-2: *Amplico;* I-I-6: *Ampliato*
   11 V: *Narcissi;* I-I-2: *Yrasciso;* I-I-6: *Narciso*
   12 V: *Tryphenam;* I-I-2: *Thyphena;* I-I-6: *Triphena*
   12 V: *Tryphosam;* I-I-2: *Triphora;* I-I-6: *Triphosa*

Have the erroneous readings *Centris, Iulia* and *Nason* of I-I-6 been corected by I-I-2, with the aid of a Vulgate? How, then, do we explain the mistaken readings *Thyphena, Triphora, Amplico* and *Yrasciso* of I-I-2, while I-I-6 is correct? The most plausible explanation, based on the evidence available, seems to be that the two Castilian versions stem from a common proto-Castilian source (PC), and commit their unique errors independently as they each copy from the common source.

This common Castilian source is readily apparent in the common additions made by I-I-2 and I-I-6 to the Vulgate. While certain additions may well reflect Vulgate textual variants, others must be assigned to Castilian, since they are glosses on the meaning of Castilian words. In some instances, the translator is not content with a literal rendition of the Latin:

9,12 V: *ex uocante;* Cast: *por la boca del llamador*
10,19 V: *primus Moses;* Cast: *Moysen, que fue el primero ensennador dellos*
14,23 V: *discernit;* Cast: *departe entre limpio e non limpio*

In other cases, the Castilian word form is related historically to the Latin word being traslated, and the gloss is needed to explain a possible semantic confusion, as in the following case, where *arquero* has another meaning 'archer, bowman:' [11]

---

[11] Corominas gives the following data:
   arquero 'cajero,' from *arca* is listed, but no first occurrence is cited.
   arquero 'el que peleaba con arco,' 'archero,' Lat. *sagittarius,* from *arco:* first occurence (c. 1300): *Gran Conquista de Ultramar.*

16,23 V: ...*arcarius ciuitatis*
Cast: ...arquero de la cibdat. Este era guardador de las
archas o metien los pechos.

Occasionally, the Castilian word appears to be a calque on the
Latin:

11,17 V: *oleaster;* Cast: *oleastro (e oleastro es azeuuch)*

Note that, a few verses later (11,24), Latin *oleaster* is translated
simply *azeuuch*. This recourse to the common Castilian term
suggests that *oleastro* may be a calque here; Corominas gives no
citation of a first occurence of the word, noting simply that it is
a "cultismo."

3,30 V: *praeputio;* Cast: *prepucio, que es la taiadura por fe.*
Here the translator has been deceived by the intricacies of the
Pauline prose at the end of chapter 2 into believing that *taiadura*
is a translation of Latin *praeputio*. Since this is an example of
both a linguistic addition and an error common to the two Castilian manuscripts, it is certainly the most significant single piece of
evidence adduced thus far.

8,29 V: *Nam quos praesciuit et praedestinauit conformes fieri*
imaginis filii eius
Cast: *Ca los que el dantes sopo que serien sanctos, aquellos*
enuio por seer conformados a la ymagen del so fiio

Praesciuit is translated literally by *dantes sopo,* and then its specific reference is explained by the gloss *que serien sanctos;* but
in 11,2 only the explanatory gloss is used:

V: *praesciit;* Cast: *auien de ser saluos*

With *praescire* we have seen attempts made on the part of the
translator to fit the literal and secondary meanings of a Latin
locution into the Spanish version; no such effort was made with
praedicere in 9,29:

V: *Et sicut praedixit Isaias;* Cast: *E assi cuemo diz Ysayas;*

Common linguistic additions of the kind just discussed are
most likely attributable to the proto-Castilian version only, the

translator, working from a Latin text, making such explanations as he sees fit. When the number of such common additions is large, it is not possible that such explanations, made independently, should be identical. Although it was common practice for the scribe to make such additions as well, the fact that neither I-I-2 nor I-I-6 contains a single independent addition [12] leads us to conclude that the scribes were, in this case, remarkably conservative.

Having accepted the existence of a proto-Castilian version PC, from which both I-I-2 and I-I-6 stem, we ask next whether the two Castilian versions are direct copies based on PC. If not, how far removed are they? Two facts indicate that I-I-6 may well be a direct copy from PC: 1) its ten erroneous readings (*guarnida* for *guardada,* for example) seem few enough, even if we attribute them all to a single copy; to spread the same errors over two or more lineal copies seems less likely; 2) it makes no independent omissions. An "omisio ex homoeoteleuto" [13] might be considered as likely as a reading error; I-I-6 is guilty of no such independent omission, while in I-I-2 there are forty-odd; [14] it seems quite

---

[12] There are two cases which at first glance might appear to be independent Castilian additions to the Vulgate: 1) 15,25 V: *In hierusalem ministrare sanctis*; I-I-2: *A Jherusalem a pensar de los sanctos que son en Jherusalem*; I-I-6: *A Iherusalem a pensar de los sanctos*; 2) 4,16 V: *ideo ex fide*; I-I-2: *por ende es padre de la fe*; I-I-6: *por ende es padre de los de la fe.* Rather than try to account for these examples as independent additions, it seems more plausible to attribute the full addition, as seen in one or the other of the Castilian texts, to PC or to the Vulgate, and then to say that one or the other omits part or all of the addition as it appears in PC.

[13] i.e., an omission caused by the fact that two phrases, following each other more or less closely, end with the same word or words; I am borrowing the term from Raúl A. del Piero, "La *Corónica de Mahomad* del Arcipreste de Talavera," NRFH, XIV (1960), 21-50. Professor del Piero (p. 34) cites A. C. Clark, *The Descent of Manuscripts* (Oxford, 1918).

[14] An examination of these omisions in I-I-2 will reveal 1) that the opportunities are numerous for a scribe to make such mistakes; 2) that such omissions are, with reasonable certainty, from Spanish, not from Latin. It might be argued that such omissions could very well be from Latin; the examples adduced here furnish evidence that such was not the case in many instances, because differences in the Vulgate have been made uniform in Spanish:

8,12 V: *Ergo fratres debitores sumus non carni ut secundum carnem uiuamus;*

possible that I-I-6 is, it self, a direct copy from PC, while I-I-2 appears to be several steps distant, in lineal descent, from the Castilian original. The most informed speculation concerning the dates of the two manuscripts places I-I-2 thirty to fifty years after I-I-6.

Where I-I-2 and I-I-6 exhibit omissions in common, we must hesitate to assign such readings to PC, for the possibility increases that we are dealing with a variant in the Vulgate text, "omissio ex homoeoteleuto" being eminently possible in the Latin as well as in the Spanish. Because of this possibility, common omissions are often of little value as evidence.

One common omission does point conclusively to PC, and is the last bit of evidence pertaining to the Castilian text. 10,11-13: Verse 11 of the Vulgate ends ...*non confundetur,* which is *saluo sera* in both Castilian texts; verse 13 of the Vulgate ends *saluus erit; saluo sera* seems the only plausible rendition in Castilian, and we may attribute this reading to PC, which would have had *saluo sera* in verses 11 and 13. I-I-2 and I-I-6 both exhibit an "omissio ex homoeoteleuto" from the end of verse 11 to the end of vere 13. The omission cannot be based on a reading of the Vulgate, which would have different verbs in verses 11 and 13; therefore we must assign it to a reading of PC. This omission might, of course, have occurred in two independent readings of PC, but it seems much more plausible to postulate the existence of a second copy of PC, to which a unique omission from the first copy can be ascribed, and from which I-I-2 and I-I-6 could have inherited the omission in common.

I-I-6: *Pues, hermanos, non somos debdores a la carne por uiuir segund la carne;*

I-I-2 omits *por uiuir segund la carne,* an "omissio ex homoeoteleuto," based on the Castilian original; such an omission is less likely in the Vulgate because of the different forms *carni* and *carnem,* and because of the post-position of *uiuamus.*

8,25 V:*Si autem quod non uidemus, speramus; per patientiam exspec-tamus;*

I-I-6: *Si lo que non ueemos esperamos, por paciencia lo esperamos;* I-I-2 omits *por paciencia lo esperamos,* certainly an omission from Castilian, since the Vulgate has two different verbs. Other examples are: 2,22; 5,5; 9,8; 11,31; 14,1; 14,7; 15,19; in each case the omission involves identical words in the Castilian text, where the forms are different in the Vulgate.

All collational arguments from the preceding discussion may now be summarized in the following minimal *stemma*:

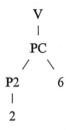

This *stemma* is, let us repeat minimal, the possibilities of additional steps at any juncture having been explored in the preceding discussion.

Now, let us turn to a consideration of the Vulgate original from which PC comes. The common omissions of I-I-2 and I-I-6, some twenty in number, offer little aid in exploring the Vulgate tradition; only two of them apear as significant variants in the W-W collation. (These two, in verses 4,12 and 9,26, connect the two Castilian texts with *Codex Toletanus*.)

In the common additions (i. e., readings not found in the text of the Vulgate as established by Wordsworth and White) we find more substantial evidence. Some thirty-five common additions to the Vulgate appear in the two Castilian texts. Approximately ten of these have already been shown to stem from PC. (They are linguistic glosses of some kind.) Most of the rest are patently doctrinal in nature, and apparently belong to the Vulgate; of these readings, some twelve appear in one or another of the manuscripts cited in the Wordsworth and White collation. The volume of the data is not overwhelming, but it is nevertheless sufficient to indicate a probable Vulgate textual ancestry for I-I-2 and I-I-6.

The principal sources indicated for the Castilian original are 1) *Codex Toletanus,* extremely important as a leading example of the very important Spanish tradition of the early Vulgate; 2) the Scholastic text, originating in France, and achieving a position of pre-eminence among the later medieval Vulgates; this Paris Bible reflects the influence of burgeoning Biblical exegesis, and draws from (among other sources) the Spanish Vulgate, and from English and Irish texts (the latter were brought to France along with

British Biblical scholars);[15] 3) the various 13th century *correctoria*, especially the so-called *Correctorium Vaticanum*, a document which seems to be the only source for certain readings found in the two Castilian texts.

The common additions of I-I-2 and I-I-6 which are listed as significant variants in the Wordsworth and White collation are now arranged in such an order as will illustrate the proposed textual ancestry:

1) Variant found only in *Codex Toletanus*: 5,6: *el iusto por nos pecadores*; *Toletanus* (cf. W-W, 84 n.): *iustus pro iniustis*.

2) Variants found in *Codex Toletanus* and in an important Scholastic text, *Sangermanensis:*

a) 8,26: *que por palaura no podrien seer contados; Toletanus, Sangermanensis,* and a few other Vulgates (cf. W-W, 104 n.): *quae uerbis exprimi non possunt*

b) 16,24: Wordsworth and White omit this verse from their text, apparently because it cannot be found in the Greek on which St. Jerome's work is based (150 n.); however, many medieval Vulgates included it, among them *Toletanus* and *Sangermanensis.*

3) Variants reflecting the Scholastic tradition generally:

a) 16,27: *e gloria* is added after *onra*; W-W, 151 n., indicates that the formula *honor et gloria* is in the Scholastic tradition.

b) 8,38: *ni uertudes*; (cf. W-W, 107 n.): *neque uirtutes*

---

[15] The textual ancestry here proposed for I-I-2 and I-I-6 is traced against a general background of the history of the Vulgate, drawn primarily from the following sources: 1) Samuel Berger, *Histoire de la Vulgate pendant les premiers siècles du moyen âge* (Paris, 1893) [repr. (New York, 1958)]; 2) H. H. Glunz, *History of the Vulgate in England from Alcuin to Roger Bacon* (Cambridge, 1933). Glunz cites evidence from the Gospels only, but his general observations on the history of the Scholastic text are the most lucid I have seen, and my data conform very well to his observations; it is hoped that eventually a more extensive collation of I-I-6 with the Wordsworth and White Vulgate can be carried out, and that the additional data can be compared in more detail with Glunz; 3) P. Ceslaus Spicq, *Esquisse d'une histoire de l'éxégèse latine au moyen âge* (Paris, 1944); 4) Beryl Smalley, *The Study of the Bible in the Middle Ages* (Oxford, 1952). Spicq and Smalley write from the points of view of the theologian and the historian, respectively, thereby producing two quite different books on essentially the same material.

c) 7,21: *la ley que es bona;* (cf. W-W, 97 n., which cites a late Scholastic manuscript which has *legem bonam;* all others have *legem* alone.

4) Variants found in some Vulgates and in the *Correctorium Vaticanum*:

a) 14,22: *tu que as fe...;* (adds *que*); most Vulgates and *Corr. Vat.* (cf. W-W, 138 n.): *tu qui fidem habes*

b) 19,9: *la cosa de to uezino;* two Vulgates and *Corr. Vat.* (cf. W-W, 132 n.): *rem proximi tui*

5) Variants found only in the *Correctorium Vaticanum*:

a) 11,36: *a el sea onra e gloria;* W-W, 126 n.: the Scholastic formula *honor et gloria* is recorded in this particular verse only in the *Corr. Vat.*

b) 9,10: *Rebeca ouo dos fiios de un ayuntamiento; Corr. Vat.* (cf. W-W, 110 n.): *geminos filios*

The probable ancestry of I-I-2 and I-I-6 can be conveniently summarized in connection with an interesting common addition at the end of 4,18: *Cuemo las estrellas del cielo e cuemo el arena del mar.* Wordsworth and White present a lengthy discussion of this variant (82 n.), from which the following points can be extracted:

1) *Sicut stellae caeli uelut arena quae est in litore maris; Codex Toletanus* (8th century)

2) *Sicut stellae caeli et arena maris; Codex Theodulfianus* and *Codex Hubertianus,* two important 9th century Vulgates, showing the influence of the Spanish (*Toletanus*) tradition of the early Vulgate, but omitting *quae est in litore* and *uelut.*

3) *Sicut stellae caeli et sicut arena maris; Codex Colbertinus* (probably 12th century; mixed text: Gospels are Old Latin; rest of N. T. is a Vulgate); omits *quae est in litore* with *Theodulfianus* and *Hubertianus;* retains *uelut* (but in the form of a repetition of *sicut*)

4) The *Correctorium Vaticanum* documents the readings of both *Toletanus* and *Colbertinus*

The data here seem to indicate an early Spanish source of the Vulgate tradition from which I-I-2 and I-I-6 eventually stem;

the line of descent then moves into France with *Codex Theodulfianus,* and joins the Scholastic tradition; influenced by the *correctoria,* it then returns to Spain with the 13th century Paris text.

Berger appears to be in error concerning the Vulgate sources of I-I-2: "Nous ne pouvons pas conclure grand'chose des sommaires, qui paraissent tirés du latin, et qui sont traduits librement, mais les arguments suffisent à nous indiquer, comme original, un ms. d'origine espagnole, peu éloigné du *Codex Toletanus.*" [16]

Our evidence is based on the examination of a limited amount of material, and the conclusions drawn therefrom must be somewhat tentative; it has been the aim of this study to suggest only the general outline of a textual ancestry. A more extensive collation of I-I-6 and the Wordsworth and White Vulgate (the Gospel of St. John, the Apocalypse, and one or two of the heavily glossed Epistles, for example) would permit a more definitive statement; it is hoped that such a collation can soon be completed.

---

[16] Samuel Berger, "Les Bibles castillanes," *Romania* XXVIII (1899), p. 397.

THE VOICES OF PLANTS AND FLOWERS AND THE CHANGING CRY OF THE MANDRAKE

ALFRED G. ENGSTROM
University of North Carolina

> "*As I wander'd the forest,*
> *The green leaves among,*
> *I heard a wild flower*
> *Singing a song.*"
>
> WILLIAM BLAKE

Through the literature of many centuries one can hear now and again the voices of trees and plants and flowers. It may be in ancient myth, in allegory, in medieval or later folklore, in fairyland, in the mystic's or drug-addict's vision, or in the rapt experience of the poet; but plant voices arise over wide areas of time and place, and they survive for us today with continuing fascination. In these few pages we shall bring together characteristic examples of this phenomenon and seek to relate them pertinently to the changing voice of the mandrake, one of the most memorable of all the plants in ancient folklore and tradition.

I

In the old tales of King Midas's reeds and of Pan and Syrinx we hear already plant voices and plant music. Talking and singing trees are recurrent in the literature of the East; and Stith

Thompson notes a Hawaiian tree with two singing blossoms and cites, from Plummer, tree leaves making melody for Irish saints. [1]

French folklore has numerous plant voices, and often these voices sing. J. F. Campbell cites, for example, "a singing apple... which the Princess Belle Étoile, and her brothers and her cousin, bring from the end of the world after all manner of adventures"; [2] and Paul Sébillot has various similar references in a lengthy passage on the blue plant that sings by day and night, a flower that sings like a nightingale, and the Fleur Dorée (in a tale from Gascony) that sings at sunrise. [3] Sébillot cites also a talking bean-vine, [4] and he shows that plant voices are at times closely linked with human lives:

> Des plantes chantent pour dénoncer un coupable ou pour révéler un secret: un enfant assassiné par son frère est enterré dans un jardin rempli de fleurs magnifiques; un berger qui passe un peu après, cueille la plus belle, et elle se met à chanter aussitôt que ce n'est pas lui qui l'a tué. Dans un conte de la Haute-Bresse, la fosse d'un petit garçon tué par sa soeur se couvre de plantes, parmi lesquelles sont des roseaux qui chantent sans intervention humaine; une bergère en coupe un; dès qu'elle l'a porté à ses lèvres il parle du crime, et quand la soeur coupable est forcée de l'approcher à son tour de sa bouche, il l'accuse du meutre. [5]

References in literature are even more memorable. In *Le roman d'Alexandre* (late 12th century) by Lambert le Tors and Alexandre de Bernay there is a strangely beautiful passage on the flower maidens who dare not venture beyond the deep shadow of the forest. One of them cries out to Alexander:

> "...gentius rois, ne m'ocis, france cose ounorée;
> quar s'estoie plain pié de la forest jetée

---

[1] *Motif-Index of Folk-Literature*, revised and enlarged ed., III (Indiana University Press, 1956), F979.21, F979.3.

[2] *Popular Tales of the West Highlands* (4 vols.; London, 1890-1894), I, lxxvii.

[3] *Le folk-lore de France, III: La faune et la flore* (Paris: E. Guilmoto, 1906), pp. 526-27.

[4] *Ibid.*, p. 527.

[5] *Ibid.*

> que euise des ombres une seule passée,
> tantos seroie morte, tele est ma destinée." [6]

Later in the same work a talking tree prophesies Alexander's death.[7]

Early in the 14th century Dante offers a sombre passage in the dark wood of the suicides (*Inferno* XIII) when he breaks a twig from the tree of the wretched Piero delle Vigne and the trunk cries, "Perchè mi schiante?" and tells its story in words mingled with blood.

In the Middle French period a talking flower appears in the dawn after May-day in a dream of Charles d'Orléans:

> Le lendemain du premier jour de May,
> Dedens mon lit ainsi que je dormoye,
> Au point du jour m'avint que je songay
> Que devant moy une fleur je veoye
> Qui me disoit: 'Amy...' [8]

Some two centuries later La Fontaine writes in the first poem of Book II of his *Fables* ("Contre ceux qui ont le goût difficile"):

> J'ai fait parler le loup et répondre l'agneau;
> J'ai passé plus avant: les arbres et les plantes
> Sont devenus chez moi créatures parlantes.
> Qui ne prendrait ceci pour un enchantement? [9]

It is not hard to find an example: "Le Chêne un jour dit au Roseau..."

The Grimm brothers in Germany continue the plant colloquy in "Strohhalm, Kohle und Bohne"; but a new tone comes into the voice of plants and flowers with the mystics and semi-mystics of the late 18th and early 19th centuries. We have already cited the song of William Blake's wild flower as an epigraph. One

---

[6] *Li romans d'Alixandre par Lambert li Tors et Alexandre de Bernay,* ed. Heinrich Michelant (Stuttgart, 1846), pp. 345-46.

[7] *Ibid.,* p. 355.

[8] Charles d'Orléans, *Poésies,* ed. Pierre Champion (2 vols.; Paris: Honoré Champion, 1923-1924), I, 87 ("Ballade LXII").

[9] La Fontaine, *Fables, contes, et nouvelles* (Bibliothèque de la Pléiade, 1954), p. 51.

of the French Illuminati, Louis-Claude de Saint-Martin ("Le Philosophe Inconnu"), claimed that he "heard flowers that sounded, and saw notes that shone." [10] Goethe, in his poem "Gefunden," is addressed by a beautiful little flower he is about to pluck. Most important of all, perhaps, is the "Blue Flower" which appears on several occasions in Novalis's novel, *Heinrich von Ofterdingen*. Though the Blue Flower never talks or sings, it becomes a famous symbol of dream and romantic longing and undoubtedly influenced the later poetic treatment of plants and flowers. Novalis first cites the Blue Flower in the second paragraph of his novel, where he refers to the old belief that flowers once spoke to men and tells of his being haunted by the conviction that they have something to tell him that he could understand.

Balzac's Séraphîta in the tale of that name (1834) claims with a smile to know "où croît la fleur qui chante." [11] Poe describes in *Silence—A Fable* the water-lilies that "shrieked within their beds..."; and Poe's great disciple, Baudelaire, in "La chambre double" (*Petits poèmes en prose*) writes in depicting what seems to be an opium dream: "Les meubles ont l'air de rêver; on les dirait doués d'une vie somnambulique, comme le végétal et le minéral. Les étoffes parlent une langue muette, comme les fleurs, comme les ciels, comme les soleils couchants." [12] Some years later, Rimbaud's *Illuminations* afford memorable examples of similar situations, in which a flower tells its name ("Aube"), the flowers of dream on the edge of the forest "tintent, éclatent, éclairent" ("Enfance" I), and magic flowers hum or murmur ("Enfance" III).

In the present century the voices of flowers recur with special power in writers who have a deep sense of the worlds mystery and sadness. Georg Trakl, the tragic Austrian drug-addict and suicide, writes in his "Gesang der Abgeschiedenen" of the harmonies of bird-flight "und die Blumen des Sommers, die schön im Winde läuten..."; and Rainer Maria Rilke introduces the singing

---

[10] Cited in Evelyn Underhill, *Mysticism* (N. Y.: Meridian Books, 1955), p. 7.
[11] Honoré de Balzac, *Séraphîta,* in *La comédie humaine,* X (Bibliothèque de la Pléiade, 1950), p. 535.
[12] Charles Baudelaire, *Petits poèmes en prose (Le Spleen de Paris)* (Paris: Éditions Garnier Frères, 1962), p. 24. See also reference in "Élévation" (*Les Fleurs du Mal*) to "le langage des fleurs et des choses muettes."

plant (in his poem beginning "Ausgesetzt auf den Bergen des Herzens") as a symbol of a last touch of sensibility "exposed upon the mountains of the heart."

In the first *tableau* of Maeterlinck's *L'oiseau bleu,* the Fée Bérylune appears with a question on her lips: "Avez-vous ici l'herbe qui chante ou l'oiseau qui est bleu?" But she is more concerned with the Blue Bird of Happiness than with possible echoes of the Blue Flower. A few years later, Guillaume Apollinaire introduces the song of a rose into the strange surrealist ball of "Les Collines." Paul Éluard, in "Après moi le Sommeil," sings of "le cri de la fleur amie"; and in *La poétique de l'espace,* Gaston Bachelard cites René-Guy Cadou's *Hélène ou le règne végétal,* in which "toutes les fleurs parlent, chantent, même celles qu'on dessine." [13]

Finally, turning to the Celts, we find the author of *Finnegans Wake,* that remarkable depository of innumerable lyric motifs, writing of "talkingtree and sinningstone" and exclaiming: "Padma, brighter and sweetster, this flower that bells..." [14]

Thus, over the years, from ancient times to the present, in enduring myth and folk tradition and significant literature, we hear the memorable and haunting voices of numerous plants and flowers. But what of the mandrake and its changing cry?

II

So far as we can tell, the earliest mandrakes had no voice at all. [15] The mandrake or mandragora has been identified with the fruit *dudaïm,* which apparently helped both Leah and Rachel to conceive sons by Jacob (Genesis XXX.14-16) and which is mentioned in the Song of Solomon (VII.13) in connection with the joys of physical love. From Greek times the plant has been cited

---

[13] *La poétique de l'espace* (Paris: PUF, 1957), p. 163.

[14] James Joyce, *Finnegans Wake* (N. Y.: The Viking Press, 1939), p. 598.

[15] For extensive discussion of the mandrake, see C. J. S. Thompson, *The Mystic Mandrake* (London: Rider and Co., 1934) and Albert-Marie Schmidt, *La mandragore* (Paris: Flammarion, 1958). There are also bibliographical notes of unusual interest on the subject in the English *Notes and Queries,* 8th Series, III (June 24, 1893), 498 and IV (Aug. 26, 1893), 174.

as providing relief from depression or worry when taken in wine (Hippocrates) and as a soporific (Aristotle). Because of its supposed aphrodisiac powers, the mandrake's fruit is said to have been called "apples of love" by the Greeks and "Devil's apples" by the more severe Arabs. [16] The suggestive and at times wildly obscene shape of its root doubtless accounts for the plant's supposed aphrodisiac and fertilizing powers, in accordance with the "doctrine of signatures," and this oddly human form enhanced the aura of strangeness that developed around it.

As early as the 3rd century B. C. Theophrastus gives a ritual procedure for getting the mandrake from the earth:

> ...It is said that one should draw three circles round mandrake with a sword; and cut it with one's face towards the west, and at the cutting of the second piece one should dance round the plant and say as many things as possible about the mysteries of love. [17]

The supposed erotic powers of the mandrake seem to animate this ritual; and it is of interest that the epithet *Mandragoritis* or "She of the Mandrake" has been sometimes applied to Aphrodite and that pieces of the root are apparently still carried as love charms by young men in Attica. [18]

In the first century A. D., Dioscorides and Pliny both cite the mandrake and refer to male and female species. [19] According to Pliny:

> Persons when about to gather this plant take every precaution not to have the wind blowing in their faces, and after tracing three circles around it with a sword, turn toward the west and dig it up. [20]

Apparently mandrakes were already dangerous.

---

[16] Thompson, p. 31.

[17] *Enquiry into Plants,* Bk. IX, Chap. VIII. 8 (Loeb Classical Library ed.), II, 259.

[18] Thompson, pp. 55, 57.

[19] Thompson (p. 47) notes that "as late as 1640 John Parkinson, in his *Theatrum Botanicum,* mentions that in England there were mandrakes and womandrakes."

[20] Cited by Thompson, p. 98.

Before the end of the first century, the Jewish historian Josephus gives details about the plant he calls *baaras,* generally identified with the mandrake, noting that the *baaras* can kill those who touch it. Josephus describes a safe way of obtaining the plant which has become a lasting part of mandrake lore:

> They dig a trench round about it till the hidden part of the root be very small. They then tie a dog to it, and when the dog tries hard to follow him that tied him, this root is easily plucked up, but the dog dies immediately, as if it were instead of the man that would take the plant away, nor after this need anyone be afraid of taking it into their hands. [21]

At this date, the mandrake apparently had no voice, and for many centuries thereafter it seems to have remained mute; but by the early 12th century a terrible cry is reported in a passage on the mandrake in the *Bestiaire* of the Anglo-Norman Philippe de Thaün which describes in detail the approved manner of gathering this lethal plant:

> ...Par engin est cuillie, / Oëz en quel baillie. / Om ki la deit cuillir / Entur la deit fuïr / Suavet, belement, / Qu'il ne l'atuche nient; / Puis prenge un chien lïé, / A li seit atachié, / Ki bien seit afamé, / Treis jurz ait jeüné; / E pains li seit mustrez, / De luinz seit apelez / Li chiens a sei trarat / La racine rumprat, / E un cri geterat, / Li chiens morz en charat / Pur le cri qu'il orat, / Tel vertu cele erbe at. / Rien ne la pot oïr / Ne l'estoce murir; / E se li om l'oeit / Eneslepas mureit. / Pur ço deit estuper / Ses oreilles, guarder / Qu'il n'en oie le cri. / Qu'il ne morge altresi / Cume li chiens ferat / Ki le cri en orat. / Ki at ceste racine, / Mult valt a medicine; / De trestute enferté / Pot trametre santé, / Fors seulement de mort, / U il n'at nul resort. / N'en voil or plus traitier... [22]

---

[21] Cited, *ibid.,* p. 90. Thompson (p. 93) quotes "the Arab Dioscorides," Ibn Beithar, as saying that the Arabs thought an evil jinn dwelt in the mandrake root "and that when being gathered the demon leaves the plant as it is raised from the ground and passes into the dog and kills it, so that the root may be handled in safety."

[22] Emanuel Walberg, ed., *Le bestiaire de Philippe de Thaün* (Suède: HJ. Möller; Paris: H. Welter, 1900), lines 1579-1613. The bestiary was probably completed by 1125 (see Urban Tigner Holmes, Jr., *A History of*

From the 12th century to the age of John Donne the traditional lore of the mandrake seems to have flourished on the con-
tinent and in Britain. Godefroy in his *Dictionnaire de l'ancienne
langue française*, V (1888), gives the spelling *mandegloire* for the
mandrake (with twelve variants, including *maindegloire*, and
the notation: "mot conservé sous la forme mandragore"); and he
cites the mandrake's appearance from the 12th and 13th centuries in *Le roman d'Alexandre*, *Fierabras*, the *Bestiaire divin* of
Guillaume de Normandie, the *Bestiaire* of Gervaise, and the *Livre dou tresor* of Brunetto Latini. Godefroy notes also the plant's
appearance in 1429 in the *Journal d'un bourgeois de Paris*, citing
a passage denouncing a current superstition that one would never
suffer poverty so long as he kept a mandrake wrapped "nettement
en beaux drapeaux de soye ou de lin."

From the late 16th century in England one hears the recurrent
shrieks, shrikes, lethal *groans,* and *hideous howles* of the mandrake in significant literature. [23] All this has left so grim a mark
upon the plant that one finds the following terse entry under "The
Vocabulary" in the back of a 19th-century volume on flower

Old French Literature from the Origins to 1300 [revised ed., N. Y.: Russell
and Russell, Inc., 1962], p. 60). Thompson (pp. 111-12) offers the following
translation of these couplets:

> "[The mandrake] is gathered by stratagem. Listen in what manner.
> "The man who is to gather it must fly [more likely, *dig*] round about
> it. Must take care he does not touch it. Then let him take a dog, bound.
> Let it be tied to it—which has been close shut up and has fasted three
> days and let it be shown bread and called from afar—the dog will draw
> it to him—the root will break—it will send forth a cry—the dog will
> fall dead at the cry which he will hear.
> "Such virtue this herb has, that no one can hear it but he must die
> and if the man heard it he would directly die. Therefore, he must stop,
> his ears and take care that he hear not the cry, lest he die as the dog
> will do which shall hear the cry.
> "When one has this root it is of great value for medicine, for it cures
> every infirmity—except only death where there is no help.
> "I will say no more about it."

[23] See for *shrieks*: Shakespeare, *Romeo and Juliet* (1595), IV.iii.47;
Heywood, *2nd Pt. Edw. IV* (1600), Wks. 1874, I.154; Webster, *The White
Devil* (1612), V.vi; for *shrikes*: Dekker, *Dreame* (1620), Wks. (Grosart),
III.39; for lethal *groans*: Shakespeare, *2nd Henry VI* (1592), III.ii.310; and
for *howles*: [Glapthorne] *Lady Mother* (1635),V.ii in Bullen, O.Pl.II.196.
(For some of these and other mandrake references, see *The Oxford English
Dictionary* under "Mandrake.")

symbolism with colored roses on its cover: "Mandrake... *Horror.*" [24]

Yet, already in the 17th century, mandrake groans are heard in terms of sorrow or suffering rather than as instruments of death. Thus John Donne, in "Twicknam Garden" (in his *Songs and Sonnets* [pub., 1633]), comes "blasted with sighs, and surrounded with tears" and pleads:

> ...Love let mee
> Some senslesse peece of this place bee;
> Make me a mandrake, so I may groane here,
> Or a stone fountaine weeping out my yeare. [25]

This is a far cry from the mandrake's hideous shriek that ends in the hearer's death. Two centuries later, Carlyle writes in this same tradition of "Ariel Melodies, and mystic mandragora Moans." [26] By this time interest in the "horror" of the mandrake seems to have much abated.

In the first half of the 19th century, imaginative literature on this most fascinating of plants turns in a new direction; and the once-terrifying mandrake, whose deadly cries had echoed over the centuries, undergoes a startling change in nature and in voice as well. Something of the Blue Flower of Novalis may have been at work along with something of French folklore and folk-song.

So far as I know, the singing mandrake appears first in literature in 1832 in *La Fée aux Miettes* (The Crumb Fairy) by Charles Nodier. The tale is told on St. Michael's Day by a youth in a Glasgow lunatic asylum. Michel, a young carpenter from Normandy, is seeking *la mandragore qui chante* (the only one of its kind in the world), whose story is in the secret books of Solomon. Michel claims to be the husband of La Fée aux Miettes, an ancient dwarf who becomes the Princess Belkiss (the Queen of Sheba) by night in his arms. A horoscope has prophesied that La Fée aux Miettes will not live more than a year after the first happiness of marriage, unless her husband can find the singing mandrake

---

[24] John Ingram, *Flora Symbolica* (London and New York, n.d.), p. 359.

[25] John Donne, *Complete Poetry and Selected Prose,* ed. John Hayward (Bloomsbury: The Nonesuch Press, 1929), p. 20.

[26] *Corn-law Rhymes* (1832): Misc. 1857.III.161. (See *The Oxford English Dictionary* under "Mandragora.")

which will give her life and youth. It will present itself voluntarily
to the hand made to pluck it. If Michel is worthy of his love, as
the last ray of the sun disappears on St. Michael's Day, he will
find the flower unfolding fresh and crimson under his fingers and
singing in unearthly tones a refrain from his childhood in Normandy:

> C'est moi, c'est moi, c'est moi,
> Je suis la mandragore,
> La fille des beaux jours qui s'éveille à l'aurore,
> Et qui chante pour toi!

As the sun goes down, Michel thinks he hears exquisite music
in his cell above the dying flowers. He runs to the mandrakes and
is never seen again in the asylum. Inmates claim that they saw
him at sunset balancing for a moment on the towers of the Catholic church with a flower in his hand and singing so sweetly
they could not tell whether the song came from him or from the
flower.

The mandrake sings again, at daybreak in J.-X. Lirou-Bastide's
Mandragores (1844), [27] and near the end of Flaubert's *Tentation
de Saint Antoine* (1872) in the ecstatic vision when Anthony sees
motion begin and life born under his eyes, and in "Amycus et
Célestin" of Anatole France's *L'étui de nacre* (1892). More recently,
there is a "mandrake music from the marrowroot" in the Celtic
world of Dylan Thomas ("Foster the Light"). But it is still Charles
Nodier who gives us the most memorable fragment of the mandrake song.

In *La Fée aux Miettes* the voice of the mandrake has changed
from the lethal cry of Philippe de Thaün's 12th-century bestiary,
and from the later *shrieks, shrikes, groans* and *howles,* to a lovely
music. It seems to have acquired meaning in common with the
wild flower of Blake and with the Blue Flower of Novalis, and
it joins the other singing plants and flowers of myth and folklore
and literature with a song that is all its own.

---

[27] Cited by Albert-Marie Schmidt. *La mandragore*, p. 114.

SOME OBSERVATIONS ON SYNTAX AND MORPHOLOGY IN THE *SOTTIE DES RAPPORTEURS* AND THE *SOTTIE DES SOTS FOURRÉS DE MALICE*

ROSALYN GARDNER
Gallaudet College

The *Sottie des Rapporteurs* and the *Sottie des Sots fourrés de malice,* numbers 6 and 33 of the Trepperel collection, are both dated by Eugénie Droz as having been composed around 1480. [1] The language is that of the *sots* and should be fairly representative of the common spoken language of the last quarter of the fifteenth century. Since the *sotties* are in verse, and the exigencies of rhyme and meter naturally affect the word order, care must be taken in drawing conclusions concerning the syntax. However, certain practices are discernible.

The definite article in Old French and early Middle French was used principally to particularize the noun. The use of the definite article with generalized nouns was well established in the fifteenth century. Yet, in the *Rapporteurs* and the *Sots fourrés,* the common practice was to omit the article before nouns used in the general sense, as well as before abstract nouns.

> Marchans tiendront tous loyaulté   (R 233)
>
> Moynes ne parlent plus aux dames   (R 179)
>
> Jacobins ont a Dieu promis   (R 167)

---

[1] Eugénie Droz, *Le recueil Trepperel. Les sotties* (Bibliothèque de la Société des Historiens du Théâtre, Vol. VIII; Paris: E. Droz, 1935), pp. 53, 73.

On ne verra plus chappellains
Tromper femmes a leur paroissains (R 205-06)

Et aultre chose ne pourchase
Que deduit et esbatement (Sf 8-9)

Soient gens de ville ou de court (Sf 169)

Vous lairés chappon et oyson
Pour menger de la venaison (Sf 25-26)

A few exceptions occur throughout the two plays.

Normans ayment bien les Bretons (R 243)

Les chatz ont fait a Dieu promesse (R 217)

Puis qu'ilz vivent des pouvres femmes (Sf 271)

The indefinite article in the fifteenth century more or less continued the practices of Old French; that is, it was generally used only to restrict the meaning. Otherwise it was omitted. In the texts under discussion here, one sees the indefinite article employed more frequently and not necessarily with any restriction of meaning.

Pour me trouver en ung combat (R 90)

C'est un grant confuion (R 122)

De la grandeur d'ung viel tonneau (R 143)

J'avoue Dieu, ilz ont sur le nez
Ung aulne de rouge esquarlate (R 148-49)

Ung mouton ne sera plus beste (R 250)

Qu'elle prent, c'est une nourrice (Sf 27)

(Aus)si ay je ouy dire a ung sot (Sf 78)

Ung grant tas de sotz estourdis (Sf 228)

J'estoye droicte comme ung jon (Sf 244)

Of twenty-three possibilities in the *Sots fourrés,* the article was used ten times, omitted thirteen. In the *Rapporteurs,* it was used eight times and omitted thirteen out of a possible twenty-one. The omissions are noted usually, though not without exception, after prepositions or negative expressions.

Je doubte qu'i ait jeu sans bourde (R 312)

Onc chien puant de passe passe (R 177)

Pour ne dire mot (342)

Il n'y a beste, soit serf ou bisches (Sf 19)

Et metre en chanbre com on fait (Sf 249)

Et j'eusse femme ung peu mignonne (R 186)

Les chatz ont fait a Dieu promesse (R 217)

Je scay bien de quoy moyne sert (R 192)

The treatment of the partitive in these two plays is variable. To express the concept of multiplicity of objects in an affirmative sentence, in a majority of cases the partitive construction was not considered necessary. Three examples of *de* alone were found in the *Rapporteurs*. The *Sots fourrés* continues the Old French usage.

Premier, nous avons veu chevreaulx (R 130)

J'ay veu cordenners faire toilles (R 288)

Toutes celles qui ont maris (Sf 154)

Mais qu'il y fauldra de chappeaux (R 43)

Vecy de bons petis langaiges (R 220)

Qu'il est de paiges macquereaulx (R 57)

J'ay de bons chiens parfaictement (Sf 13)

As a general but no means invariable rule, in the *Rapporteurs*, the preposition *de* is used before plural nouns after a general negation. It is omitted in the *Sots fourrés*. In line with current practice in the latter part of the fifteenth century, *de* regularly follows adverbs and nouns of quantity. Exceptions are rare.

Il n'est plus de larrons cousturiers (R 227)

Ha! je n'en vids jamais de telles (R 45)

Et ne boyvent plus mais que bieres (R 136)

Procureurs ne vueil ne advocatz (Sf 348)

Et vous doit autant de ducatz (R 109)

Sont marris qu'il n'est assez vins   (R 161)

Peu de gens sont au temps qui court   (Sf 167)

Ung grant tas de sotz estourdis   (Sf 228)

Omission of the partitive is noted after the prepositions *en, par,* and *sans.* For example, one sees *en cendres* (R 247), *par faulcetez* (Sf 126), and *sans avoir elles* (R 285). [2]

The true partitive, which in the fifteenth century expressed an indeterminate fraction of a quantity (as differentiated from the plural of the indefinite article), was not often expressed. This use of *de* with the definite article is still rarer in our texts. In the affirmative singular it is normally absent. Only one possible true partitive was found (in the *Sots fourrés*), and that is questionable because of the verb *donner.*

Desquels ilz ont aide et support   (R 34)

C'est par Dieu, de faire grant chere   (R 154)

Lequel m'a donné du tourment
De l'ennuy et douleur amere   (Sf 310-11)

After a general negation and adverbs and nouns of quantity, the use of *de* is favored in the *Rapporteurs.* It is usually omitted in the *Sots fourrés*

En serpent qui mord,
N'a point d'asseurance   (R 322-23)

Cloches ne feront plus de bruit   (R 258)

En Romme n'est plus simonye   (R 238)

Yvrongnes ne bouront que biere   (R 241)

Ne boit point la moitié tant d'eau   (R 144)

Qu'a luy venez s'il n'y a ame   (Sf 71)

Hay, tais toy et n'en dis plus mot   (Sf 76)

En chat qui repplique
Ne donne asseurance   (R 319-20)

---

[2] Here *elles* means "wings."

Subject pronouns, so often and regularly omitted earlier, are in general use in the *sotties*. In one hundred examples in the *Rapporteurs,* the pronoun was used eighty-five times; in the *Sots fourrés,* it was omitted only forty-eight times out of one hundred eighty-one. It is probable that many of the omissions were due to the number of syllables required by the meter.

The distinction between *tu* and *vous* in the singular seems well defined. The *sots* use *tu* when speaking to an equal, *vous* to a superior.

> It te part d'ung maulvais couraige
> De t'armer contre ton seigneur   (R 101-02)

> Propter quos, le vray chief d'onneur,
> Jesus vous doint joye et sancté   (R 106-07)

> Hay, tais toy et n'en dis plus mot   (Sf 76) [Captain to *sot*]

Any confusion is rare.

> Cappitayne, Dieu vous benye.
> Tu soye tresbien venu vrayement.   (Sf 110-11)

Direct and indirect object pronouns occur in their normal position, with two exceptions. When two object pronouns precede the verb, the direct object precedes the indirect object (except *se* which is always first in order), and *en* precedes *y.*

> Vien ça, vien, nous le te diron   (Sf 82)

> Sainct Jehan, il en y a plusieurs   (Sf 123)

> Il vauldroit bien mieulx
> Soy grater les yeux
> Que soy les hors traire   (R 336-38)

When a pronoun is the direct or indirect object of an infinitive which in turn depends upon a modal auxiliary or other verb, the pronoun precedes the latter. In few instances, following Old French procedure, *me, te, se* appear in the construction in their strong or disjunctive forms.

> Proserpine le debroit bien scavoir   (R 21)

> Qu'ils les y feront bien chauffer   (R 201)

Vous ont ilz voulu efforcer?   (Sf 234)

Sa, G[a]ultier, va les moy hucher   (R 30)

Que servir ne s'en pouvoient plus   (Sf 265)

Ou senglier, qui eschapper luy puisse   (Sf 20)

Rarely the strong form serves as the subject where one would expect the weak form. The reverse is also possible.

Et si ne scay moy qui le poist   (R 155)

Le vela, c'est il vrayement   (Sf 52)

The modern forms (with variant spellings) of the demonstrative pronouns and objectives are firmly established in these works. Gone is any distinction in meaning between the *cel* and *cest* forms. The reinforcing *-là* has become necessary when the need for differentiation between near and far is felt.

Comme ce fol me rapportoit?   (R 153)

Habillee m'ont de cest habit   (Sf 260)

A ces povres frans musequins   (R 60)

Les sergens de ceste ville   (R 211)

Je l'interprecte en ce point la   (Sf 285)

Qui est celluy qui crie ainsi?   (Sf 97)

Toutes celles qui ont maris   (Sf 154)

Laissez moy ceulx la, c'est assez   (R 118)

The invariable *ce* appears in its stronger form *cela* and with the relative pronoun *que*.

Laissons cela, ilz sont infames   (R 181)

Ce sont ilz, bien je les entens   (Sf 48)

Font ce qu'il veuillent a tous coups   (Sf 127)

Par ma foy, je croy bien cela   (Sf 286)

De tout ce qu'on ot   (R 343)

One might note use of both *que* and *qu'est-ce que* among the interrogative pronouns. The usual fifteenth-century contraction of *est-ce* to *esse* is made.

> Que luy as-tu dit au destroit? (Sf 65)
>
> Mais qu'esse qu'il faisoit? (Sf 62)

The relative adjective occurs, only in the *Sots fourrés,* but not to the extent that it appears in the non-conversational literature of the period.

> Durant lequel temps m'ont pillee (Sf 356)
>
> Lequel bon gouvernement oncques
> N'euz dessoubz luy que gens de bien (Sf 298-99)

It is difficult to make any statement concerning the position of adjectives in these two *sotties.* The rhyme often demands that the adjective be placed in a certain position. On the whole, allowances being made, it would seem that the position is more or less the same as in the modern language: *mauvais gouvernement* (Sf 252), *grant personnage* (R 103), *marchans fourrez* (Sf 141), *trosne imperial* (R 1). If this is true, the treatment of adjectives is more consistent that found in other fifteenth-century texts.

The adjectives *grand, fort, tel,* and the interrogative adjective and pronoun *quel* were neutral in gender in Old French; that is, there were no feminine form. The authors of the two *sotties* retained the Old French neutral form of *grand* with feminine nouns, although in the *Evangile des quenouilles,* written some years earlier, almost half of the feminine examples were feminine in form. [3] *Tel* regularly agrees in the feminine, as does *fort* in the single example found. On the other hand, the authors were a little more reluctant to renounce the neutral forms of *quel.* One finds *grans oreilles* (R 298), *grant chere* (R 154), *grant forfaicture* (Sf 205), *telle maniere* (R 151), *tellement quellement* (Sf 196), *forte et puissant* (Sf 243), *quel chose* (R 113), *quel plaisance* (Sf 184), *quel creature* (Sf 186), *quelle maniere* (Sf 67).

---

[3] Rosalyn Gardner and Marion A. Greene. *A Brief Description of Middle French Syntax* (University of North Carolina Studies in the Romance Languages and Literatures, No. 29; Chapel Hill: The University of North Carolina Press, 1958), p. 28.

Little can be said concerning the agreement of the present participle because of the paucity of examples. In the *Rapporteurs*, it appears generally to follow the common usage of the period by agreeing in number (but not in gender) with its noun or antecedent, whether the participle is a true adjective or verbal adjective. There is only one occurrence (in the *Sot fourrés*) of the participle as part of a progressive tense.

> Jacobins ont a Dieu promis,
> Mectans tous es enffers leurs ames.   (R 167-68)

> Sus, sus, mes suppostz qu'on vous voist
> Procedans en ceste matiere.   (R 156-57)

> Et chevauschons sans selle, et pour le mieulx,
> Disant adieu, tant a mont com a val. (Sf 388-89)

> Qu'elle va ainsi boyteusant   (Sf 221)

The adjective *puissant* does not appear with a feminine form.

> Leurs femmes ont grosses ceintures
> Et en sont riches et puissans.   (Sf 144-45)

> Forte et puisant com ung lyon   (Sf 244)

Among locutions to be mentioned, one might point out the presence of such negative constructions as *ne ... plus mais que* (R 136), *ne ... que* (R 241, Sf 151), *ne ... ja* (Sf 171), *ne ... onc, oncques* (R 177, Sf 300), and *nenny* (Sf 134).

There is one survival of the archaic determinative complement: *Aux pourceaulx monseigneur saint Anthoine*. (R 269)

Because of rhyme and meter requirements, it is difficult to perceive the factors that determine uncommon word order. One can only note tendencies and interesting variation. Popular with the authors of both texts is the practice of placing the past participle before the subject and auxiliary verb in the past indefinite tense and passive voice.

> Englouty l'eust de tenebreure male   (R 14)

> Deffait tu as cest huys, tien, tien   (Sf 99)

> Car gastee m'ont totalement   (Sf 232)

Divisay fut le siecle vivement (R 5)

Car traictee suis trop desordonnement (Sf 198)

Habillee m'ont de cest habit (Sf 260)

Inversion of subject and verb after an adverb or short conjunction occurs in the *Rapporteurs* twice as often as the regular order. It will be noticed that short adverbs and conjunctions have a stronger influence than longer ones. For example, *puis, si, et si, et, aussi, tant,* and *encore* account for all the inversions noted; whereas, such adverbs as *toutesfois, vrayement, auffort, tant plus,* and *oncques* apparently had no effect. Such inversions occur less frequently in the *Sots fourrés.*

Et si ont juray tous les sains (R 263)

Tant portent ilz la cuille verd (R 190)

Puis n'a on pas tout emporté (R 67)

Si m'en fuiray je du debat (R 87)

Et dit en qu'il n'en est pas trop (R 180)

Vrayement ilz ont bien tempesté (R 70)

Aussi scauray je bien (Sf 379)

Ains que passe la sepmaine (Sf 181)

Mais vray[e]ment c'est grant dommaige (Sf 220)

Qu'oncques en ma vie je visse (Sf 121)

Et n'y a il nul qui dire puisse (Sf 176)

Et is also strong enough to hold the object pronoun before the verb in an affirmative imperative construction.

Et me dicte, sans tromperie
De quels lieux vous venez tous? (Sf 115-16)

Another word order encountered is the position of the infinitive before the modal auxiliary in such sentences as *Mectre y fault une tente* (Sf 382). In negative locutions, both negative words appear at times before the verb, especially in the beginning of a sentence: *Pas ne dit* (Sf 217); *Point ne l'ont frappée* (Sf 235).

It would seem that, in their syntax and morphology, the texts examined are somewhat more conservative than other writings of the period and more conservative than one would expect, considering the popular and oral nature of the two plays.

THE DEPRECIATORY COMPARISON:
A LITERARY DEVICE OF THE MEDIAEVAL FRENCH EPIC

A. Robert Harden

Victoria College, University of Toronto

During a moment of justifiable wrath, Aalais, the mother of Raoul de Cambrai, in the *chanson de geste*[1] hearing her son's name, cries scornfully:

> 1184 "Hom d'Aroaise ne vaut une cinele
> "Trop par sont bon por vuidier escuele
> "Mais au combatre, tex en est la novele,
> "Ne valent mie .j. froumaje en fissele."

The noble lady's outburst interests us here because of her use within four lines of two derogatory comparisons. Generally such comparisons are uttered by males, since they comprise the majority of characters in the *chansons de geste*. But, whether expressed by a male or a female, such depreciatory observations form a primary ingredient of the imagery found in this type of mediaeval literature. It is our purpose to examine firstly the elements which motivated the popularity of these devices and secondly the objects which frequently provided the comparison.

---

[1] P. Meyer et A. Longnon, *Raoul de Cambrai, chanson de geste du XIII siècle* (Paris: Société des Anciens Textes Français, 1882). In order to avoid the repetition of the term *op. cit.*, the bibliographical information concerning each work is given when it appears for the first time and is not repeated. Each citation is preceded by the name of the source of origin. Although many other *chansons de geste* were read in pursuit of these comparisons, the choice for purposes of citation has been limited.

It will be seen, when citations are made to illustrate them, that these derogatory comparisons occur generally in the speeches of the chief protagonist and that an examination of the more established characteristics of the latter make such devices almost inevitable. For *chanson de geste* heroes are almost invariably distinguished by a propensity to boast whether it be about their God, their king, their audacity, their armour, their virtue, their horse or their sword. The author of *Le Pèlerinage de Charlemagne,* to select a noteworthy example, underscores his satiric intent by overplaying magnificently this very quality in his epic figures. Of course, such self-appreciation leads the typical epic hero to depreciate roundly similar objects of personal veneration in his attitude which provides the motivation for the depreciatory comparison. It becomes a sort of conventional braggadocio reminiscent of the utterances of modern day sports enthusiasts as they either participate in or observe a game of competitive skill. Obviously then as now the more defamatory the comparison, the more soothing it is to the hero's vanity or perhaps to his hidden anxiety, and the less palatable to his adversary's pride. The authors of the *chansons de geste* in utilizing them are no doubt recording some very authentic and familiar speech practices which harmonize well with the swagger, bravado and scornful arrogance they permit their heroes.

Turning now to the precise nature of these comparisons, two elements must be borne in mind. Firstly the position in the line of Poetry of the object with which the enemy, his weapons, his beliefs or his choice of values are to be compared and secondly the mediaeval concept of what objects are considered sufficiently suitable for scornful comparison. Since the majority of these expressions occur in the second half of the line of poetry the objects of comparison are usually the final words. As a result it could be suspected that they might become a sort of *cheville,* a convenient ending which satisfies the desire for a rhyme or an assonance. However they are consistently so apt, as we shall see, that the intended insolence is usually most effective and the use of the word justified. As to what objects are considered pertinent in the mediaeval mind for use in depreciatory comparisons, an examination of numerous *chansons de geste* reveals that they are confined to some six categories: cloth and clothing, food, money, plants, small armour and finally, creatures of the animal kingdom. The general policy in the selection of a suitable object is to choose something which underlines the inadequacy of a person or thing because it is too soft, too small, too old or so altered as to be incapable of self-preservation.

Beginning with the first category, cloth and clothing, the *chanson de geste, Fierabras,*[2] provides, by way of an introduction, three disparaging comparisons of enemy armour with cloth:

> 1658 L'aubers ne li valut le double d'un samin...
>
> 1795 Ne li valut l'aubers le taille d'un samis...
>
> 5734 Amont parmi son heaume ala ferir Milon
> Ne li valut li cercles vaillant .l. auqueton...

The first two materials are forms of silk, the third is a type of cotton. *Les Narbonnais*[3] contains a comparison, under similiar circumstances, with buckram:

> 7534 Par mi l'escu d'un bon espié trenchant
> Ausi le perce com un viez boquerant...

There are in *L'Entrée d'Espagne,*[4] in this same connection, two rather singular references to specific cloths which seem to be designated not so much to denigrate the particular type of material as to indicate its unsuitability as a protection in warfare. The first of these is to cloth of Flanders, the traditional home of excellent weaves:

> 8698 Escuz ne obers n'i valt une toile de Flaindre...

The second is to the unadorned and simply dyed cloth used by mountain dwellers:

> 10161 Me li vaut son obers un dras gris de montaigne...

[2] A. Kroeber et G. Servois, *Fierabras* (Paris: Anciens Poètes de France, 1860).

[3] H. Suchier, *Les Narbonnais, chanson de geste* (Paris; Société des Anciens Textes Français, 1898).

[4] A. Thomas, *L'Entrée d'Espagne, chanson de geste franco-italienne* (Paris; Société des Anciens Textes Français, 1913).

Leather, more especially the fine soft leather from Cordova, suitably provides this simile, again from *L'Entrée d'Espagne*:

10050 Les eschuz trencherent come fust cordevaire...

Garments themselves are also used to illustrate the inadequacy of enemy material. Here are two examples also from the last-mentioned *chanson de geste*. A long, sleeveless coat which descended to the calves of the leg, called a *gone*, is very aptly used to illustrate the ineffectiveness of certain armour:

10693 Ne escuz ne obers ne li vaut une gone...

In another passage the poet employs the more general term *mantel*:

10720 Que ne escuz ni obers ne li vaut un mantel...

Closely related to clothing are the following accessories and objects of personal hygiene: gloves, shoes, buttons and combs. To indicate the popularity of the first of these, here are three examples. First, from *Raoul de Cambrai*, comes the following:

3090 Qe sa proiere ne li valoit .j. gant...

Then in *La Chevalerie Ogier de Danemarche* [5] are these lines:

9804 Il ne cremoit en France nule gent.
Ne mais Ogier cremoit sor tote gent;
De tos les autres ne donast un besant.
Il ne les prise la mantance d'un gant...

And finally in *Otinel* [6] there occurs:

86 Ne vallent pas la couture du gant

---

[5] J. Barrois, *Le Chevalerie Ogier de Danemarche, chanson de geste de Raimbert de Paris* (Paris, 1842).

[6] F. Guessard et H. Michelant, *Otinel, chanson de geste publié pour la première fois d'après les mss. de Rome et de Middlehil* (Paris: Anciens Poètes de France, 1859).

In *Doon de Maience* [7] the author chooses to use an old shoe for his unflattering purposes:

3079 Mès il ne (le) prisa vaillant uns soulers viés...

Both *Otinel* and *Raoul de Cambrai,* amongst many others, provide illustrations of derogatory comparisons to buttons. In the former the reference is to a human being:

61 Dist Otinel, "Ne vos prise .11. bouton...

In the latter it is to war:

3951 "Qe ceste guere ne vaut pas .j. bouton...

Les Quatre Fils Aymon [8] offers this comparison to a comb:

15855 Li haubers de son dos ne li vaut .l. viez paigne...

Turning from clothing to food the choice for comparison becomes more elaborate. In dealing with edible objects consideration is given by the poet not only to their smallness and malleability but also, as might be expected, to their flavor. Probably the most abused object is the egg. The mediaeval author, however, is not content with underlining the mere fragility of this food as a source of scathing comparison but he seems to enjoy the addition of an adjective or two to his description. For some curious reason these eggs are usually "peeled." This refers, perhaps, to hard-boiled eggs which, having lost their shells before being consumed, are doubly vulnerable to being crushed. In *Huon de Bordeaux* [9] the expression appears in the following:

6544 La cercle fent, ne vaut .l. oef paré...

[7] A. Rey, *Doon de Maience, chanson de geste* (Paris: Anciens Poètes de France, 1858).

[8] F. Castets, *Les Quatre Fils Aymon, chanson de geste* (Montpellier, 1909).

[9] F. Guessard et C. Grandmaison, *Huon de Bordeaux, chanson de geste publiée pour la première fois d'après les manuscrits de Tours, de Paris et de Turin* (Paris; Anciens Poètes de France, 1860).

In *Raoul de Cambrai* it takes this form:

> 8706 Car n'i forfirent vaillant .i. oef pelet...

The following variation is to be found in *Horn*: [10]

> 1451 La bataille en avras ja de mei per a per
> Que la lei de Mahun ne vaut d'oeuf un quarter...

Garlic is treated with similar disdain in these comparisons. First from *Otinel* comes:

> 1385 Tot son pooir ne vaut .ll. aux pelez...

Then in *Huon de Bordeaux* we find:

> 5740 "Je ne le pris vaillant .l. ail pelé...

Fruit also contributes to the subject matter of these comparisons. Interestingly enough not only its smallness but also its gastronomic utility, or lack of it, obviously recommends it for this purpose. An example of small fruit utilized for derogatory comparison is provided by the author of *Les Quatre Fils Aymon* who notes that a coat of mail is not to be valued at the worth of a gooseberry:

> 15921 Li haubers de son dos n'i vaut une grossele...

Larger but equally soft fruit also inspire unflattering comparisons, as for instance, the apple, a fruit which in the two instances cited here, both from *Raoul de Cambrai,* is qualified by adjectives which contribute to its malleability:

> 3005 "Ne'en puis mais, sire, tex est ma destinée
> "N'i vaut desfense une poume parée."

and

> 1907 "Ce nel desfen a m'espie forbie.
> "Je ne mepris une poume pourie...

---

[10] M. K. Pope, *The Romance of Horn by Thomas* (Oxford: Basil Blackwell, Anglo-Norman Texts Society, 1955).

The pear, more particularly the medlar, a fruit which quite appropriately is eaten in a decomposed state, finds its way into a similar expression. The author of *La Chanson de Guillaume*[11] writes in this fashion:

> 2115 Cele baptisterie ne valt mie une nife...

Two types of berries which no doubt draw depreciatory comment because although handsome to observe are so bitter in taste as to make them inedible and consequently ideal objects for derogatory comparison are those of the service tree and those of the oak apple The first of these, the *alisier,* botanically resembles the mountain ash. Its greenish-brown berries, know as *alies* frequently become objects of derision. In *Gaufrey*[12] this line occurs:

> 178 "Que nul n'i mefferoit la monte d'une aillie...

The second of the fruits is the *cine.* In all probability this is the modern French word *cenelle,* as Godefroy indicates, a term for the hawthorne or the holly, trees whose reddish berries are attractive but unpalatable to humans. However there is another French word *cinelle* which could be applicable here and perhaps be even more ironic. This is what is known in English as the oak apple or sometimes oak gall. It is the large, fleshy excrescence produced by the sting of the gall-fly on the oak leaf and, of course, is no fruit at all. Its pretentions to gustatory satisfaction both in shape and name make it a first-rate choice for something superficially appealing but pragmatically useless. But it little matters to which one reference is precisely made. The mockery of the comparison is evident and its frequency would indicate its popularity. In *Gaufrey* it occurs in these lines:

> 3661 A .ll. mains, si grant coup et de tele ravìne,
> Que la pel du serpent n'i valut une cine...

---

[11] D. McMillan, *La Chanson de Guillaume* (Paris: Société des Anciens Textes Français, 1949-1950).

[12] F. Guessard et P. Chabaille, *Gaufrey, chanson de geste* (Paris: Anciens Poètes de France, 1859).

In *Raoul de Cambrai* it is discovered in the citation with which this article began and also in the following:

4689 La bone coife ne valt une cinele...

Several humble vegetables are victimized in a similar fashion to the fruit. Matamar, the pagan king, urges on his men with this contemptuous comparison of a shallot to the French defense the *Moniage Guillaume*:[13]

4229 "Ferés, paien! Franchois erent ja outre,
    La lor defense ne vaut une excaloigne...

Similarly, a related and common vegetable, the leek participates often in a derisive comparison. *Les Quatre Fils Aymon* offers this example:

9448 Ne priseroie tout vaillant .l. porion...

In *Gaufrey* another product of the garden represents the quality of military defenses in this manner:

6856 Bien voit que sa deffense n'i vaut une leitue;...

The author of *Aymeri de Narbonne*,[14] as did many others, finds the chestnut an ideal vegetable for comparative comment. This citation is from his poem:

1781 Ne li valut l'escu une chastengne...

Bread and cheese, such noble, every-day staples of a generally soft quality also seem convenient for abuse. The author of *Huon de Bordeaux*, for example, prefers to have the contrast further underlined by having the bread in a crumbled form:

5082 Ne poise pas .l. blanc pain buleté...

---

[13] W. Cloetta, *Les deux rédactions en vers du Moniage Guillaume, chanson de geste du XII siècle* (Paris: Société des Anciens Textes Français, 1906-1913).
[14] L. Demaison, *Aymeri de Narbonne, chanson de geste* (Paris: Société des Anciens Textes Français, 1887).

An illustration of the use of cheese for a similar treatment can be drawn from *Les Narbonnais*:

> 164 Foi que Dieu qui nos fist a s'ymaje
>   Ja n'en avroiz vaillesant un fromaje...

From the point of view of meat, curiously enough, it is fowl which seem to suffer most from the indignities of these comparisons. In *Doon de Maience* there are two examples. The first involves the chicken under quite drastic circumstances:

> 11455 "On ne le doit prisier .1. pouchin escaudé...

The second concerns the partridge, or really a portion of its anatomy:

> 8482 Mès il ne li valut l'ele de .ll. pertris...

Apparently the reference to the wing is quite popular for it is found also with regard to other poultry as in these lines from *Horn*:

> 1663 Horn brandist sun espié, dunt l'enseigne traine,
>   Si ferit un paien, Turlin de Taberine —
>   Parent iert Gudelaf, nez iert de sa cosine ...
>   Que l'escu ne li vaut l'ele d'une geline...

Even a duck, perhaps not for its food value but rather for its soft down, becomes the object of contempt. In *Gaufrey* one of the heroes comments:

> 3334 Il ne me doutent mie vaillissant un mallart...

Moving from food to plants we observe that it is the delicate, brittle nature of the branches or the tender nature of the flowers and their leaves which lend them admirably to derogatory comparison. The elder-berry bush, the modern French *sureau,* is a notable example of a plant which becomes a symbol of weakness. It is particularly appropriate because the centre of each of its branches is composed of a soft pulp which when removed, as is often done by young children to make pea-shooters, further reduces its ability to withstand aggression. In *Gaufrey* the example is the following:

> 3230 La cuignie trestourne, s'a le cheval feru,
>   En ll. moitiez le coupe comme un raim de séu...

The *Moniage Guillaume* offers this unhappy commentary on a French defeat:

> 4815 Muerent Franchois a duel et a tristor
>   Toute la force ne lor vaut une flor...

The leaf of the rose fulfils a similarly melancholy function in this line from *Doon de Maience*:

> 7020 Qu'autresi li derout comme .l. feul de rosier...

The leaf of the lily in *Les Narbonnais* is also utilized in related circumstances:

> 7015 Desoz la bocle li a fret et malmis,
>   N'i vaut l'auberc une foille de lis...

Vine shoots and branches of common trees frequently represent hopelessly inadequate weapons or individuals. *Les Quatre Fils Aymon* has, for example:

> 17476 Et vos ne vales mie .l. rainsel de sarment...

Another very effective branch for use in such comparisons because of its extreme pliability is the water willow or *osier*. In *Aymeri de Narbonne* the enemy inspires this observation:

> 504 "N'en tandront mès vaillisant une osiere...

A piece of straw is a more obviously suitable and an often used object in these defamatory phrases Here is an example from *Doon de Maience*:

> 3108 Que tout li a derout comme .l. festu de blé...

Sometimes the militant shape of a plant's leaf provides a most apt comparison to ineffective armour. In this instance it is the arrow-head, *la fléchière* a plant whose leaves, although shaped like its namesake are as incapable of preventing or inflicting destruction as the helmets found in this comparison. It comes from *Aliscans*:[15]

> 605 Elmes ni haubers (n'i) vaut me flekire...

It is curious to find that weapons which themselves are so frequently the subject of comparisons can also become the object of them. Generally, however, they are small accoutrements which have no destructive ability. A favorite is the spur. An example is to be noted in this angry outcry of the protagonist in *La Chevalerie Ogier de Danemarche*. He reacts to his banishment with this expresión of despair:

> 7259 De tote France bani par mesprison
> Ne m'as laissieé qi vaille un esperon...

Closely related to this is the stirrup which the author of *Gui de Bourgogne*[16] employs in this speech of his hero:

> 2582 Quant l'enfes Guis l'entent, si dist parole fiere:
> "Vos mentes. Se Diex plaist, qui est voirs justiciere,
> "N'enporterés du mien qui vaille une estriviere,
> "Que del sanc de ton cors ne soit bien esligiée...

A particularly scornful reference is that to the *quintaine*, the manikin which is the helpless object of attack in jousting. This construction which consists of armour arranged to represent a man makes an admirable choice to portray inadequacy. This example occurs in *L'Entrée d'Espagne*:

> 8760 Son escu ne li vaut li cor d'une quintaine...

Also to be included with military accoutrements is the drum. Allusions to it in a derogatory sense are very frequent. As this

---

[15] F. Guessard et A. de Montaiglon, *Aliscans, chanson de geste* (Paris: Anciens Poètes de France, 1870).

[16] F. Guessard et H. Michelant, *Gui de Bourgogne, chanson de geste publiée d'après les manuscrits de Tours et de Londres* (Paris: Anciens Poètes de France, 1859).

instrument is associated with the enemy in the *chanson de geste,* it would seem natural that its worth would be discounted by the French. However since the terror struck into the hearts of the non-infidel by these drums is well-known, this attitude on the part of the French knights would appear to be something akin to genuine braggadocio. [17] *L'Entrée d'Espagne* contains this reference:

> 10143 Ne L'escuz ne l'obers ne li vaut un tambor...

One of the most telling sources of derogatory comparisons is to be found in money. A particularly interesting sidelight on this is the use that is often made of currency which came from areas where under certain conditions the silver or gold content could be so debased that the money could frequently be suspect. One has only to handle some of this mediaeval money to discern the high copper content in some of the coins, a quality which would, of course, automatically reduce their worth in comparison to purer currencies. Such conditions usually reflect either economic difficulties or conscienceless minters. Under the circumstances we are discussing references are made, naturally enough, only to money of the lower denominations. There are, of course, numberless allusions to *denier* and *denrée* without any source of origin being specified. Of singular note, however, are the references to these coins when they are qualified with the adjective *abatu.* This word, it seems, could apply either to poorly minted money or perhaps money from which a portion had been removed to fabricate illegal currency. One of many such uses of this abused *denier* is found in the *Moniage Guillaume:*

> 3938 Et dist Guillaumes: "Synagon, que dis tu?
> Toute ta force ne vaut mie un festu
> Envers Franchois, un denier abatu...

Amongst some of the specified coins frequently mentioned under unflattering conditions are the following:
the *mensois,* money from Le Mans as in *Girart de Vienne:* [18]

---

[17] See note to line 852, *La Chanson de Roland* (New York: D. C. Heath, 1929), ed. by T. A. Jenkins.

[18] G. Yeandle, *Girart de Vienne, chanson de geste, according to Ms. B XIX Royal of Brit. Mus.* (New York: Columbia University Press, 1930).

154 Tote no terre nos tient en tel defois
Que n'i prenons vaillissant .ll. mensois...

the *balois,* money from Bâle as in *Raoul de Cambrai*:

2466 Toutes ces armes ne valent .j. balois...

the *parisi* also from *Raoul de Cambrai*:

1618 Ne lor laira[i] qi vaille .j. parisi...

the *pavois,* money from Pavie as in *L'Entrée d'Espagne*:

10186 Ni escuz ni obers valisant un pavois...

the *angevin,* currency from Anjou which suffers particularly from derogatory comparisons as in *Gui de Bourgogne*:

4209 Quant or voit Aquilant qu'il estoit si sorpris
Que ne lui vaut desfendre vaillant .ll. angevins...

Strictly foreign coins, especially those which add something of the oriental atmosphere of the Saracen world, often appear in the texts. The most common are the *besant* and the *mangon.* Even though both of these are gold coins they receive the same contemptuous treatment in these comparisons as that endured by French money of baser metal. The *besant* is a coin of ancient ancestry. Constantine the Great had minted a gold coin which was called a *solidus.* When a similar coin appeared much later in Western Europe it was known as a *bezant* or *byzant* because of its association with the Eastern Empire. The *mangon,* [19] a coin whose etymology is not precisely known—DuCange believes it is related to the word *marca* but one wonders it if would be too extreme to find it related to the currency known as *mancusus,* because of the representation of a hand on it—also occurs in unfelicitous comparisons. This coin is apparently equivalent to two *besants.* In *Gui de Bourgogne* this line is illustrative of the *besant*:

[19] A. R. Frey, *Dictionary of Numismatic Names* (New York: Barnes and Noble Inc., 1947), p. 142; see also; F. F. V. Schrötter, *Wörterbuch der Münzkunde* (Leipzig und Berlin: Walter de Gruyter and Co., 1930), p. 366.

7566 Mes ne lor vaut la monte d'un besant...

Les Narbonnais contains this example of the *mangon*:

980 Con nos n'avom vaillesant un mangon...

Another coin of low value repeatedly found in the *chansons de geste* under the circumstances we are discussing is the English farthing. This line is from *Aymeri de Narbonne*:

> 394 "Que encor tienent .XX. mile Sarrazin
> "Qui ne vous doutent vaillisant .j. ferlin...

Leaving monetary comparisons we come to the final group, that involving the animal kingdom. Very often the references are not to the total creature but only to some portion of the anatomy. At one point in the story of the *Moniage Guillaume,* the hero is about to go on a perilous journey to collect fish for Lent. He has earned the hatred of his fellow monks because of his boisterous, non-academic behaviour. Before his departure he is asked to leave behind his civilian garments. He willingly does so. When mention is made of his *bliaut,* the abbot makes this contemptuous observation

> 697 "Sir Vuillaumes, Par l'ame de mon paire,
> Jou nel vauroie por une vace vaire...

L'Entrée d'Espagne alludes in a similar fashion to a cow horn:

10777 Anc ne le puet forfere vallant un cor de vace...

A de-horned sheep, comes to symbolize something worthless, no doubt because of its inability to defend itself. *Doon de Maience* presents this version:

11461 Ne prison vostre don .l. mouton escorné...

The dog also provides as might be expected many opportunities for unflattering comparisons. *Gaufrey* offers a typical example with descriptive adjectives:

8756 "Que Mahon ne vaut pas .l. ort mastin puant...

Another version from the *chanson de geste* is the following:

> 8599 "Que Mahommet ne vaut vaillant .l. chien tués...

The soft and handsome skin of the stoat or ermine inspires this comparison from *Horn*:

> 1666 Que l'escu ne li vaut l'ele d'une geline
> Ne l'auberc dublentin la pel d'une hermine...

A product of the animal world, wax, provides this comparison which is both apt and modern. In *L'Entrée d'Espagne* it appears in this fashion:

> 4939 A le frer Corsabin fait il un tel colp rendre
> Que li trence li heume cum se fust cire tendre...

Birds and creatures of the sea are also victimized. This example for the former coming from *Raoul de Cambrai* involves the swallow:

> 4662 "Je ne me pris vaillant .j. arondel...

From the ocean comes this source for a scornful comparison. The citation is drawn from *La Mort Aymeri de Narbonne*: [20]

> 2439 Auberc ne broine ne li vaut .ll. coquilles...

Finally, to keep within the animal kingdom and yet to move from its lowest common denominator to its highest we discover the following comparison. In this instance the inspiration for the depreciatory reference is a wife. In almost all previous examples we have been dealing with men and their military relationships with the enemy. We now come to a situation which involves male relationships within the hierarchy of the feudal state. The scene comes from the *L'Entrée d'Espagne*. A rebellious knight, regretting his treasonous conduct appears before Charlemagne, beseeching the king's pardon for his actions. He kneels before the monarch and his gestures draw this comparison from the author:

---

[20] J. Couraye du Parc, *La Mort Aymeri de Narbonne* (Paris: Société des Anciens Textes Français, 1884).

7048 Cil vient au roi por le comant Naimon
     Le duch Herbert se mit en çenulon
     Ausi cum dame quant oit feit mesprison
     Ver son mariç e vout querir pardon...

Thus, from humble articles of clothing to the distaff side, the author of the mediaeval epic ranges in his search for the suitable depreciatory comparison. As we have seen, this literary device developes primarily from his hero's exalted appreciation of his own material and spiritual values, and his correspondingly low opinion of the same qualities in his enemies. It is symptomatic of his boastful, noisy speech as he attempts to intimidate his opponent and buttress his own courage. In addition, it provides, by its very nature, an insight into those elements of mediaeval life which, justly or unjustly, could be seized upon as objects of contempt.

ON THE INFLUENCE IN ENGLAND OF HENRI ESTIENNE AND BONAVENTURE DES PERIERS: THE SOURCES OF SCOGGINS JESTES (1613)

J. WOODROW HASSELL JR.
University of Georgia

Since an article on international literary influences is almost always addressed to at least two categories of specialists, the author must be particularly careful to identify clearly the persons and works with which his essay deals. It will be useful, therefore, to indicate here that the present article is concerned principally with Henri Estienne and his *Apologie pour Hérodote*, Bonaventure des Périers and his *Nouvelles récréations et joyeux devis,* and the English jestbook the *Jestes* of Scogin.

Henri Estienne (1531-1598), it will be recalled, was perhaps the most distinguished of the eminent Estienne family of printer-scholars, and the *Apologie pour Hérodote* (Geneva, 1566) is a commentary on the morals of his times, in which we find a vast amount of narrative material.

Bonaventure des Périers (1510[?]-1544[?]) was a *valet de chambre* of Marguerite de Navarre. He is best remembered for his *Cymbalum mundi* (1537) and the work that concerns us here, *Les Nouvelles récréations et joyeux devis,* published posthumously by Robert Granjon in Lyon in 1558. This short story collection was translated in part into English and published in London in 1583 and again in 1592 (this time in abbreviated form) under the title *The Mirrour of Mirth and Pleasant Conceits.*

Apparently the *Jestes* of Scoggin appeared for the first time in the sixteenth century, although only fragments of the early printings survive. The first complete, or nearly complete, edition of this early text is that of 1626. Probably in an effort to capitalize on the popularity of the older redaction of the *Jestes* the London printer R. Blower published in 1613 a collection also entitled *Scoggins Iestes* but differing radically in content from the earlier work. It is with this edition, or rather different jestbook, of 1613 that we are concerned here.

In his monograph entitled *Eulenspiegel in England*, Friedrich Brie included a study of the *Jestes* of Scogin (or Scoggin). [1] In adition to a general discussion, in which he showed convincingly that the *Jestes* of 1613 is almost completely different from the edition of 1626, Brie presented a study of the sources of the tales in the 1613 edition. Although a creditable piece of work, his study is incomplete and not always entirely accurate. It is the purpose of this essay to correct and to add to the data presented by Brie.

The inspiration for this article stemmed from two statements by earlier scholars. The first was F. P. Wilson's observation that the compiler of *Scoggin's Jestes* (1613) had "clearly consulted the [English] translation [of Des Périers' tales] of 1583 [*i.e., The Mirrour of Mirth*]." [2] That Wilson had not applied this idea to a general study of the sources of the *Jestes* was enough to arouse one's curiosity. The second statement was Brie's assertion that twelve of the *Jestes* were derived from Des Périers' collection. [3]

A preliminary investigation of Des Périers' contribution to the *Jestes* of 1613 produced the material for the following table (the letter B precedes the entries supplied by Brie; question marks in the left-hand column indicate pairings which in my opinion are incorrect; the interrogation point in the right-hand column belongs to Brie; the letter M indicates those of Des Périers' tales which appear in *The Mirrour*):

---

[1] Friedrich W. D. Brie, *Eulenspiegel in England* (Berlin, 1903), pp. 81-91 (Palaestra XXVII). The discussion by Ernst Schulz (*Die englischen Schwank-bücher bis herab zu "Dobson's Drie Bobs"* [1607] [Berlin, 1912], p. 66) adds nothing of significance to what Brie said about *Scoggin's Jestes* (1613).
[2] F. P. Wilson, "The English Jestbooks of the Sixteenth and Early Seventeenth Centuries," *The Huntington Library Quarterly*, II (1938-39), 140, n. 45.
[3] *Eulenspiegel in England*, p. 88.

TABLE I

	Scoggin's Jestes (1613)								*Les Nouvelles récréations...*	
1.	B no.	4	appears to be derived from				no.	3	M
2.	B "	5	"	"	"	"	"	"	34c	M
3.	B "	6	"	"	"	"	"	"	34d	M
4.	B "	15	"	"	"	"	"	"	15 (?)	M
5.	B "	16	"	"	"	"	"	"	7	M
6. ?	B "	20	"	"	"	"	"	"	2c	
7.	B "	22	"	"	"	"	"	"	41	M
8. ?	B "	31*	"	"	"	"	"	"	103	
9.	B "	39	"	"	"	"	"	"	58	M
10.	B "	40	"	"	"	"	"	"	40c**	M
11.	B "	50	"	"	"	"	"	"	12	M
12. ?	B "	63	"	"	"	"	"	"	36	
13.	B "	65	"	"	"	"	"	"	33	M

* Brie erroneously listed this as no. 32.
** Brie should have omitted the letter *c*.

This table served as the basis for further study of Des Périers' contribution to the English collection. It should be noted that I added one pair of entries to those provided by Brie and that the validity of three of the pairings which he had proposed was questioned.

The next problem to be considered was that of the immediate provenance of these tales. Had the compiler of the *Jestes* borrowed from the French text of Des Périers, or was Wilson correct in believing that he had consulted *The Mirrour of Mirth*? [4] A confrontation of the texts [5] proves conclusively that *Jestes* 4, 5, 6, 15, 16, 22, 39, 40, 50, and 65 were adapted directly from *The Mirrour*.

At this point in our investigation the validity of pairing 1-5, 7, 9-11, and 13 in Table I had been established (we must not forget that the borrowings were from the English translation of Des Périers' tales, not from the French text). Remaining to be considered were the other three, those involving *Jestes* 20, 31,

---

[4] While Brie was aware of the existence of an English translation of Des Périers' tale collection (or of a part of it, to be exact), he apparently did not consider the possibility that this translation, *The Mirrour of Mirth*, might have served as a source for *Scoggin's Jestes* (1613).

[5] The texts used were: (1) *Scoggins Iestes...* (London: Raph [*sic*] Blower, 1613); (2) Bonaventure des Périers, *The Mirrour of Mirth and Pleasant Conceits*, tr. T. D., ed. J. W. Hassell, Jr. (Columbia: University of South Carolina Press, 1959).

and 63. That versions of these tales appear in the *Nouvelles récréations et joyeux devis* (but not in *The Mirrour of Mirth*) made it necessary to consider the possibility that these *Jestes* might have been derived from the French text of Des Périers' tales, but the hypothesis seemed improbable for two reasons. In the first place, as Brie had shown in regard to several of the *Jestes*[6] and as I had just demonstrated with respect to ten more, the compiler of the English collection seems to have had a predilection for English-language sources. In the second place, *Jestes* no. 20 differs significantly from Des Périers' version but adheres to a well-defined narrative tradition which goes back to Poggio.[7]

From earlier studies of Des Périers' tales we knew that versions of the three narratives in question (*Jestes* 20, 31, and 63) also occur in Henri Estienne's *Apologie pour Hérodote*.[8] It was distinctly possible, therefore, that the compiler of the *Jestes* had borrowed from the *Apologie,* or, more probably, from an English translation of Estienne's work. At first, however, this line of investigation did not prove fruitful. A comparison of *Jestes* 20, 31, and 63 with the corresponding passages in the *Apologie* produced what seemed to be inconclusive results, as did the comparison of those *Jestes* with the corresponding passages in the early seventeenth century translation of the *Apologie,* the *World of Wonders.*[9]

And then, in a collection of bibliographical data I found listed under Henri Estienne's name a work entitled *The Stage of Popish Toyes* ([London], 1581), which proved on examination to be an anti-Catholic propaganda work derived in large part from the *Apologie.* Here at last was the solution to the problem of the origin of *Jestes* 20, 31, and 63 (and much more besides, as we shall see). The parallel passages given below prove conclusively that the three *Jestes* in question were adapted directly from *The Stage of Popish Toyes*:

---

[6] *Eulenspiegel in England,* p. 88.

[7] See J. W. Hassell, Jr., *Sources and Analogues of the* Nouvelles récréations et joyeux devis *of Bonaventure des Périers* (Chapel Hill, 1957), I, 32-34.

[8] Henri Estienne, *Apologie pour Hérodote,* ed. P. Ristelhuber (Paris: Liseux, 1879), II, 346, 252, 253.

[9] Henri Estienne, *A World of Wonders...* (London: Norton, 1607), pp. 321-322, 285.

Scoggin's Jestes (1613), sig. C3[v].

How Scoggin Tooke a Frier Tardie.

In Rome there was one Frier Thomas, who to observe the straigt lawes of their religion, had his concubine close in his bed to help him say his mattens at midnight now Scoggin... comming up of a sodaine into the chamber in the morning (by chance they both a slepe) he saw foure naked feete hang out of the bed, whereat he seemeth greatly to wonder, and sodainly put his hand [sic] out of the window and mainely cryed, what ho, come see a miracle, come see a miracle for Frier Thomas hath foure legges: whereupon they were so ashamed that they knew not how to excuse the matter.

The Stage of Popish Toyes, pp. 71-72.

...a Jesuite, who, to observe the straight lawes of their religon, had his Concubine close in his bed to help him say his Mattins at midnight: And his boy or Novice comming up in the morning (by chance they both asleepe) he saw foure naked feete hang out of the bed, whereat he was so amazed, as he sodainely put his head out at the windowe, and mainely cryed: ho, come see a myracle, for my Mayster hathe foure legges.

Scoggin's Jestes (1613), sig. C8[v].

Of a Jesuite That Spake Against Scoggin.

After this Scoggin grew in hate among the Friers, because he many times made Jestes upon them, whereupon there was a Jesuite that would always speake mightily against Protestants, thinking Scoggin to be one, affirming that he would proove a Protestant worse then a Divell, for (said he) if I meete

The Stage of Popish Toyes, p. 51.

But a Jesuite... used his sermon in playner termes who made it no conscience to sweare by God, in despight of the Protestantes: affirming that he woulde prove, how they were worse then the Divel. For (said he) if I meete with the Divel, & blesse my selfe but with the signe of a Crosse, he wil straight flye from me: But if I make the signe of

with a Divell, and blesse my selfe but with the signe of the crosse, hee will straight flie from me: but if I make the signe of the crosse to a Protestant, by God he will flie upon me, and be ready to strangle me.

a Crosse to a Protestant, by God he will fly upon me, & be redy to strangle me.

Scoggin's Jestes (1613), sig. F2.

How Scoggin Excommunicated His Parishioners.

Within a while after this, Scoggin received a certaine scroule from the Cardinall and a Bishop, wherein was written the names of sundry men and women, that hee should excommunicate, the which scroule by chaunce hee let falle into a little hole of his pocket, for remedy whereof he helped himselfe in this order, for with the losse of the paper, hee had lost the remembrance of all the names hee should have then excommunicated, and therefore thus he said, I excommunicate all those that are within that hole, whereupon remembring himselfe better of the matter, he excepted the Cardinall and Bishop who had thereunto set their hands and seales, else had the Bishop and Cardinall bin both of them excommunicated.

The Stage of Popish Toyes, p. 54.

This same Doctor, that in one yeere was become so wyse, receyved a certayne scedule or little scroll, from the Byshoppe of Paris and the Officiall, wherein was written the names of sundry that he shoulde excommunicate, which (by chance) he let fall into a little hole of hys Pulpit, for remedie whereof he helped himselfe with this pestilent practize, as one that with the losse of the Paper, had lykewise lost the remembrance of their names whom he shoulde excommunicate. And therefore sayde, I excommunicate all those, that are within that hole: and yet in the ende (remembryng himselfe better of the matter) he excepted the Byshoppe, and the Officiall, who had subscribed to the same.

A further comparative study of *Scoggin's Jestes* of 1613 with the document of 1581 produced equally convincing evidence that *Jestes* 1, 2, 3, 17, 18, 19, 21, 23, 24, 25, 30, 32, 33, 45, and 60 were derived directly from *The Stage of Popish Toyes*. In this group there is one entry, no. 45, about which a difference of opinion could exist. Brie maintains [10] that it was derived from *Mery Tales, Wittie Questions and Quicke Answeres*, no. 102 (actually his reference is not correct; the story which Brie had in mind must surely be the one numbered 122 in the Hazlitt edition [11]). However, a comparison of the text of the *Jestes*, no. 45, with that of the *Mery Tales* and then with that of *The Stage of Popish Toyes* (pp. 50-51) provides convincing evidence that the story in the *Jestes* was adapted directly from the latter, not from the *Mery Tales*.

This brings us to the question of the origin of the other one of the *Jestes*, no. 54, which according to Brie was derived from the *Mery Tales* (no. 58). It is true that these are both versions of the story of the numskull who is persuaded by tricksters that he is dead, but a comparison of the two texts does not convince one that the variant in the *Jestes* was taken from that of the *Mery Tales*.

On the other hand, Brie was entirely correct in asserting [12] that eleven of *Scoggin's Jestes* (1613) were borrowed directly from *Tarlton's Jests*, [13] and he may well have been right in attributing [14] the ultimate origin of *Jestes*, no. 2, to Morlini, although, as we have seen, its immediate source was *The Stage of Popish Toyes*.

Brie also maintained that four of the *Jestes* of 1613 were derived from the other redaction of *Scoggin's Jestes*. A comparison of the texts [15] shows clearly that three of the four pairings proposed by Brie are correct, that nos. 41, 44, and 64 of *Scoggin's Jestes* (1613) were lifted almost word for word from the older version. However, no. 35, which Brie also considered derived from the

---

[10] P. 88.

[11] *Shakespeare Jest-Books...*, ed. W. Carew Hazlitt (London: Sotheran, 1881), pp. 134-136.

[12] P. 88.

[13] The editon which I consulted was the following: *Old English Jest Books. Tarlton's Jests...*, ed. W. Carew Hazlitt (London, 1866).

[14] Pp. 88-89.

[15] The editions used were that of 1613, cited above, and the following: *Old English Jest Books. Scoggin's Jests...*, ed. W. Carew Hazlitt (London, 1866).

earlier redaction (apparently he had in mind no. 3, "How Scogin Deceived the Skinner"), was probably taken from another source.

Since it has not been possible for me to examine the problem of the contribution made by *Howlglass* to the *Jestes* of 1613, I accept provisionally, but without vouching for it, Brie's view [16] that eight of the *Jestes,* nos. 7-14, were derived from the collection of stories about Eulenspiegel.

The data presented above may be summarized in tabular form as follows (in the table abbreviated titles are used; thus *"Jestes"* indicates *"Scoggin's Jestes* (1613)"; after references to *Popish Toyes* I have indicated in parentheses the location, in the Ristelhuber edition, of the corresponding passages in the *Apologie*):

TABLE II

Jestes	no.	1	was	adapted	directly	from	*Popish Toyes*		pp. 30-31*	
"	"	2	"	"	"	"	" "		p. 47	(II, 242-243)
"	"	3	"	"	"	"	" "		pp. 66-67	(II, 200)
"	"	4	"	"	"	"	*The Mirrour*	no.	1	
"	"	5	"	"	"	"	" "	"	26	
"	"	6	"	"	"	"	" "	"	26	
"	nos.	7-14	were	derived	from	*Howlglass,* according to Brie.				
"	no.	15	was	adapted	directly	from	*The Mirrour*	no.	10	
"	"	16	"	"	"	"	" "	"	5	
"	"	17	"	"	"	"	*Popish Toyes*	p.	12	(II, 366)
"	"	18	"	"	"	"	" "	pp.	8-9	(II, 77)
"	"	19	"	"	"	"	" "	p.	74	(I, 202-204)
"	"	20	"	"	"	"	" "	pp.	71-72	(II, 346)
"	"	21	"	"	"	"	" "	p.	61*	
"	"	22	"	"	"	"	*The Mirrour*	no.	31	
"	"	23	"	"	"	"	*Popish Toyes*	p.	60	(II, 206)
"	"	24	"	"	"	"	" "	p.	13	(II, 140)
"	"	25	"	"	"	"	" "	p.	51	(I, 106)
"	"	26	— — — — — — of unknown origin — — — — —							
"	"	27	was	adapted	directly	from	*Tarlton's Jests*	no.	25	
"	nos.	28 and 29	— — — — — of unknown origin — — — — —							
"	"	30	was	adapted	directly	from	*Popish Toyes*	p.	14	(II, 364)
"	"	31	"	"	"	"	" "	p.	51	(II, 252)
"	"	32	"	"	"	"	" "	p.	46	(II, 191)
"	"	33	"	"	"	"	" "	p.	46	(II, 191)
"	"	34	"	"	"	"	*Tarlton's Jests*	no.	42	
"	"	35	— — — of unknown origin (see comment made above) — — —							
"	"	36 §	was	adapted	directly	from	*Tarlton's Jests*	no.	61	
"	"	37	"	"	"	"	" "	"	62	
"	"	38	— — — — — — — of unknown origin — — — — —							
"	"	39	was	adapted	directly	from	*The Mirrour*	no.	38	
"	"	40	"	"	"	"	" "	"	30	
"	"	41	"	"	from	*Scoggin's Jestes* **		"	58	
"	"	42	"	"	directly	from	*Tarlton's Jests*		"	71	

---

[16] P. 89.

Jestes	no.	43	— — — — — — — of unknown origin — — — — — — —				
,,	,,	44	was adapted from *Scoggin's Jestes* **		no. 29	
,,	,,	45	,, ,, directly from *Popish Toyes*		pp. 50-51	(II, 245-246)
,,	,,	46	,, ,, ,, ,, *Tarlton's Jests*		no. 50	
,,	,,	47	,, ,, ,, ,, ,, ,,		,, 41	
,,	,,	48	,, ,, ,, ,, ,, ,,		,, 51	
,,	,,	49	— — — — — — — of unknown origin — — — — — — —			
,,	,,	50	was adapted directly from *The Mirrour*		no. 8	
,,	,,	51	,, ,, ,, ,, *Tarlton's Jests*		,, 60	
,,	,,	52	— — — — — — — of unknown origin — — — — — — —			
,,	,,	53	— — — — — — — of unknown origin — — — — — — —			
,,	,,	54	— — — — — of unknown origin (see discussion above) — — — —			
,,	,,	55	— — — — — — — of unknown origin — — — — — — —			
,,	,,	56	— — — — — — — of unknown origin — — — — — — —			
,,	,,	57	was adapted directly from *Tarlton's Jests*		no. 4	
,,	,,	58	,, ,, ,, ,, ,, ,,		,, 5	
,,	,,	59	— — — — — — — of unknown origin — — — — — — —			
,,	,,	60	was adapted directly from *Popish Toyes*		p. 51	(II, 372)
,,	,,	61	— — — — — — — of unknown origin — — — — — — —			
,,	,,	62	— — — — — — — of unknown origin — — — — — — —			
,,	,,	63	was adapted directly from *Popish Toyes*		p. 54	(II, 253)
,,	,,	64	,, ,, from *Scoggin's Jestes* **		no. 70	
,,	,,	65	,, ,, directly from *The Mirrour*		,, 25	
,,	,,	66	— — — — — — — of unknown origin — — — — — — —			

* I have not been able to find a version of this story in the *Apologie pour Hérodote.*

§ Cf. *The Stage of Popish Toyes*, p. 32, and the *Apologie pour Hérodote,* ed. cit., II, 16.

** The older redaction.

From the foregoing discussion the following conclusions are indicated:

1. The compiler of the *Jestes* of 1613 was indebted to Des Périers for ten of his stories, which were all taken, almost word for word, from *The Mirrour of Mirth.*

The three *Jestes* the origin of which was incorrectly attributed by Brie to Des Périers were actually derived from *The Stage of Popish Toyes,* as were fifteen others of the *Jestes.* Of these eighteen tales, sixteen apear to have been adapted by the compiler of *The Stage of Popish Toyes* from the *Apologie pour Hérodote* of Henri Estienne.

Thus, through English translations or adaptations of their works, Des Périers and Estienne contributed twenty-six of the *Jestes,* or about forty per cent of the collection.

2. Contrary to Brie's view, it is doubtful that the compiler of the *Jestes* utilized the *Mery Tales* as a source.

3. Brie's statement that eleven of the *Jestes* were taken directly from *Tarlton's Jests* is correct, as is his view that three of the *Jestes* of 1613 were derived from the other redaction of *Scoggin's Jestes*. It is doubtful that the fourth tale attributed by Brie to the last named work was actually taken from it.

4. It is probable that, as Brie believed, eight of the *Jestes* of 1613 were adapted from *Howlglass*.

5. These data warrant the further conclusions that the *Jestes* (1613) was a product of the most outrageous plagiarism and that its compiler, who clearly had a taste for foreign works in English translation, seems to have borrowed most of his material, probably all, from English-language sources. [17]

[17] I should like to offer my sincere thanks to the Director and to the staff of the Folger Shakespeare Library for making available texts without which this article could not have been written.

SOME ASPECTS OF THE TROUBADOUR CONTRIBUTION TO THE *DOLCE STIL NUOVO*

Elliot D. Healy
Loissiana State University

The influence of the troubadours of Provence on the development of Italian poetry is universally recognized. It is immediately obvious, for example, that the poets of the Sicilian school are in all essentials a group of transplanted troubadours writing in a different idiom. Their poetic modes, *genres,* aproach to love, attitudes and postures constitute a clear continuation of the procedures of the poets of the *langue d'oc* who had been highly esteemed in Italy since the late twelfth century.

With the Tuscan school, however, beginning toward the end of the third quarter of the thirteenth century, and culminating in Dante himself, we are faced with a different matter. Here opinion is divided. Some would say positively that the poetry of the sweet new style owes nothing to the singers of Provence, indeed that Dante and Dante alone is the creator of the *dolce stil nuovo.* Thus Francesco Biondolillo in a study of Dante's poetic art states categorically, "Il creatore del 'dolce stil nuovo' è Dante, soltanto Dante," adding that Dante not only recognized that he was different from the poets of the Sicilian school and the early Tuscans, but also from his immediate predecessors who are usually classified as *stilnovisti* poets, men such as Guido Guinizelli, Guido Cavalcanti, Cino da Pistoia, Lapo Gianni, Dino Frescobaldi, and Gianni Alfani. [1] This is simply another way of saying that there are

---

[1] *Poetica e poesia di Dante* (Messina, 1948), p. 23.

differences in gradation in the work of the poets of the *dolce stil nuovo* group. No one would be inclined to question the superiority of Dante with respect to his predecessors in the sweet new style. It may seriously be questioned, however, that Dante would have "created" a new poetic doctrine without the example of those who had begun before his time to construct the framework of the *dolce stil nuovo.*

Luigi Tonelli in his highly interesting treatment of the subject put it somewhat differently. He makes a distinction between the *stil nuovo* and the *dolce stil nuovo,* the first being the new poetry of the Tuscan School (Guinizelli, Cavalcanti and others), no longer Sicilian or provençalizing, but clear, original, with realism of subject matter and approach, and still attached to the earth, whereas the term *dolce stil nuovo* is not applicable until the advent of Dante who represent a further stage in which poetry is impregnated with *dolcezza e soavità.* [2]

The other extreme of this point of view was well expressed by the late Joseph Anglade, a French provençalist who, almost alone in his generation, fully appreciated the literary qualities of troubadour poetry. Anglade saw Dante as simply a troubadour of stature and his Beatrice as another troubadour "lady". "L'immortelle Béatrice de Dante n'est que la femme idéale de la poésie méridionale chantée par un troubadour de génie." [3]

Somewhere between these two extremes lies a more reasonable and demonstrable evaluation of the relationship between the work of the troubadours and of their celebrated heirs, the poets of the *dolce stil nuovo,* which it will be the purpose of this study to consider briefly.

It might be well to indicate the principal differences most often noted between troubadour poetry and the creations of the *stilnovisti.* It will be conceded at once that both school wrote what is essentially a love poetry dedicated to singing the praises and virtues of woman. It is in the basic love concept and approach that the two currents are seen as being most widely divergent. The troubadour are regarded as having their feet, and their thoughts, close to mother earth, whereas the *stilnovisti* inhabit a

---

[2] *Dante e la poesia dell' ineffabile* (Firenze, 1934), pp. 88-89.
[3] *Les Troubadours de Toulouse* (Toulouse et Paris, 1928), p. 8.

more rarefied stratum between earth and heaven. The troubadours are essentially a product of the feudal system, and their worship of womankind is part and parcel of the homage which a man owes to his overlord and which he expresses by singing the praises and virtues of his lord's wife. He is highly imitative in his compositions, accords maximum importance to the formalized metrical system which is his by tradition and inheritance, and is devoted at one and the same time to a perpetuation of the poetic platitude of his fellows and to a deliberate literary obscurity which he proudly labels *trobar clus* and which has as its aim the exclusion of the uninitiated from participation in the intricacies of his thought and verbal pyrotechnics. Such, at any rate, is a picture of troubadour poetry quite frequently presented.

In contrast to this somewhat depressing description of a vital period in the poetic history of the western world, the poets of the *dolce stil nuovo* are credited with developing a poetry freed of contact with mundane matters, imbued with a new philosophy and intellectualism which embarks upon a quest for the meaning of love, eternally seeking an answer to the question: "Che è amore? Donde e como nasce?" It is deeply concerned with the essential kinship between love and the gentle heart, for as Dante himself put it, "Amore e'l cor gentil sono una cosa." It involves a learned approach to the problem of love, and basically it reflects the thirteenth century preoccupation with learning. It owes much, in effect, to the wave of fervor for knowledge which swept through Italy in this stimulating period of its literary and intellectual history. The most remarkable creation, however, of the *dolce stil nuovo* is its concept of the *donna angelica*. Maurice Valency has a piquant description of the ladies of the *stilnovisti* poets: "These ladies are infinitely more mysterious than the ladies who inhabit the troubadour songs. We have no idea of where they come from or where they go; their very nature is in doubt, whether human or divine." [4] This statement may be open to question with respect to the "dame" of the troubadours, and we make a slight reservation concerning it. Toward an understanding of the phenomenon of love inspired by such ladies the poets of the *dolce stil* brought an almost scientific type of investigation. They were interested not

---

[4] *In Praise of Love* (New York, 1958), pp. 209-210.

in the physiology of the ladies themselves, but in the physiology of the amorous sentiments aroused, in the mechanical and even anatomical devices by which love was created from the sight of the lovely object which was the lady. But in his avid interest toward an understanding of the mechanics of love's birth, the poet is not so much concerned with the lady as he is with a projection of himself into the metaphysical aura which surrounds the lady. Physical desire is so remote as to be almost non-existent. The poet's unflagging interest centers upon an attempted explanation of the phenomenon of beauty which confronts him and of his reaction to it. I can do no better than to cite Maurice Valency again in this connection, in a pithy, if somwhat exaggerated observation, wherein he says, "Ultimately, this poetry has little to do with women." [5]

If the two preceding summaries of the basic procedures of the troubadours and of the *stilnovisti* poets seem oddly disparate in substance, it is probably because few have tried, until quite recently, to analyze the philosophic purport of troubadour poetry. It is demonstrable that the gap which exists between the two schools, though definite and tangible, is far less wide than is generally assumed. In fact, the *rapprochement* is so close that I have no hesitancy in urging that the troubadours and the *stilnovisti* poets represent in a clear and continuous process of evolution a poetic development which links the Middle Ages and the Renaissance.

It is generally recognized by provençalists that following the flourishing years of the twelfth century a change in the tone of troubadour literature took place early in the thirteenth century, and particularly in the wake of the Albigensian crusade which occupied the two decades between 1209 and 1229. There can be no question that the devastation of the flourishing civilization of southern France by the crusading armies of Simon de Monfort had an equally devastating effect on the morale of the troubadours. Their singing became less joyous, less permeated with the things of this earth, and more concerned with the spirituality of life. As Antoine Thomas put it very neatly, "Les derniers troubadours ont pris très sérieusement le change, et, ayant une fois

---

[5] *Ibid.*, p. 210.

lâché la proie pour l'ombre, ils se sont acharnés à faire de cette ombre une réalité ...on émascula le dieu (de l'amour) et on put alors brûler sans crainte et sans scrupules de l'encens sur ses autels..." [6] This would seem to suggest that the troubadour concept of love underwent a sudden change of direction and emphasis at a given point of time. It is indeed true that the period following the Albigensian Crusade did see an accentuation of the change in the direction of troubadour love poetry, but it would be too much to expect that a single political event, even such a shattering one as disastrous civil war, would be the sole explanation of what actually took place.

As a matter of fact there were many indications even in the work of troubadours of the classic period (i.e. the second half of the twelfth century) to indicate that the tendency toward a gentler and more ethereal concept of love was already in full evolution. Bernart de Ventadorn, to cite one notable example, was convinced that poetry existed for the sake of expressing love, and that neither poetry nor love is of any avail unless both come from the sincere heart:

> Chantars no pot gaire valer,
> Si d'ins dal cor no mou lo chans;
> Ni chans no pot dal cor mover,
> Si no i es fin'amors coraus.
> Per so es mos chantars chabaus
> Qu'en joi d'amor ai et enten
> La boch'e·ls olhs e·l cor e·l sen.[7]

And in another passage, one incidentally which Dante himself must have noted, for he expresses the selfsame thought in the twentieth canto of the *Paradiso,* Bernart expresses that sense of ineffable joy which brings love and death close to each other in

---

[6] *Francesco da Barberino et la littérature provençale en Italie au moyen âge* (Paris, 1883), p. 54.

[7] Carl Appel, *Bernart von Ventadorn, Ausgewählte Lieder* (Halle, 1926), p. 11. "Singing can hardly be of worth, if from within the heart the song does not move; nor can a song come from within the heart if a sincere love does not dwell there. For this reason is my singing excellent, and in the joy of loving do I place my mouth, my eyes, my heart and my understanding."

the well known image of the lark which out of the very sweetness
of flight allows itself to fall to earth:

> Can vei la lauzeta mover
> De joi sas alas contral rai,
> Que s'oblid' e·s laissa chazer
> Per la doussor c'al cor li vai,
> Ai! tan grans enveya m'en ve
> De cui qu'eu veya jauzion,
> Meravilhas ai, car desse
> Lo cor de dezirer no·m fon. [8]

It seems to me that this is precisely the *dolcezza* and *soavità*
which Luigi Tonelli mentioned as Dante's chief contribution to
the new style. If this were an isolated example of this kind of
poetic imagery in the work of a single troubadour, mention of it
would be meaningless. But one has only to go beyond the an-
thologies, and scan the works of some of the less often cited
troubadours, as for example Aimeric de Belenoi, Albertet de Sis-
teron, Lanfranc Cigala, Aimeric de Pegulhan, Guilhem de Montanhagol, Bertran Carbonel and Guilhem d'Olivier d'Arles to find
an abundance of passages in which the increasing gentleness of
the later troubadour concept of love is made evident. Even in the
twelfth century many troubadours had sung of love in the same
gentle fashion as did the Tuscan poets and seen in it a mystic
element whose nature it was to uplift man and plant his feet upon
a path of honor. But it is in the thirteenth century that the tendency toward the ideal becomes the rule rather than the exception,
and it is no exaggeration to say that for a time the poetry of
the troubadours and that of the Tuscans run parallel until that
moment arrives at which the lyric strain of Provence exhausts
itself, and its Italian counterpart goes on to the achievement of
even greater stature. It is, therefore, among the later troubadours
that we must seek the parallels which established the close relationship between the two poetries. It is of this period that

---

[8] *Ibid.*, p. 21. "When I see the lark joyously moving his wings against
the sun so that he forgets himself and allows himself to fall out of the
sweetness which penetrates his heart, oh such great envy comes to me of
him whose happiness I see that I marvel that my heart does not at once
melt from desire."

Joseph Anglade is speaking when he says, "Elle n'eut pas de peine à s'élever de plus en plus au-dessus de la terre, où est en somme son vrai domaine, pour remonter vers le ciel et s'y transfigurer." [9]

One of the most noteworthy innovators among the thirteenth century troubadours was Guilhem de Montahagol of Toulouse. This troubadour flourished in the middle years of the thirteenth century, and thus is a near predecessor of Guinizelli and Cavalcanti. He was doubtless already a promising young poet in 1233 when Gregory IX turned the administration of the Inquisition in Southern France over to the Dominicans, who took their mission seriously enough to stimulate a transformation in the emphases and direction of the troubadour doctrine of courtly love. Since the latter was considered by the Church to be an immoral doctrine it became necessary for poets either to renounce their time honored tradition, or to seek some way in which to reconcile it with the austerities of Christian morality now on the point of being enforced with some rigor. Montanhagol at first expressed his vexation with the clergy for attacking the very principle of *la vie courtoise,* but he adopts nevertheless a new approach and as his editor Jules Coulet puts it, he says, "aux riches, aux nobles dames qui n'osent plus aimer, que l'amour n'est pas un péché; aux clercs, que le véritable amour est un principe de vertu." A few lines will demonstrate what he meant by true love:

> Anz es vertutz que·ls malvatz
> Fai bos, e·lh bon son melhor,
> E met om' en via
> De ben far tot dia;
> E d'amor mou castitatz,
> Quar qui·n amor ben s'enten
> No pot far que pueis mal renh. [10]

No troubadour of the early period would have dreamed of asserting that "d'amor mou castitatz" and the fact that Guilhem de

---

[9] *Les Troubadours de Toulouse,* p. 144.
[10] Jules Coulet, *Le Troubadour Guilhem de Montanhagol* (Toulouse, 1898), p. 70. "Rather is it a virtue for it makes the evil good, and those who are good are better, and it puts a man in the path of doing good always; and out of love grows chastity, for he who understands love well can not do that which later causes ill."

Montanhagol can and does say it serves to underline in somewhat dramatic fashion the fact that a revolution is occurring in troubadour thinking about love.

In this conection, however, it should be remembered that the thirteenth century witnessed the flowering of a special cult of the Virgin Mary in western Europe, and that this cult would spill over into the love poetry of the time and color it to some extent is to be expected and reckoned with in any study of woman's rôle in the new poetry. There was in effect a double cult, overlapping in nature. Many songs to the Virgin are love songs in a literal sense, and many *cansos d'amor* read as if addressed to a saint, so that the lady celebrated, spirit of the highest good, is identified with the spirit as a masterpiece of God's creation.

Guilhem de Montanhagol takes the position that a man who treats love in careless fashion does not really love or deserve to be loved, for genuine love does not seek to persuade a lady to any indiscretion, nor must a lover desire anything which may lead to his lady's dishonor:

> Qu'amors non es res mas aysso qu'enansa
> So que ama e vol ben lialmen,
> E qui·n quier als, lo nom d'amor desmen. [11]

As tempting as it may be to multiply examples of this kind, and they are by no means rare, it is perhaps more pertinent to note that among the troubadours who most nearly approach the sweet new style are a number who sojourned at some length in Italy, as well as the majority of the native Italians who composed in the Provençal tongue. Here there seems to be at least a suggestion that later troubadour poetry may in a certain measure have been influenced by attitudes and trends of thought existing in the air of the times in northern Italy. A few examples will serve to illustrate.

Representative of those troubadours who lived in Italy in the second quarter of the thirteenth century is Peire Raimon de Toulouse. Peire Raimon is indeed a poet of the heart, and the

---

[11] *Ibid.*, p. 140. "For love is nothing but that which uplifts what it honors, and wishes it every good in loyal wise, and he who seeks aught else belies the very name of love."

delicacy of his thought and phraseology is always pleasing. In words which call to mind the sonnet of Dante some seventy years later in the *Vita Nuova* beginning, "Tutti li miei penser parlan d'amore" he assures us:

> De fin'amor son tot mei pensamen
> E mei desir e mei meillor jornal
> E pres d'amor voill aver mon ostal... [12]

In him we find many echos of the increasing air of gentleness and subtlety which is infiltrating troubadour poetry and endowing it with a freshness and feeling which all but conceal the fact that it is a slowly dying art. With little originality, perhaps, but with genuine charm and a touch of unselfishness which is relatively rare in the utterances of earlier poets, Peire Raimon likens himself to a candle in this pleasing image:

> Atressi com la candela
> Que si meteissa destrui
> Per far clartat ad autrui,
> Chant, on plus trac greu martire
> Per plazer de l'autra gen. [13]

Elsewhere he speaks of his lady as a "flower, a mirror, and a light, the leader and the guide of all good breeding," [14] and he feels that if the service of love did not exist, that if courtship were not, there would be on this earth no goodness or serving or honoring. Here we find expressed in effect that equation which is more and more coming to be a troubadour conviction, namely, that love and courtesy, love and gentleness are necessary to each other. Is this not much the same as Dante's "Love and the gentle heart are one same thing?"

---

[12] Joseph Anglade, *Les Troubadours de Toulouse,* p. 68. "All my thoughts are of perfect love and all my longings and all my best days, and near unto love I wish to take my dwelling..."

[13] Joseph Anglade, "Poésies du troubadour Peire Raimon de Toulouse," *Annales du Midi,* XXXI (1920) ,p. 179. "Like unto the candle which destroys its very self that it may give light unto others, do I sing there where I suffer great martyrdom to give happiness unto others."

[14] *Ibid.,* XXXII, p. 285. "La bella qu'es flors e mirailz e lutz / E caps e guitz de tot ensegnamen..."

A few verses gleaned here and there from other thirteenth century troubadours who sojourned in Italy will serve as further indication of the growing *dolcezza* and *soavità* of the troubadour style. Guilhem d'Olivier d'Arles, for example, speaks eloquently of the ennobling and uplifting effects of love:

> Fals' amor no si pot dir
> Per dreg c'amors la nomnes
> C'amors autra res non es
> Mas can benvolen dezir. [15]

Peire Vidal thinks to see God himself when he looks upon his lady and insists that God when he created her fixed his entire mind upon the task, paying attention to no other thing. Aimeric de Belenoi, who dwelt for some years in Italy and who was one of a number of troubadours to be praised by Dante in the *De Vulgari Eloquentia* or in the *Divine Comedy,* expresses the somewhat novel thought that there where he loves the most he thinks to love but little. He feels himself too insignificant to love so perfect a being as his lady, too lacking in honor and nobility before the perfection which she represents. This sort of humility was not characteristic of the earlier troubadours, and it leads Aimeric to declare further that beauty, lineage and wealth are of no matter to him if they are not accompanied by inteligence and knowledge, for these latter qualities alone protect from fault and wrong a woman and the man who pays court to her. All good conduct, he believes, comes from loving sincerely.

Several Italian-born troubadours of this period write in much the same vein. Chief among them are Mantuan Sordello, and the Genoese Bonifazio Calvo and Lanfranc Cigala. Lanfranc Cigala, who died just as Guido Guinizelli was reaching maturity, is recognized as possessing so many *stilnovisti* qualities that we can hardly enumerate them here, while Sordello and Bonifacio Calvo, unequal though they were in poetic skill, both subscribe to the concept

---

[15] O. Schultz-Gora, "Die *Coblas Triadas* des Guilhem de l'Olivier d'Arle," Provenzalische Studien I, in *Schriften der Wissenschaftlichen Gesellschaft in Strassburg,* 1919, pp. 24-82. Cobla II, 1-4. "It may not be said that false love be rightly named as love, for love is no other thing than that which desires goodness."

that love is life's most ennobling influence, and the lady's peculiar rôle is to support man's faltering progress toward a higher good.

Another trait which the troubadours and the poets of the *dolce stil nuovo* share is their common interest in how love is born through the impact of beauty upon the eyes which in turn transmit the "sweet pain" to the heart. While these notions go back to antiquity and were to endure well into the sixteenth century there can be little doubt that the Italian poets inherited them directly from the troubadours. Aimeric de Pegulhan among many others offers an interesting treatment of this theme:

> Quar li huelh son dragoman
> Del cor, e l'huelh van vezer
> So qu'al cor platz retener;
> E quan ben on acordan
> E ferm tuit trei d'un semblan,
> Adoncas pren veray' amor nasquensa
> D'aisso que l'huelh fan al cor agradar,
> Qu'estiers no pot naysser ni comensar... [16]

Dante himself uses such conceits often. In the magnificent *canzone* from the *Vita Nuova* which begins, "Donne ch'avete intelletto d'amore" he speaks of the effect of love emanating from the eyes of his lady in this fashion: "From her eyes, as she turns them, there issue forth flaming spirits of love, which strike the eyes of those who look upon her, and enter so that each one finds the heart..." [17] And again in the equally impressive sonnet to which we have already referred and which begins "Amore e'l cor gentil sono una cosa" he says, "Beauty then appears in a lady of wisdom,

---

[16] William P. Shepard and Frank M. Chambers, *The Poems of Aimeric de Peguilhan* (Northwestern University Press, 1950), p. 74. "For the eyes are the interpreters of the heart, and they hasten to see what it pleases the heart to retain. And when they are in good accord and all three firmly of one mind, then does true love take its birth from that which the eyes cause the heart to find pleasing; for in no other wise can it begin or be born."

[17] *Vita Nuova (Opere di Dante*, M. Barbi *et als.,* Firenze, 1921), pp. 22-23.

> De li occhi suoi, come ch'ella li mova,
> escono spirti d'amore inflammati,
> che feron li occhi a qual che allor la guati,
> e passan sì che'l cor ciascun retrova...

which is so pleasing to the eyes, that within the heart there is born a desire for the pleasing thing, and it lasts long enough therein that it causes the spirit of love to awaken." [18]

Thus far we have touched upon the troubadour attitude toward woman as a being and as an object of courtship or adoration only indirectly. Here again we can observe the evolution of the poetic concept from the joyous carnality of Guillaume de Poitiers, earliest known poet of the *langue d'oc,* to the idealization of Montanhagol and his contemporaries who urge that the true lover would not only do nothing, but would desire nothing in any way harmful to his lady or to her honor. One of the basic misconceptions about troubadour poetry has been precisely the tendency to extend the physical aspects of courtship which we find among the first generations of Provençal poets over the entire range of their compositions, and thus to obscure the changes which took place after the Albigensian Crusade. The later concept of the *domna,* therefore, is well worth observing in its relationship to that of the *stilnovisti* poets.

Jacques Wettstein, in a Zurich dissertation of 1945, [19] saw the concept of the lady as an aspect of the troubadour ideal of *mezura.* *Mezura* we define as a sense of proportion, moderation and restraint. Wettstein sees the troubadours as attributing three aspects to *mezura.* There is the *mezura* of wisdom, which is the purest and highest form. Then there is the *mezura* of the knight, in which is involved the concept of nobility, and in which gentleness, courage and Christianity combine to create the chivalric ideal, and, thirdly, there is the *mezura* of the lover, or for that matter the *mezura* of the poet. Following this reasoning we may establish the equation that *mezura* is to the man of wisdom what nobility is to the knight, and what courtly love is to the lover. All are special aspects of the ideal of restraint. From this point of view the lady is seen

---

[18] *Ibid.,* p. 24.

> Bieltate appare in saggia donna pui,
> che piace a gli occhi sì, che dentro al core
> nasce un disio de la cosa piacente;
> e tanto dura talora in costui,
> che fa svegliar lo spirito d'Amore.

[19] *Mezura. l'idéal des troubadours* (Zurich, 1945), pp. 100-102.

as representing a *summum bonum,* a transcendent ideal, to which all the attributes of *cortezia* and all the qualities of goodness and benevolence are applied.

This equation is of considerable interest because we are accustomed to thinking of the *donna* of the *stilnovisti* poets, as an ethereal creature, removed from earth, an image and an ideal to be worshipped, who, in effect, descends from some remote and nebulous heaven to become a divinity guiding the steps of faltering man, still earthbound, into the higher realm of being and union with the infinite. The later troubadour concept differs from this attitude only in minor degree. The *domna* of the troubadours is possibly even more of an abstraction than the *donna* of the *stilnovisti* poets. We can create in our minds an image of Dante's Beatrice, however generalized it may be. No such image is possible for the vast majority of the ladies of the *cansos d'amor.* They are almost never individuals, but rather the collective representation of an ideal. Beatrice may be only half real, but she is an individual. The *domna* of the troubadours is the perfection of medieval *cortezia* created by the poet through a process of contemplation, and *cortezia* is for the troubadours above all a social quality. For Dante it is more profound and less social, and it results not in the *joi* of which the troubadour sings, but in *virtù.* For the troubadours it leads to happiness, to *joi*; for the *stilnovisti* poets it leads to beatitude. But despite this difference in degree and direction — the troubadour lady having come up from the earth and the lady of the Tuscan poets having come down from heaven — they all but meet in a common abstraction in which an ideal, rather than a woman, is sung in both *cansos* and *canzoni.*

It is my belief, therefore, that the gap which is commonly seen as existing between troubadours and *stilnovisti* poets is far less wide and far less profound than is so often assumed. For the later troubadours were moving rapidly toward a sweet new style of their own in their changing attitude toward love, in the sweetness and suavity of their verse, and in the increasing tendency toward a transfiguration of the image of the lady. Why they did not arrive at a complete achievement of a new poetic doctrine is a subject for further study. One reason which has always seemed significant to me, and which has also been noted by others, lies in the peculiar quality of the developing Italian language for clothing poetic images in a delicate, provocative and luminous language, in which the concepts of the poet are enveloped in a melodic verbal beauty which is the undying glory of the *dolce stil nuovo*. More than a hundred years earlier the *language d'oc* had been the only neo-Latin language deemed capable of the expression of the ultimate in poetic subtlety and imagery, but by the time of Guido Guinizelli the Provençal decline was imminent, and by Dante's time it was well under way. In part this decline is certainly the inability of the troubadours to shake off the shackles of formal versification and to modify the rigidity of their poetic tradition. It is gratifying to think that in dying this same tradition was able to pass on to illustrious successors much of the accumulated poetic wisdom of two centuries of literary creation.

THE CHARACTER *"FIGURA"* IN *LE MYSTÈRE D'ADAM*

R. E. KASKE
Cornell University

In the famous stage direction prefacing the twelfth-century Anglo-Norman *Mystère d'Adam,* the Deity is first introduced under the title *salvator,* and then immediately referred to as *figura*: "Tunc veniat salvator indutus dalmatica, et statuantur coram eo Adam [et] Eva. Adam indutus sit tunica rubea, Eva vero muliebri vestimento albo, peplo serico albo, et stent ambo coram figura..." [1] After the opening lesson and chant, His initial speech is accompanied by the direction, "Quo finito dicat FIGURA"; and in the rest of the play as we have it, He is consistently called *figura.* [2] This unusual designation is dismissed by Marius Sepet as "ce nom mystérieux," which "représente, croyons-nous, plus particulièrement le *Verbe,* qui doit plus tard s'incarner en Jésus-Christ." [3] To the best of my knowledge, it has received no further clarification in print; and a few casual inquiries among contem-

---

[1] Latin lines 6-10, ed. Paul Studer (Manchester, 1918), p. 1.

[2] Latin line 21, *ibid.,* p. 2; and Latin lines 22, 23, 27, 32, 70, 73, 74, 77, 79, 81, 82, 86, 89, 93, 154, and 156, besides the constant use of *Figura* to identify His speeches.

[3] *Origines catholiques du théâtre moderne* (Paris, [1901]), p. 139 n. 1. See also his *Le drame chrétien au Moyen Âge* (Paris, 1878), p. 128; and *Les prophètes du Christ* (Paris, 1878), p. 116. Some rather inconclusive suggestions are added by Hermann Breuer, "Untersuchungen zum lateinisch-altfranzösischen Adamsspiel," *ZfrPh,* LI (1931), 635-36; and Gustave Cohen, *Le Jeu d'Adam et Éve: Mystère du XIIe siècle* (Paris, 1936), p. 21 n. 1.

porary scholars seem to confirm a general unawareness of the explanation which follows. [4]

The opening verses of the Epistle to the Hebrews contain an explicit reference to God the Son as the *figura* of the Father:

> (1) Multifariam multisque modis olim Deus loquens patribus in prophetis, (2) novissime diebus istis locutus est nobis in Filio, quem constituit heredem universorum, per quem fecit et secula. (3) Qui cum sit splendor glorie et figura substantie eius, portansque omnia verbo virtutis sue, purgationem peccatorum faciens, sedet ad dexteram maiestatis eius in excelsis.

This concept of the Son as *figura* finds at least one other clear echo in twelfth-century ecclesiastical literature, at the beginning of Adam of St. Victor's best-known Christmas sequence:

> Splendor Patris et figura
> Se conformans homini,
> Potestate, non natura,
> Partum dedit Virgini. [5]

It seems all but certain, then, that our *figura* in the *Mystère d'Adam* must somehow reflect the "figura substantie eius" of Hebr. 1:3—a certainty further confirmed by the thematic parallel between His role as creator at the beginning of the play, and the statement "per quem fecit [Pater] et secula" in verse 2; and by the similar parallel between His initial appearance as *salvator,* and "purgationem peccatorum faciens" in verse 3. If so, what further significance can be found in this precise rather uncommon Scriptural allusion?

In medieval commentary on Hebr. 1:3, the words "splendor glorie et figura substantie eius" are conventionally explained as a reference to the divine nature of Christ, expressing His equality in Godhead with the Father as well as His personal distinctness

---

[4] An analysis of traditional Christian imagery in the *Mistère d'Adam* as a whole will be presented by Charles E. Hodges of Fordham University, in his dissertation on the use of hexaemeral material in the English mystery plays (University of Illinois).

[5] St. 1, ed. Léon Gautier, *Oeuvres poétiques d'Adam de Saint-Victor* (3rd ed.; Paris, 1894), p. 9.

from the Father. The interpretation is stated concisely, for example, in the *Glossa ordinaria*:

> *Qui cum sit splendor glorie, etc.*: Hic secundum divinam naturam commendat Christum, ostendens eum coeternum et coequalem Patri, eiusdemque cum eo substantie, sed alterum in persona....*Figura substantie*: Ecce aliter personaliter, ut figura ab eo cuius est figura; sed equalis, quia non parum dissimilis, sicut ipse ait: "Pater in me est [John 14:10,11] et "Qui videt me, videt et Patrem meum"" [*ibid.*, v. 9]....*Splendor* autem et *figura* (sicut et *imago*) proprie ad personam Filii referuntur et relative dicuntur. [6]

The twelfth-century exegete Hervé of Bourgdieu, with some help from Gregory the Great, offers a detailed analysis of this meaning in the word *figura*:

> ...addit, *et figura substantiæ ejus,* per quod ostenditur consubstantialis Patri. Quia est *figura substantiæ ejus,* id est expressa similitudo ejus, non secundum exteriora, sed secundum substantiam. *Figura subtantiæ ejus* est, id est forma et imago substantiæ ejus, quia quantus est Pater, tantus est ipse; qualis est Pater, talis est ipse, cujus substantiæ est Pater, ejusdem et ipse, quod est Pater, hoc est ipse. Filius enim, qui est sapientia Patris, per hoc quod ipsum revelat et facit cognosci, figuram substantiæ ejus exprimit....Cum enim æternitas Patris cernitur a nobis, prout infirmitatis nostræ possibilitas admittit, imago ejus mentis nostræ oculis antefertur, quia, cum vere in Patrem tendimus, hunc quantum accipimus per suam imaginem, id est per Filium, videmus, et per eam speciem, quæ de ipso sine initio nata est, eum aliquo modo cernere, qui nec coepit, nec desinit, conamur; et hæc est figura expressa

---

[6] *Biblia cum glosis ordinarijs et interlinearibus...* (Venice, 1495), fol. 1291^{r-v} (*PL* 114, col. 643). Besides the commentaries quoted immediately, see also Chrysostom, *Hom. in Hebr.*, I, 2 (frequently repeated by Latin exegetes), *PG* 63, cols. 20-22; ps.-Primasius, *PL* 68, col. 688; Luculentius, *PL* 72, col. 856; Alcuin, *PL* 100, cols. 1033-34; Rabanus Maurus, *PL* 112, col. 713; Haimo of Auxerre (ps.-Haimo of Halberstadt), *PL* 117, col. 823; Hatto of Vercelli, *PL* 134, col. 730; Lanfranc of Cantebury *et al.*, *PL* 150, col. 376; ps.-Bruno the Carthusian, *PL* 153, col. 492; ps.-Hugh of St. Victor, *PL* 175, 610; eter Lombard, *PL* 192, col. 405; and Alain de Lille, *Distinctiones, PL* 210, col. 791.

substantiæ Dei. Unde idem Filius dicit: "Nemo venit ad Patrem nisi per me" [John 14:6] .... [7]

Equally thorough is the exposition by an anonymous twelfth-century follower of Abelard, whose commentary survives in a Cambridge manuscript:

> *Et figura*: Omnis figura est similitudo, sed non omnis similitudo figura. Et non est aliqua creatura, que similitudinem quamcumque cum creatore suo non habeat. Corpu enim, etsi esse incepit, non deficit, in quo cum Deo convenit. Anima quoque rationalis est quemadmodum Deus. Et ita, cum tam corporea substantia quam incorporea aliquam cum Deo habeat similitudinem, ideo sepe per aves sive eitam per inanimata se significari voluit. Unde dicitur: "Petra erat Christus" [I Cor. 10:4]. Petra enim firme nature, que ideo in fundamento ponitur. Ita Deus in se firmus est nec deficere potest, a quo omnia sustentantur. In creaturis tamen, etsi similitudo aliqua reperiatur, numquam figura illius reperitur. Est enim figura similitudo illa, que rem representat secundum corporis lineamenta, quia videlicet et tale caput habet, tales oculos, talem nasum, toracem talem et talia omnia. Dicitur ergo Filius figura Patris, id est expressa eius similitudo, quia ei equalis est per omnia. Quippe eternus est sicuti ille et immensus sicuti ille. Eodem quoque modo in ceteris equalitatem habet. Unde ipsa veritas: "Qui videt," inquit, "me, Philippe, videt et Patrem" [John 14.9], id est in me potest cognosci Pater. Qui enim cognoscit meam substantiam, cognoscit et Patris, quia eiusdem sumus substantie; qui vero meam immensitatem, et Patris; qui eternitatem meam, et illius. [8]

Such exegeses suggest strongly that to the playwright of the *Mystère A'dam,* the character *figura* was essentially a dramatic device through which God the Father, and by implication the triune Godhead, could be presented without loss of theological

---

[7] *PL* 181, cols. 1522-23. Gregory (whose contribution extends from "Cum enim æternitas Patris" to the end), *Mor. in Iob,* V, xxxv, 64 (Job 4:16), *PL* 75, col. 714.

[8] Ed. Artur Landgraf, *Commentarius Cantabrigiensis in Epistolas Pauli e schola Petri Abaelardi* (Publications in Mediaeval Studies, II; Notre Dame, 1937-45), IV, 665-66.

accuracy under the image of the Son, Who is in turn visible to mortal eyes only as Christ. A device of this kind would agree closely with the statement of Gregory repeated by Hervé (quoted above) that "...the image [of God the Father] is placed before the eyes of our mind, in that when we truly strain toward the Father, we behold Him — insofar as we do perceive Him — through His image that, is, through the Son." An even more explicit basis for it might be found in the Cambridge commentary, in the explanation that "a *figura* is that kind of likeness which represents a thing acording to its bodily features, since it does in fact also have just such a head, just such eyes, just a nose, just such a chest, and all things just so. Therefore the Son is called the *figura* of the Father — that is, the express likeness of Him — because He is like Him in all respects." The occurrence of so allusive a device entirely within the stage directions seems to imply either that the playwright was indulging in a bit of learned by-play for his own amusement or more probably that he was composing a play to be read as well as acted, and so anticipated in his own fashion the "literary" stage directions of modern dramatists like Shaw and Barrie — a suggestion that does not seem implausible in itself, though I cannot recall that it has been made before in connection with medieval drama. The introductory *salvator* may be part of the playwright's original stage direction; or it may, I suppose, result from an incorporation of a later explanatory note by some less poetic mind concerned with (let us say) costuming, who had had difficulty with the playwright's term *figura.* In either case, it seems quite likely that the familiar title *salvator* was inserted here at the beginning for the practical purpose of indicating that the Deity on stage should resemble Christ, thereafter to be called *figura.* If *salvator* is the playwright's own word, *figura* and *salvator* together may constitute also a kind of composite definition of the *Deus-homo,* with the former emphasizing Christ's divine nature and the latter His human nature. However that may be, this very presentation of the God of the Old Testament under the appearance of Christ is clearly paralleled in medieval iconography, where Christ — evidently to be understood as the co-eternal Word of the Father — often appears as creator of the world including Adam and Eve (*Myst.,* lines 1-20,) author of the prohibition concerning the Tree (lines 89-104), as judge of Adam and Eve after the Fall (lines 391-518), and even a judge of Cain after the killing of Abel (lines 723-44). [9]

This connection between the Deity in the *Mystère d'Adam* and the imagery of Hebr. 1:3 may have some bearing also on the dispute concerning the original length of the play, which in our single manuscript copy appears to be incomplete. It seems a reasonable enough conjecture that in choosing *figura* as a name to be used for Christ, the playwright may have intended to call attention to certain other significant parallels between the subject of this play and that of the opening passage of Hebrews. With this possibility in mind, let us notice the inevitable thematic relationship between the *processus prophetarum* with which the *Mystère* breaks off (lines 754-942), and Hebr. 1:1, "Multifariam multisque modis olim Deus loquens patribus in prophetis..."; and the completion of the drama that would, in these terms, be implied by the words which follow immediately in Hbr. 1:2: "...novissime diebus istis locutus est nobis in Filio." A more striking possibility of this kind is presented by Hebr. 1:2-3, which contain a sort of capsulized account of the history of mankind through the completion of the Redemption: "...per quem [*i.e.*, Filium] fecit [Pater] et secula. Qui...portansque omnia verbo virtutis sue, purgationem peccatorum faciens, sedet ad dexteram maiestatis eius in excel-

---

[9] As a single example of this medieval commonplace, see the illustrations of the opening chapters of Genesis in MS. Oxford, Bodl. 270b, ed. A. de Laborde, *La Bible moralisée illustrée* (Paris, 1911-27), I, pl. 1-8 (1, Christ as creator; 2-4, creation of the world; 5-6, creation of Adam and Eve, and the prohibition; 7, the Fall; 8, the judgment of Cain), where the portrayal of the Deity corresponds exactly to that of Christ in the accompanying New Testament scenes; the MS is probably from the first half of the thirteenth century (*ibid.*, V, 30). Note particularly Tertullian, *Lib. adv. Praxeam*, 16 (*PL* 2, cols. 174-75), "Ipse [*i.e.*, Filius] enim et ad humana semper colloquia descendit, ab Adam usque ad Patriarchas et Prophetas... Ita semper ediscebat, et Deus in terris cum hominibus conversari non alius potuit quam Sermo, qui caro erat futurus." Further pertinent references to early writers are assembled in *PL* 41, col. 508, note (*a*), on *Civ Dei* XVI, 29. For the Son as creator see Hervé on Hebr. 1:2 (*PL* 181, col. 1522), "Et *per quem,* secundum quod Verbum Patris est, ipse Pater *fecit* non solum æterna...*sed et sæcula*...Et cum sæcula per Filium facta sint, manifestum est eum esse Creatorem hominis..."; and for the role of the Son as judge, Luculentius (*PL* 72, col. 855), "*Per quem fecit et sæcula* ... Sicut enim neminem judicat Pater, sed omnia dicitur [dicit, *ed.*] judicare per Filium [cf. John 5:22-3], quem judicem genuit, sic etiam dicitur operari per Filium, quem constat opificem genuisse."

sis." [10] Did the original *Mystère d'Adam* perhaps fulfill this same pattern, with the *figura* of Hebr. 1:3 as its "hero"?

Finally, there is a tantalizing hint that the playwright's initial inspiration for the character *figura* may have been an association from the liturgy. As Sepet pointed out long ago, the opening lesson IN PRINCIPIO CREAVIT DEUS CELUM ET TERRAM (Latin line 19), the opening chant *Formavit igitur dominus* (Latin line 20), and the three subsequent chants (Latin lines 26, 92, 153), all seem closely dependent on the *lectiones* and *responsaria* of Matins for Septuagesima Sunday. [11] Though the history of the relevant liturgical books in twelfth-century England (collectar, ordinal, lectionary, and the like) is admittedly more obscure than one could wish, it is clear enough that for the time between the feast of the Epiphany and Septuagesima Sunday, the lessons or readings in such books are as a general rule drawn largely from the Pauline Epistles, in something like their canonical order—an arrangement which theoretically would bring the "figura substantie eius" of Hebr. 1:3 in rather close proximity with the Matins for Septuagesima. Explicit instances of this proximity are in fact difficult to find, since in medieval liturgies—which normally provide for only five Sundays after the Epiphany, ignoring the infrequent occurrence of a sixth Sunday and its following week—the series of lessons from the Epistles is nearly always terminated by Septuagesima Sunday before reaching the Epistle to the Hebrews. [12] At

---

[10] Hervé (*PL* 181, col. 1523): "Qui et portat *omnia,* id est sursum tenet ne decidant, et in nihilum revertantur, unde creata ab ipso fuerant et sustentat ea non labore, nec difficultate, sed *verbo virtutis suæ,* id est imperio suæ potentiæ, hoc est sola volutate sua, quæ in eo virtus est et omnipotentia, per quod patet, quia Patri compotentialis est. Et est *purgationem peccatorum faciens,* quia sanguine suo nos a peccatis mundat. Commonet Apostolus crucis ejus et mox resurrectionis et ascensionis. Nam, postquam fudit in cruce sanguinem, ut faceret peccatorum nostrorum purgationem, suscitatus est de sepulcro, et elevatus est in coelum."

[11] *Les prophètes,* pp. 104-10. Studer, *ed. cit.,* pp. 2, 6, 25, 36.

[12] For example, in the *Breviarium ad usum insignis Ecclesiae Sarum,* ed. Francis Procter and Christopher Wordworth (Cambridge, 1882-86), I, cccclxxiv, these lessons end with I Thess. 2; in the *Breviarium ad usum insignis Ecclesie Eboracensis* (Surtees Society, 71; Durham, 1880-83), I, 228, they end with Eph. 3; and in *The Hereford Breviary,* ed. W. H. Frere and L. E. G. Brown (Henry Bradshaw Society, 26; London, 1904-15), I, 234, they end with Eph. 4. In their extant forms, of course, all of these breviaries are considerably later than the twelfth century. The eleventh-century "Wulfstan

least one clear juxtaposition of this kind does survive, however, in the ordinal and customary of St. Mary's Abbey in York (preserved in a manuscript of around 1400), where the Matins for Septuagesima are immediately preceded by the services for the fifth Sunday after Epiphany, including lessons from Hebr. 1:1ff.: "Ad Matutinas. Omnia ut supra Dominica prima, exceptis lectionibus que sunt ad Hebreos: *Multipharie*." [13] This belated bit of evidence, the flexibility which obviously prevailed in the use of the Pauline Epistles as lessons, and the inviting silence of the liturgy itself about any time which might follow the fifth Sunday after Epiphany, leave one wondering whether some such liturgical pattern may not have furnished our twelfth-century playwright the suggestion for his *figura* as well as for his lesson and chants—a question whose complexities, if they do not defy research altogether, are at least beyond the scope of the present study.

Collectar," ed. E. S. Dewick in *The Leofric Collectar* (Henry Bradshaw Society, 56; London, 1914-21), II, 515ff., continues the lessons from the Pauline Epistles beyond Septuagesima, but shows no significant placing of Hebr. 1-1ff. For the quite common use of 1:1ff. at Christmas and its season, see for example the "Wulfstan Collectar," *ibid.,* II, 509, 510; the "Leofric Collectar," *ibid.* (HBS, 45), I, 22, 36; the sequence by Adam of St. Victor quoted above at note 5; the *Institutions liturgiques de l'Église de Marseille (XIIIᵉ siècle),* ed. Ulysse Chevalier (Bibliothèque liturgique, 14; Paris, 1910), p. 27; and *The Sarum Missal,* ed. J. Wickham Legg (Oxford, 1916), p. 29.

[13] Ed. Abbess of Stanbrook and J. B. L. Tolhurst, *The Ordinal and Customary of the Abbey of Saint Mary, York* (Henry Bradshaw Society, 75; London, 1936-51), II, 232, with the Matins for Septuagesima on the following page; for the date of the MS, *ibid.* (HBS, 73), I, vii. (*Multipharie* is a common medieval variant for the opening word of Hebr. 1:1.) Instead of prescribing specific lessons from the Pauline Epistles, medieval breviaries sometimes present a complete text of the Epistles, ending with Hebrews — thus placing Hebr. 1:3 in the near vicinity of the Septuagesima Matins; see for example a fourteenth-century breviary of Padua, MS. Cornell University B.39, fol. 64ʳ. The modern Roman Breviary employs Hebr. 1:1-4 as the first lesson of Matins for the infrequent sixth Sunday after Epiphany.

FRENCH PRINTED VERSIONS OF THE TALE OF APOLLONIUS OF TYRE

FLORENCE MCCULLOCH
Wellesley College

One of the popular Latin adventure stories of the middle ages is the tale of Apollonius of Tyre which begins with incest in Antioch, continues with beheadings, shipwrecks, separations, and pirates, to conclude with a family reunion in the temple of Diana at Ephesus! Existing in many mediaeval Latin manuscripts, it is natural that this episodic story with its happy dénouement was translated into most European languages. [1] Though several references to Apollonius appear in Provençal and French writings of the late twelfth and thirteenth century, no complete poem has survived in Old French; [2] the oldest manuscripts of the French translations date from the fourteenth and fifteenth century. It is the extremely rare printed editions of Louis Garbin of Geneva (ca. 1482) and of Gilles Corrozet of Paris (1530, ca. 1543), along

---

[1] The best general study is that of Elimar Klebs, *Die Erzählung von Apollonius aus Tyrus* (Berlin, 1889). For bibliographical references see Robert Bossuat, *Manuel bibliographique de la littérature française du moyen âge* (Melun, 1951), 1241-1250. Although some scholars have attributed a Greek origin to the Apollonius tale, Klebs believes that it was first written in Latin before the fourth century, and that the rare Christian elements are later additions (pp. 216-218). For a useful summary of the various views on the origin of the story, see Charles B. Lewis, "Die altfranzösischen Prosaversionen des Apollonius-Romans," *Romanische Forschungen,* XXXIV (1915), pp. 153-159.

[2] A list of citations in Romance referring to Apollonius is found in the *Libro de Apolonio,* ed. C. Carroll Marden (Baltimore, 1917), pp. XXV-XXIX.

with the curious account attributed to the latter in the eighteenth century, that will be investigated here. Two other reworkings of the ancient tale are relevant to this study: that of François de Belleforest published in his *Histoires tragiques* (Volume VII, 1582); and the largely forgotten tragi-comedy of Bernier de la Brousse, *Les Heureuses infortunes,* which appeared in 1618. Although the story remained basically the same in its successive appearances, each writer, by the nature of his additions or modifications, gave it a particular character. Essential to the analysis of these variations, however, is an outline of the original plot with its profusion of incidents, so typical of complicated late Greek romances. [4]

> After the death of his wife, Antiochus, king of Antioch conceives a criminal passion for his daughter and overcomes her horrified resistance. All her suitors, unable to solve the ambiguous question set by the king, are beheaded except a youth from Tyre, Apollonius, who correctly interprets the enigma. Temporarily spared by the king who of course denies the truth, Apollonius returns home, but fearing for his life, he loads his ships with supplies and leaves for Tharsus, vainly pursued by the king's steward, Thaliarchus. In Tharsus, Apollonius learns from a fellow countryman, Elanius (Hellenicus),

---

[3] The French manuscripts have been edited by Lewis, *op. cit.,* pp. 1-277. A complete list of French manuscripts, containing two that were unknown to Lewis and which belong to his version A, appears in Brian Woledge, *Bibliographie des Romans et Nouvelles en prose française antérieurs à 1500* (Genève and Lille, 1954), n. 17. The version of particular interest to this study is the one which Lewis calls A, based on Paris, Arsenal 2991, fourteenth century. A is a translation of the earliest Latin account generally known as the *Historia Apollonii Regis Tyri,* and is closely related to the version of the *Historia* designated by Klebs as RB (*op. cit.,* p. 25). This has been edited by Alexander Riese, *Historia Apollonii Regis Tyri* (Bibliotheca Teubneriana, Lipsiae, 1893), who based his text on Oxford, Magdalen Coll. 50, eleventh century, and gave it the siglum *B*. Riese's volume also contains the edition of Klebs' RA (*op. cit.,* p. 18; Riese's sigla AP), based on Florence, Laurentian Lib., plut. LXVI tenth century, and Paris, Bibl. Nat., lat. 4955, fourteenth century. In the present study the word *Historia* will refer to Riese's edition.

[4] The Latin proper names are those of RB as they appear in the *Historia*; where there is a marked difference, those of RA are given in parentheses. After this outline of the plot the spelling of proper names and places will conform with that of the work under discussion.

that he has been outlawed by Antiochus. By the sale of grain Apollonius proceeds to relieve the suffering caused by a famine, then, after the citizens erect a statue in his honor, he leaves Tharsus for Pentapolis, where his ships are lost in a storm and he alone is cast on the shore of Cyrene. There an aged fisherman shows him the way to the city where the king, Archistrates, impressed by Apollonius' dexterity in athletic games, invites him to dinner. The king's daughter, Archistratis (Lucina), charmed by his skill in music, begs her father to keep Apollonius as her teacher. After a time, sick with her secret love for him, Archistratis rids herself of importunate suitors by declaring that she will marry none other than the man who has been shipwrecked. Meanwhile Antiochus and his daughter having been killed by lightning, and Apollonius named king of Antioch, he and his wife sail off to take possession of the kingdom. At sea Archistratis gives birth to a daughter and apparently dies. When the ship's captain refuses to have a dead body on board, Apollonius places his wife in a coffin with money and a note, and casts it into the sea. The coffin floats to Ephesus where it is found by a doctor, Chaeremon. As the body is being prepared for burning, signs of life appear, and Archistratis regains consciousness. She is then allowed to retire to the temple of Diana at Ephesus where she becomes a priestess. In the meantime the grieving Apollonius returns to Tharsus to entrust his daughter, Tharsia, to Stranguilio and his wife, Dionysiada, and, vowing not to cut his hair, beard or nails until Tharsia is married, he sails to Egypt. In Tharsus the nurse, Lycorida, dying, reveals to the young girl her parentage. However the foster mother, Dionysiada, jealous of Tharsia's beauty compared to that of her own daughter (Philomusia), plots to kill her ward. A slave, Theophilus, is bribed to slay Tharsia, but at the crucial moment, pirates arrive, carry off Tharsia to Mitylena, and sell her to a procurer named Leoninus, who places her in a bordello. Because of her entreaties and her wit she preserves her virginity and is protected by the king, Athenagora.

Fifteen years pass before Apollonius returns to Tharsus where Dionysiada tells him that Tharsia has died, and shows him the monument erected in her memory. Disconsolate, Apollonius again sets out to sea. This time the winds drive him to Mitylena where he refuses to participate in the festivities in progress. Athenagora, hoping to cheer the grieving Apollonius, sends the beautiful and talented Tharsia to his ship. Her song and riddles have no effect on the unconsolable king, but when Tharsia recounts her unfortunate life, Apollonius recognizes his daughter, who is soon married to Athenagora. Then, told by an angel to stop at the temple of Diana at Epheus on his way home, Apollonius is recognized by his wife. After punishing the procurer and Dionysiada and rewarding those who had help him, Apollonius records all of his adventures in two volumes, one of which is for the temple Diana at Ephesus, the other, he keeps in his library.

In Geneva around 1482, Louis Garbin (or Cruse) printed *Le romant de Appollin roy de Thir.* [5] Although Garbin's book is related to a French manuscripts version (A) which rather closely follows the text of the *Historia Apollonii Regis Tyri,* [6] the printed work was evidently intented for a public that would have been unfamiliar with either the names of the customs of antiquity contained in the original; [7] every classical reference has been omitted or changed. The results is a simplified, easily understood adventure story in which the effort to give a Christian and contemporary tone to the tale does not always hide its pagan ancestry.

A few examples will show the unknown author has modified details. Whereas in A (I) Antiochus' unlawful love for his daughter is only attributed to "l'ardeur de felon desir et plaisir," in Garbin Anthiogus "par mauvais eschauffements et par temptacion du

---

[5] Two copies of this book are known: one, to which Lewis (*op. cit.,* p. 248) assigns the date 1482, in the collection of Stanislas de Lavallaz in Sion, Switzerland; the other, undated, formerly in the collection of M. Yéméniz of Lyon, is now n. 538 of the Musée Thomas Dobrée, Nantes. See M.-L. Polain, *Catalogue de la Bibliothèque du Musée Thomas Dobrée* (Nantes, 1903), Tome II. This copy was seen on microfilm.

[6] See n. 3. The chapter numbers appearing in parentheses are those of Lewis' version A (*op. cit.,* pp. 2-46); these chapters correspond to the *Historia.*

[7] One is even tempted to think that this version was composed for a listening as well as a reading public. Not only are the syntax and the vocabulary of the greatest simplicity, but in the brief listing of contents at the beginning, the formula "vous aures" is several times repeated (i.e., "Premierement comment il [Apollonius] s'en fuyt par mer pour la paour du roy d'Antioche, comment vous aures cy ensuyant...") This supposition is strengthened by the terms used by Copland in the prologue to his translation of Garbin's edition (see below, n. 13), "I beseche all the reders and herers of this present hystorye..."

dyable fut esmeu et mist son amour en sa fille." Appollin who is
"un jouvencel de Thir, prince de son pays, ... enfourmé habon-
damment en lettreure" (A IV) becomes a king, "beau, jeusne,
joyeulx, plaisant, riche, et tresbon clerc." The Latin names of the
winds which destroy his ships (A XI) are omitted, and Appollin's
apostrophe to Neptune, beginnig (A XII), "O Neptun, robeur et
pillart, defraudeur de hommes innocens, deceveur de nefs, plus
cruel que Antiocus..." is changed to, "O fortune, ingenieuse des
hommes, as tu attendu cestuy grant peril de moy fayre tant de
mal?" After Tarcie has been abducted in a "galee coursoire," A
(XXXIII) tells how the "houillier," 'procurer' in Mitylena tries
to force the young girl to worship an idol of Priapus studded with
precious gems. Tarcie's reaction is to ask the procurer if he is
from Lapsacene. [8] The details are softened in Garbin: "Ung qui
estoit maistre des ruffiens et tenoit maintes femmes en peché ou
lieu publique ... la bouta en une chambre ou il avoit une ymaige
inhonnorable a dire et luy dist qu'elle adourast celle ymaige. Et
elle luy dist: 'Ja Dieu ne plaise que je adoure tel chose." The
celebration being held when Appollin inadvertently arrives at Mitylena is in honor of Neptune (A XXXIX), but in the Christianized
version it is for "saint Jehan, le patron de la nef." And finally,
an amusing mixture of ancient and contemporary customs and
language. Appollin stops "en la terre des Effessions" to sacrifice
to Diana, and on entering the temple he and his followers "trou-
verent une nonain qui leur dist: 'Seigneurs, pardonnez moy, car
nul n'y aouse entrer sans licence de ma dame l'abesse.'" [9] Garbin's

---

[8] This is the Greek settlement Lampsacus in Asia Minor, seat of the
worship of Priapus.

[9] This conversation is followed by:

> En celluy temple ne demouroit si non dames qui vouloient chasteté
> garder et en celuy temps Archistatres, femme du roy Appollin,
> estoit eslevée pour abbesse, laquelle Appollin tenoit pour morte.
> Et desja y avoit .x. ans qu'elle y demouroit. La portiere vint
> demander a l'abesse, et luy dist que a la parte avoit ung roy bien
> acompaigné qui vouloit faire oraison a la desse Dyana. Quant
> l'abbesse entendit que c'estoit ung roy, elle fist porter une chiere
> en l'esglise et s'en alla seoir dedens.

The wording of this passage should be compared with the unusual London
version (Brit. Mus., Royal 20 C. ii, fifteenth century) which Lewis prints,
op. cit., p. 239:

explicit corresponds to the religious spirit of the entire work:
After Appollin had written his adventures in six volumes,[10] he
and his wife died, "Et ainssi Dieu les appella en son royaulme de
Paradis, lequel nous doint le pere et le filz et le benoist saint
esperit. Amen."

In only two additions does the author of the Garbin edition
deviate markedly from the French A: one he might have incorpor-
ated from a folk-tale; the other originated in his model. To
convince Appollin of Tarcie's death, the scheming Dyonise not
only moistens her husband's and her own eyes with saliva to
simulate tears, but she places in the empty tomb a sheep, dead
for four days, and "puant a merveillez." Apparently no such ruse
exists in other versions. But one constant element of the scene
where Tarcie tries to comfort the grieving stranger is the inclusion of a varying number of riddles, originally composed by a
late Latin poet to whom the name Symphosius has been given.
Garbin's edition contains four riddles, of which three are found
in A (XLII), River and Fish, Bath-house, and Mirror,[11] and one,

---

> ... on leur moustra auquel temple comme devant avons dit estoient
> mises les femmes qui vouloient garder chasteté, et là estoient pour
> abbasse Archicastres la femme de Appolin de Thir que avoit bien
> demouré XV ans leans, la quelle son mary cuidoit qu'elle fust
> morte. Appolin et toute leur compaignie vindrent vers le temple
> et prierent a la portiere qu'elle leur ouvre sist l'eglise car ilz vou-
> loient faire leur oroyson. Lors la portiere dist 'attendez ung petit
> s'il vous plaist et je l'iray dire a ma dame l'abesse. ... Quant Archi-
> castre öyt la portiere elle commanda que on luy appareillast une
> chaiere au temple ... avecq grant compaignie de nobles dames et
> s'assist en son siege.

Although the London manuscript contains no riddles, there are resemblances
between it and the Italian version, both of which Lewis relates to a group
of Latin manuscripts in Paris, which belong in turn to the Stuttgart family
(Lewis, *op. cit.*, pp. 236-242).

[10] The six books were destined for: "l'ung fut ou temple de Dyana,
l'aultre en la terre des Effessiens, l'aultre en Anthyoche, l'aultre en Terme
[a corruptio of Cyrene], l'aultre en Tarcie, et l'aultre en son royaulme gentil
de Thir."

[11] The one riddle left unanswered by Appollin is that of the Mirror;
its corrupt form explains his silence: "dedens se monstre resplendissant, et
se tu t'approuchez lune semble le souleil et ne monstre si non ce que est
devant luy." A (XLII), approximating the Latin, reads: "En moy n'a point
de certain figure ne d'estrange, anssi j'ay en moy resplendisseur par dedens
aussi comme ce se feust une estuelle divine, la quelle ne demoustre rien

less common, the Reed, appears in the Spanish and Italian versions of the tale. [12] On the whole, the principal interest of the version printed by Garbin is its classical impoverishment and Christian coloring, its unusual additions, and the fact that it was the basis for Robert Copland's English translation, entitled *Kynge Appolyn of Thyre,* published in London in 1510 by Wynkyn de Worde. [13]

---

fors ce qui par avant ly est demoustray." Copland (see below, n. 13) compounds confusion by translating the beginning of Garbin's tests, "Within this monster shining, approcheth alway an endynge..."

[12] See Marden, *op. cit.,* Str. 507, 508, and *La Storia di Apollonio di Tiro,* ed. Carlo Salvioni (Bellinzona, 1889), p. 30, 1.5. In the Latin riddle found in RA (Riese, *op. cit.,* p. 91, l. 3) Tharsia says:

> Dulcis amica ripae semper vicina profundis,
> Suave canens Musis, nigro perfusa colore
> Nuntia sum linguae digitis signata magistri.

> .Et ait ad eam Apollonius 'dulcis amica dei, quae cantus suos mittit ad caelum, canna est, ripae semper vicina, qui iuxta aquas sedes collocatas habet. Haec nigro perfusa colore nuntia est lingua [ex ea natum, quod per eam transit].

Because the author of Garbin's version or his source did not realize that the last detail was referring to the use of black ink and a reed pen, his riddle is transformed, but in a plausible manner: 'l'eau du fleuve qui yroit a la rive de laquelle musicque et doulz chant se sont. Et n'est de noire coulleur. Messaigier est de allegrance quant l'on la touche avecques les doiz.' Lors le dit Appollin respondit et dist: 'La doulce amye de la rive du fluve [sic] c'est la cane qui tousjours veult estre prez de l'eau. De laquelle musicque et doulz chant ce sont, c'est quant on a des fleuctes ou aultres instrumens. Et n'est point de noire coulleur, car elle est blanche. Massaigier est d'allegrance quant on la touche avecques les dois sur les partuis, car on luy fait dire ce que l'on veult.'" For the source of these riddles, see Raymond Ohl, *The Enigmas of Symphosius* (Philadelphia, 1928).

[13] This book is in the British Museum, C. 132.i.35; there also exists one copy of an extremely limited reprint in 1870, C.34.1.18. Heretofore the exact origin of Copland's translation has not been certain, though Klebs surmised a relationship with Garbin (*op. cit.,* p. 472) but a comparison of his text with Garbin's now leaves no doubt. In his prologue Copland states:

> ... my worshypful mayster Wynkyn de Worde havynge a lytell boke of an auncyent hystory of a kynge somtyme reygnynge in the countree of Thyre, called Appolyn, concernynge his malfortunes and peryllous adventures right espoventables, bryefly compyled and pyteous for to here. The which boke I, Robert Coplande, have me applyed for to translated out of the Frensche language into our maternal Englysche tongue. ... Wherfor I beseche all the reders and herers of this present hystorye yf there be any thyng amysse in the translacyon to pardon myn ignoraunt youth...

Very different in composition and tone is Gilles Corrozet's *Histoire du roy Apolonius prince de Thir en Affricque et Roy d'Antioche lequel apres avoir souffert plusieurs & diverses calamitez & adversitez retourna en plus gros honneur et joye que devant,* to give the entire title. [14] Laden with extraneous characters and episodes and suffering from an excess of moralizing and sentimentality, Corrozet's work is a strange combination of traditional material and cumbersome additions. The edifying nature of the story is emphasized in the prologue:

> ...en lisant ladite hystoire on pourra eviter oysiveté, cause, comme disant les saiges, de tous maulx. Et pourront les lecteurs de ce livre grandement prouffiter en

---

Except for occasionally inflating passages like the description of the storm (A XI) or Appolyn's lament for his dead wife (A XXV), Copland faithfully follows Garbin even when his original is nonsense. The statue raised by the grateful citizens of Tharsus to Apollonius shows him, "stans dextera manu fruges tenens, sinistro pede modium calcans" (Riese, *op. cit.,* p. 19, l.1). This Garbin translates: "laquelle ymaige tenoit en sa main du blé, et avecques le pied senestre mettoit du blé en la mesure," and Copland: "in his ryght hande a shefe of whete & with his lyft fote he put corne into the mesure."

In his remarks on the relationship of the Apollonius tale found in Book VIII of Gower's *Confessio amantis* with Shakespeare's play *Pericles,* G. C. Macaulay states that Shakespeare had sources other than Gower alone (see *The Complete Works of John Gower,* ed. G. C. Macaulay (Oxford, 1901), Vol. III, p. 538). It is certain that Copland's translation is not one of these.

[14] One Copy of this book (in-4°, nine woodents), printed in Paris by Jean Bonfons without date (ca. 1543), is known; it is Oxford, Bodleian, Douce A. 275, and is probably the copy from the Hibbert Sale, 16 March 1829, when it was lot 383 (not 382 as Brunet incorrectly indicates, *Manual du Libraire* (Paris, 1860), I, 351). In speaking of this edition Brunet says that it might be a reprinting of the volume cited by La Croix du Maine with the title: "*Plaisante et agréable histoire d'Apolonius, prince de Thir en Afrique et roi d'Antioche,* traduit par Corrozet en ses jeunes ans, imprimée à Paris par Alain Lotrian et Denis Janot," without indication of date or format (see La Croix du Maine and Du Verdier, *Les Bibliothèques Françaises* (Paris, 1772), Vol. I, p. 287). G. Panzer, *Annales Typographici,* Vol. VIII, p. 139, n. 1968, states that the book is in-8°, printed in 1530, and refers to Henning, p. 99. The present writer has been unable to verify the latter reference. In any case, no copy is known of the 1530 edition which would have been one of the first coming from the press of Alain Lotrian who began printing in 1528 (see the handwritten catalogue of Philippe Renouard, *Bibliographie parisienne XVIᵉ siècle*), and the first work in prose of the twenty-year old Corrozet. For a study of Corrozet, best known for *La Fleur des antiquitez* (1532), the *Hecatomgraphie* (1540), and *Le Compte du Rossignol* (1546), see S. M. Bouchereaux, "Recherches bibliographiques sur Gilles Corrozet," *Bulletin du Bibliophile,* 1948, 1949, *passim.*

voyant la forme & maniere de vivre, la bonne patience, la prouffitable sapience, la mobile & liberalle fortune d'icelluy Seigneur & prince, lequel apres plusieurs adventures retourna en plus grande dignité que devant. Si prie, moy, indigent de sapience, a tous begnins Lecteurs, qu'ilz ne regardent point au langaige mal couché, mais cuillent le fruict de l'Hystoire. Et se quelque erreur y a, qu'il me soit remis & pardonné. Car je l'ay faict non pour cueillir le fruict de louenge qui en pourroit venir, mais pour monstrer les gestes et faitz de noz anciens antecesseurs. Plus que moins.

The first of the forty-six chapters begins with the briefest of histories of the city of Antioche, founded by "Selecus Nichanor," Alexander's heir, whose son was "Antiocus Sother," and grandson, "Antiochus Magnus," to whom Corrozet attributes the naming of the city, "a cause de ce nom Magnus qu'on luy imposa."[15] Passing over other matters, "bource [sic] que ne seroit que confusion et ennuy, nous ... viendrons a nostre principalle matiere." When the point is finally reached, we learn that Anthiocus' daughter is called Argine. Whereas seventeen characters are named in the author's source — to be discussed below — Corrozet uses forty proper names, apparently of the most heteroclite origin. [16] Moreover, the smallest incident of the *Historia* is elaborated, colored emotionally, lightly sprinkled with classical allusions, as, for example, the inception of the king's love for his daughter: "Or est mue Lychaon en loup ravyssant par la puissance Jupiter, & Anthiocus par le dard empoysonne de Cupido." Further on, amidst an involved development of Anthiocus' passion, which in contrast to some

---

[15] In chapter 32, "Comment Appolonius alla se faire couronner roy d'Antioche," Corrozet dwells long on the historical city of Tyr, "maintenant l'appelle on Sur a cause qu'elle est l'entrée de Surie," and states that he has found his material "en plusieurs hystoires." The present writer has been unable to locate them.

[16] Argine, for example, appears in Sebastien Mamerot's *Histoire des Neuf Preux et des Neut Preues* (see Marcel Lecourt, "Notice sur l'histoire des Neuf Preux et des Neuf Preues," *Romania,* 37 (1908), p. 531). Argine's "demoiselles," Florimonde and Esclarmonde are queens or princesses in *Florent et Octavien* (see Robert Bossuat, "*Florent et Octavien,* Chanson de geste du XIVe siècle," *Romania,* 73 (1952), pp. 289-331). But what can be said for the two "sathalites" of Taliarchus, Golandas and Satrapas, or Apolonius' companions, and Carabdis, whose name looks suspiciously like the whirlpool Charybdis?

fifteen lines in the *Historia* extends over the first six chapters, familiar words suddenly occur. The revealing sentence is this: "Car amour avec le venin de peché luy firent une treshorrible guerre & *son cueur estoit en continuelle bataille pour la beaulté de sa fille que follement il aymoit.*" The italicized words are identical with those in *Le Violier des histoires romaines* (Ch. 125), an early sixteenth century translation of the widely known collection of moralized tales assembled in the fourteenth century, the *Gesta Romanorum.* [17] Chapter 153, of the latter, entitled "De tribulacione temporali, que in gaudium sempiternum postremo commutabitur," is another version of the tale of Apollonius differing in some details from the *Historia.* [18] With questionable skill Corrozet has added to the *Violier* a heavy layer probably of his own invention, but revealing the influence of prose romances of his time. [19]

---

[17] See the edition published by Hermann Oesterley (Berlin, 1872), and the text of chapter 153 printed by S. Singer, *Apollonius von Tyrus* (Halle, 1895, pp. 71-105), as well as the observations of Klebs, *op. cit.,* pp. 349-361 (especially those on Singer's unreliable transcription, p. 353, n. 3).

[18] The first French edition of the *Violier* was printed in 1521. In 1529, Denis Janot printed another with the title: *Le Violier des histoires rommaines: moralitez sur les nobles gestes, faictz vertueulx, & anciennes croniques de toutes nations de gens, fort recreant et moral.* This edition was reprinted by Pierre Gustave Brunet (Paris, 1858). Were it not for two reasons one could assume that Corrozet used Janot's edition since he often took the summaries in the margin of the *Violier* as his chapter headings e.g., the *Violier*: "Grosse remuneration que fist Apolonius au pescheur qui l'avoit secouru en la necessité"; Corrozet, chapter 46: "De la grosse remuneration que Apolonius fist au pescheur...") However, in the *Violier* the name of Tharsie's nurse is Liguyde, and Dyoniside's daughter, Philomacie; the corresponding names in Corrozet are Ligozide and Philomancie. The latter are closer to the Latin forms found in the manuscript on which Oesterley based his edition of the *Gesta Romanorum* (where they are Ligozidem and Philomancia) than in the one from which the *Violier* was translated. Also differing from the *Violier* with its more common conclusion according to which Apollonius wrote two volumes of memoirs, is Corrozet's *explicit*: "et fist six volumes tous traistant de ses fortunes & de sa fille; lesquels il donna le premier a Penthapolis, le second a Machilent, et le tiers au temple des Ephesiens, le quart en Tharse, le quint en la ville d'Antioche, et le VI et le dernier retient en sa librairie en la cité de Thir. Et pour fin de l'hystoire il fina ses jours & mourut plain de bonnes oeuvres si qu'il fut saulvé comme il est a croire par les vertus qu'il eut, et la patience qui ne fut pas moindre que martire." The text beginning "il fina ses jours..." is identical with the *Violier*.

[19] See G. Doutrepont, *Mise en prose des épopées et des romans chevaleresques* (Bruxelles, 1939), pp. 467-687.

What characterizes Corrozet's contributions? Every expression of feeling — love and particularly suffering — is lengthily developed, as for example the complaints of Tharsie at sea in the chapter (34) entitled, "Comment Tharsie fut recoussé des mains du mestayer par les pirates de mer qui la vendirent a un macquereau." There are monologues, like that of Anthiocus who debates his course of action in this manner "O, Anthiocus, tu te boutes bien en une grand frenasie de vouloir ainsi maculer le lict de ta fille. Iray je? Non feray. Si feray..." Apostrophes abound, like Apolonius' to Penthapolis which begins, "Adieu, noble cité royalle en laquelle j'ay eu tant de biens & tant d'honneurs recevyz..." The author delights in detailed descriptions of palaces with their columns surmounted by golden eagles holding gleaming carbuncles in their beak, of Apolonius' triumphal entry into Antioche, of the beautiful features of Lucine, Apolonius wife. Corrozet himself sometimes intervenes with a homely proverb as when he alludes to the continued pleasure of Anthiocus with his daughter, "Car, comme on dict, il n'est que la premiere pint chere," with reference to his source, "Or dit le compte," and by introducing his name in an acrostic "complaincte" sung by Tharsie in the bordello. [20] Corrozet's work gives every sign of being a product of his youth because of its pompous erudition, rhetorical emotion, and inclusion of supernumerary persons and episodes in what is already an overburdened plot.

Until the recent discovery of Gilles Corrozet's book, its contents were only known through a detailed résumé published in 1781 by Contant d'Orville in *Mélanges tirés d'une grande Bibliothèque,* [21] the "great library" being that of the Marquis de Paulmy,

---

[20] The acrostic reads as follows:

Complaindre dois mon douloureulx exil
Duquel je suis & en tresgrant peril,
Recongnoissant la dollente fortune,
Rememorant mon amere importune,
Ouvrir je doys mon cueur plorant sans cesse
Sans regarder a ma gente noblesse,
Et a honneur on me veult deflorer
Tant ordement, dont bien je dois plorer.

[21] Volume O (Sect. VIII). The résumé, by an unidentified M.M.C.D.G. is on pp. 265-313.

one of the celebrated eighteenth century bibliophiles. In the introductory remarks to "Les Aventures d'Apollonius de Tyr," presumably written not by the Marquis de Paulmy but by his collaborator Contant d'Orville, the writer mentions a fine fifteenth century French prose manuscript in his possession, and after refering to the edition printed in Geneva, he states: "En 1530, Gilles Corrozet, Imprimeur et Auteur, ... publia une seconde édition en un volume in-8°. C'est celle que je vais extraire: elle est conforme à l'édition précédente et au manuscrit" (p. 263). Klebs correctly detects an error in the identifying of Corrozet's version with the earlier Geneva edition, [22] but he was unaware of the extent to which this preliminary notice is misleading. Although he points out the modern spirit of the work attributed to Corrozet, it is strange that his suspicions were not aroused by the tone of the résumé, particularly when characters are quoted and inscriptions transcribed. A few examples will show what we mean. Antiochus suffers excessive torment before declaring to his daughter, Cléobule, " 'Ma gloire, dit Antiochus, est de t'offrir un Amant digne de toi, qui t'aime pour toi-même, qui connaisse ... comme moi ... le prix de tous tes charmes' " (p. 274). Cléobule is visibly troubled on meeting Apollonius. Later, an old woman gives Apollonius a letter in which the princess has written: "Oubliez pour jamais l'infortunée Cléobule ... Vous frémiriez si vous saviez ce qu'un monstre ... ah! que je ne puis nommer ... a osé entreprendre sur ce coeur que vous cherchez à mériter. ... Fuyez des lieux fouillés par un crime qui fait frémir la Nature ... Fuyez, Prince, et croyez que ce n'est pas la haine qui vous donne ce conseil" (p. 279). Incidentally, in the mêlée following Apollonius' successful answer to the king's question. Cléobule is killed by a stray arrow. The statue of Apollonius in Tharse bears the following inscription (p. 293):

> Une disette horrible
> Nous affligeoit de ses rigueurs,
> Quand un Prince aimable et sensible
> Vint terminer tous nos malheurs.
> Ce monument de notre zele
> Dans les siecles futurs offrira tout à tour,

---

[22] Klebs, *op. cit.*, p. 415.

Aux Rois le plus parfait modele,
A nos enfans l'objet de notre amour.

At the court of Archistrates Apollonius falls in love with the king's daughter, Altrizade, who returns his love but suffers from no mysterious malady, while Tarsie, after her purchase by "un certain Léonis, que le Romancier nomme un Houllier," is installed not in the bordello but in the palace of the prince of Mitilene, "qui lui compose une Cour que ses vertus, sa candeur et ses talens augmentent tous les jours" (p. 306). There are no riddles in the recognition scene between Tharsie and her father, and at Ephese it is only when the weeping Apollonius pronounces the name of Altrizade that the astonished "Grande-Pretresse ... leve son voile et tombe dans ses bras" (p. 312).

Clearly this is not Gilles Corrozet's version. Not only are the discrepancies in detail too great, but the gallant speech and precious sentiments are not those of the sixteenth century, even in an eighteenth century résumé. Who then is the author of the source used by Contant d'Orville? The notice preceding the résumé contains this disparaging remark: "...en 1711, M. Le Brun, Auteur connu par quelques ouvrages poétiques, tourna ce Roman-ci à la moderne, mais y jeta beaucoup de froid et peu d'intérêt" (p. 264). A brief glance at Le Brun's novel is revealing.

In 1710 in Paris and in Rotterdam appeared *Les Avantures d'Apollonius de Tyr* by Monsieur Le Br.[23] On the first page of this turgid novel[24] we read that Antiochus' wife died "à la fleur de son âge, après avoir mis au jour une fille, nommée Cléobule, dont la Nature avoit fait son chef d'oeuvre." Further on, having answered the king's question, Apollonius is warned by Cléobule who says: "Vous frémiriez d'horreur, si vous scaviez ce que vous demandez ... fuyez l'aspect de ces lieux redoutables; fuyez, Prince malheureux, et croyez que la haine n'a point de part au conseil que je vous donne" (pp. 25,26). The similarity in wording between

---

[23] This is Antoine-Louis Le Brun, Parisian novelist, poet and playwright.

[24] When Antiochus fells whole forests to make a fleet for the pursuit of Apollonius, "ces majestueux Habitans des Bois se virent transporter sur l'humide empire des flots" (p. 40), and when the city of Tarse suffers from famine, even "la Nymphe de chaque fontaine, appuyée languissamment sur son urne, ne voit plus d'eau couler que de ses yeux baignez de pleurs" (p. 54).

Cléobule's speech here and her letter quoted in Contant d'Orville's résumé can only be explained by plagiarism. The disdain for Le Brun's novel expressed by the editor of the *Mélanges* did not prevent him from copying the major part of it with only occasional changes dictated apparently by caprice. [25] Why, for example, call the daughter of Strangulion and Dionisiade, Sophonibe, when Le Brun had used her traditional name, Philomatie, and why make her jealousy the motivation of the proposed murder of Tarsie? Contant d'Orville also omits one exotic episode whose presence in Le Brun reveals that this author too was very probably an arrant plagiarist. After long travels and numerous adventures in Egypt (he is even loved by a priestess of Bacchus, who vainly asks the help of a magician in winning his affections) Apollonius settles in Arabia where prince Aretas gives him command of the army to avenge his defeat by Silleus. Klebs indicates that this deformed version of an actual event in Arabic history is found in a novel written in Amsterdam in 1710 by an Isaac Trojel. The name of the novel? *De Wonderlyke Gevallen van Apollonius van Tyr*! According to Klebs there are reasons for assuming that Le Brun copied Trojel, rather than the contrary. [26] Thus the tale of Apollonius attributed since the publication of the *Mélanges* to Gilles Corrozet is not his at all, but a widely divergent version based largely on Le Brun's novel which in turn copies either wholly or in part a contemporary Dutch novel. The circuitous course of the tale in the eighteenth century somewhat resembles the wanderings and inconstant fortunes of its hero.

We must return to the end of the sixteenth century for another appearance of the story of Apollonius. In 1582, François de Belle-

---

[25] Two details can only be explained by the assumption that Contant d'Orville occasionally made use of the fifteenth century manuscript mentioned in the preliminary notice. Le Brun limits his identification of the procurer to "un infâme et mercénaire prostitueur," but Contant d'Orville calls him Léonis, a form of his traditional Latin name derived from the common noun, *leno*, 'pimp'. This precision could have come from a manuscript source. The same origin probably explains the name of Apollonius' wife. To create Altrizade Contant d'Orville could have taken wife's name as it appears in Le Brun's novel, Isménide, and combined it with Alcistrates, the form occurring in the Latin version closest to Le Brun's source (see Klabs, *op. cit.*, p. 418).

[26] Klebs, *op. cit.*, pp. 419, 420. Since Klebs had never seen the Dutch edition, his conclusions are tentative.

forest published volume VII of his *Histoires tragiques,* translations derived largely from the Italian *novelle* of Bandello. [27]
Histoire 118 is entitled, "Accidens divers advenus à Apollonie
Roy des Tyriens; ses malheurs sur mer, ses pertes de femme,
& fille, & la fin heureuse de tous ensemble." This account, like
Garbin's before and Le Brun's after, is based on version B (RB)
of the *Historia,* as is shown by the name of the king's daughter,
Archestrate, "la fille, portant le nom mesme du père." [28] Other
elements, however, have intruded. The similarity with Corrozet's
introduction—Belleforest speaks of "Antiochus qui fut dit Sauveur,
& dona son nom à la cité d'Antioche, bastie par son père Seleucus"
(p. 114)—is probably coincidental and can be explained by Bandello's *novella* or by the author's wide reading in history, but the
transformation of Apollonie from the laconic hero of the *Historia*
into a tender and later jealous lover is original. Apollonius' skill
with the lyre, once compared to Apollo's (A XVI), is now
superseded by his delicate songs to Archestrate: "Ces derniers
propos, comme mignardement ils furent touchez & amoureusement
chantez & departis avec un fredon languissant & tremblotant de
souspirs, detournerent les esprits de chacun de la tristesse prece-
dente..." (p. 142). When news of Antiochus' death arrives, Apollonie remains sceptical until his informant "jura par le haut Iupiter,
le blond & lumineux Apollon, par Neptune l'ecumeux & par la
grande deesse des Sydoniens, que tout ce qu'il avoit dit

---

[27] The edition of volume VII used was Rouen, 1604. For a study of
Belleforest's translations, see Frank S. Hook, *The French Bandello,* University of Missouri Studies, XXII, I (Columbia, 1948). The story told by
Bandello (*La Seconda Parte de le Novelle,* Lucca, 1554. Novela LV, p. 373)
which served as Belleforest's point of departure recounts how Antioco, son
of Seleuco, king of Babylon, having fallen in love with his step-mother
Stratonica, is mortally ill from the passion he cannot declare. To save his
son's life, Seleuco gives him Stratonica, a gesture warmly approved by
Bandello. Belleforest's reaction is the opposite. He is persuaded that examples
of unnatural love serve "au seul pervertissement de l'ordre de la nature, à
la confusion de l'homme & à l'infélicité du siècle" (p. 110), and to counteract
these pernicious examples, Belleforest, having "une histoire tirée du Grec &
icelle ancienne, comme aussi je l'ay recueillie d'un vieux livre écrit à la
main," proposes to pass rapidly over the love of a king for his daughter and
to dwell on "les jeux de la fortune sur un Prince généreux..." (p. 111).
[28] The original name of Apollonius' wife was Archistratis. Klebs (*op. cit.,*
p. 42) explains how the Latin expression *cogente Lucina* (Riese, *op. cit.,* p. 46,
l. 6), referring to the goddess of child-birth, through a scribal misunderstanding became the name of Apollonius's wife in RA.

contenoit verité." (p. 169). No longer is a corpse on shipboard considered merely bad luck. Belleforest gives the pilot a more explicit reason for casting it overboard: "s'ils laissoyent ce corps en la galere, [que] son ame vagant d'un, & d'autre costé, suyvant que le tenoyent les Platonistes, ne faudroit de les turmenter, & de causer mille fascheries au vaisseau..." (p. 174). [29] To conform to his own sense of propriety — "je n'ay plaisir à vous deschiffrer des choses tant esloignees de la modestie & honesteté requise au Chrestien" (p. 188 — Belleforest barely touches the scenes of Tharsie in the bordello, omits all mention of the infamous statue, and even eliminates the riddles. In order to remain within the pagan framework of his story, however, it is not the angel of Belleforest's Latin source which tells Apollonie to go to the "temple Ephesien de Diane," but "une grand majesté, et qu'il estimoit estre un genie" (p. 198). These illustrations of Belleforest's penchant for prolixity, sentimentality, and misplaced erudition belie the claim of fidelity to the text with which he concludes: "le stile duquel [that of Apollonnie's memoirs] suivant presque mot à mot le liseur m'excusera, & de ce que j'ay esté un peu trop long, & du peu de grace, ornement & gentillesse de langage que j'ay pratiqué en cette histoire, m'ayant suffit de la vous raconter nuement, & sans nul fard & couleur" (p. 205). The disparity between an author's statements of intention and protestations of integrity and the demonstrable reality of his text is again visible in the work of a seventeenth century lawyer from Poitiers, Bernier de la Brousse.

In the Advis au Lecteur preceeding his tragi-comedy, *Les Heureuses infortunes* (1618), [30] Bernier de la Brousse declares that he took his story from an old manuscript entitled *Gesta Romanorum cum applicationibus* etc., and that though Belleforest "l'a deduite plus elegammant," his own play was finished when he came upon the other work, "qui fait qu'il y a quelque surcroist & difference aux noms, mais tout revient à un" (p. 276). It is indeed true

---

[29] Hook, *op. cit.*, p. 12.

[30] François Bernier de la Brousse, *Les Oeuvres poétiques* (Poitiers, 1618), pp. 276-330[v]. For brief remarks concerning this play "which best exemplifies the definition of a tragicomedy as a dramatized romance" (p. 122), see H. C. Lancaster, *A History of French Dramatic Literature in the Seventeenth Century*, Part I, Volume I (Baltimore, 1929), pp. 122-124.

that the names are in some cases dissimilar, not only because another source was used — the *Gesta* rather than the *Historia* — but in the recasting of the tale as a play, additional characters were needed for the numerous *récits* and confidences; hence there are "capitaines des gardes" and "maistres d'hostels." One begins to wonder, though, when Berys, Antioque's "maistre d'hostel," in the course of lamenting the fate of the beheaded Prince d'Apamee, and after refering to "l'antique maison Du vaillant Seleuque," says of his king,

> ... le brave renom
> Qu'on te donne icy bas ne convient à ton nom.
> Tu ne fus onc Soter, ton ame est trop cruelle. (p. 281ᵛ)

Historical allusions such as these are foreign to the *Gesta*. But it is a totally insignificant detail that betrays Bernier. When Apollonie recounts in retrospect to Altistrate and Lucine his confrontation with Antioque, he quotes the latter,

> Je te cognois fort bien, me respond le tyran,
> Tu es de mes vassaux, fils du brave Emyran
> Il fut mon bon amy, & pour la souvenance
> Que j'ay de sa vertu, je pleins ta decadence. (p. 289ᵛ)

The notion of friendship between Apollonie's father and Antioque could only have been suggested by "le Roy qui avoit aimé le pere de ceste adolescent, fut marry de le voir venir à sa mort certaine," and the sentence is from Belleforest (p. 121)! Bernier obviously read and profited from Belleforest's novel before he put the final touches on his play. The psychology and style, however, are entirely Bernier's, and their nature can be judged from the following short quotations. When Apollonie arrives in Ephesus, he is recognized after some hesitation by his wife:

> LUC. Que je luy saute au col? ce divin habitacle,
> Ny mes habits sacrez n'y serviront d'obstacle.
> THAR. O dieu quel sacrilege, ah! la pauvre Nonnain!
> Elle entre en son ecstase, ou a l'esprit mal sain.

Lucine identifies herself,

> APOL. O Ciel! ô terre! ô mer! ô dieu darde-lumiere!
> (p. 329)

And this has gone on for two *journées* of five acts each! Finding a way to end this undramatic play where narration has become contorted dialogue was a difficulty that Bernier cannot be said to have overcome successfully. After sacrificing "Cent boeufs forme-gueretz & de choix cent moutons," Apollonie plans to punish Trangulion and his wife Dorade.

> Luc.   Mon amy, dites-moy qui est ce Trangulie?
> Apol.   Ailleurs vous apprendrez son estre et sa folie.

Fin

Bernier's diffuse play with its double heritage of the *Gesta Romanorum* and Belleforest exhausts both the subject and the reader; in contrast, Garbin's prose seems rough and very remote.

Thus we have followed over three centuries the diverse appearances in French books of the tale of Apollonius stemming from two Latin sources, the *Historia* and the *Gesta Romanorum,* in their various modifications and disguises. Its popularity is obvious, for a story of misfortune and multiple coincidences on sea and land always appeals to those who like to hear about the frustrations and triumph of love, about perilous situations and incredible escapes from death, at the end of which the wicked receive their just deserts and the virtuous are appropriately rewarded. The tale of Apollonius contains all of these elements together with whatever moralizing or erudition each author cared to add so that it is not surprising to find this story flourishing for a thousand years or more after Venantius Fortunatus wrote:

> Tristius erro nimis patriis vagus exsul ab oris
> Quam sit Apollonius naufragus hospes aquis. [31]

---

[31] Quoted by Klebs, *op. cit.,* p. 12.

ADVENTURES OF A CELTICIST IN THE WEST KERRY GAELTACHT

ROBERT T. MEYER

Catholic University of America

It was quite by accident that I went to Dunquin and the Blasket Islands almost fifteen years ago. * To be sure, I'd read those fascinating books in English translation, Tomás Ó'Crohan's *An t-Oileánach* (The Islandman) [1] and Maurice O'Sullivan's *Fiche Blían ag Fás* (Twenty Years a-Growing). [2] Professor Stith Thompson had written to me in 1945 that he should like to 'proselytize me into the field of Folklore,' because of my interest in Celtic languages. Later still I checked various and sundry things for the late Tom Peete Cross when he was finishing his *Motif-Index* of *Early Irish Literature*. [3] He was situated in his retirement in rural Virginia, far removed from the rich libraries of the Chicago area, and it was easy enough for me to help him with most of the books in my own seminar room at the Catholic University of America.

---

* I am under obligation to the American Philosophical Society for generous grants for the research on this project, as well as grants from the Catholic University of America. Cf. *Year Book of the American Philosophical Society*: 1954, 374; 1956, 377; 1958, 430-431.

[1] Tomás Ó Criomhthain, *An t-Oileánach: scéal a bheathadh féin. An Seabhac do chuir i n-eagar* [Dublin, 1929]. The translation is by Robin Flower, *The Islandman* [London, Chatto & Windus, 1934]; reprinted Oxford University Press, 1951.

[2] Maurice Ó Sullivan, *Fiche Blían ag Fás* [Dublin, 1933]; translated by Moya L. Davis and George Thomson *Twenty Years a-Growing* ... [New York, 1933] reprinted in the World's Classics [London, 1952].

[3] Tom Peete Cross, *Motif-Index of Early Irish Literature* (Bloomington, Ind., 1952 [Indiana University Publications: Folklore Series, no. 7].

A generous grant from my University enabled me to spend the summer in Dublin to work at the mediaeval Irish manuscripts in the Royal Irish Academy, Trinity College, and the National Library of Ireland. Everything went along very well until the last day of July when I saw posted on the door of the National Library a sign to the effect that the building would be closed 'during the month of August for cleaning and dusting.' That same day I discovered that a similar situation would prevail at the other libraries. Hopefully I went out to number 57 Upper Leeson Street that evening to see the famous Richard Irvine Best. [4] It was he who had been so good in assisting me in many ways with photostats, advice and encouragement in my early student days.

"Surely," I thought, "the man who was the Director of the School of Celtic Studies of the Dublin Institute for Advanced Studies, former Librarian of the National Library of Ireland, member of the Irish Manuscripts Commision, would do something to keep a place open for me, perhaps a desk at the Commission, a place to work during August."

However, to my surprise (and I thanked him for this later) he told me to keep away from all libraries for a month:

"Young man, you've enough in the manuscript room for awhile. You can always get photostats or microfilms of the things you need. These manuscripts and books will be here for others to work at hundreds of years from now. But go down to the country, go out to West Kerry, live in a cabin and learn Irish. Keep away from hotels and tourists out there. Read no English for a month. Learn Irish, speak Irish, read Irish. But live with the people. After awhile find an old *shanachie,* take down the stories, the poetry, the proverbs. 'Twill be good for your ear to do this. I'm telling you to do these things because I've never done them myself."

Somehow, no one who knew the late Richard Irvine Best could ever have associated him with Irish cabins, consorting with fishermen and farmers, learning to speak the common idiom. Better for him to pontificate in high places, to chair the proceedings of

---

[4] Richard Irvine Best (1872-1959), whom Prof. Eleanor Knott called the "Nestor of Celtic scholars" in his obituary notice in *Ériu* XIX (1962 123-25. A bibliography of his published work appeared in *Celtica* V (Dublin, 1960) v-x.

a learned society and afterwards to edit the papers, to point out a manuscript and say in his authoritative manner: "This is the scribe of the Book of Dimma, don't you see the tail on the letter *d*," or, "This verbal form never occurs in the prose texts."

Next day, Saturday, I busily scoured the Dublin bookstores along the quays and around Trinity College for a copy of Madame Sjoestedt's study of the speech of West Kerry. [5] My own copy was at home over 3000 miles away, and the scholars in Dublin who owned a copy which I might have borrowed were themselves out of the city and the country on holiday. Madame Sjoestedt had done her study for a degree at the Sorbonne a generation earlier. Later I was to meet some of her original informants either on the Great Blasket itself or on the mainland overlooking it.

Monday morning found me at 8 a.m. boarding the train at Westland Row without Madame Sjoestedt's book and only an Irish dictionary, a Latin-Irish missal, and a school edition of O'Sullivan's *Fiche Blian ag Fás*. [6] I succumbed at the last moment of packing and included the all-Greek Macmillan edition of the *Iliad*. At least I'd obeyed Mr. Best's injunction — no English books!

One approaches the West Kerry Gaeltacht in this wise: one rides a train out across Central Ireland past an occasional seventeenth century castle erected by some English lord. This is a modern Diesel powered train, complete with dining car, where one can have a very fine breakfast in luxury for 35 cents. This takes us past the great sugar beet plantations near Mallow and then on a single-track, as the Irish say "from there out," past the Killarney lakes and mountains on to Tralee. Everything changes at Tralee; the whole tempo of life slows down. The Slieve Mish to the south of the town is a great mountain bare of trees, a cheerless prospect on a cloudy day, but glorious with its multi-colored heather on a sunshiny day. The bus driver must be bilingual, and one is at first surprised to hear the smartly dressed secretary, homeward bound on holiday, speak excellent English

---

[5] Marie Louise Sjoestedt, *Phonétique d'un parler irlandais de Kerry* (Pa-1931) [Collection de documents linguistiques, IV].

[6] Maurice O Sullivan, *Fiche blíadhain ag Fás... eagran scoile* (Dublin, n.d.).

in answer to some query of a fellow passenger, then fluent Irish to the old grannie who came into town to sell a few eggs and buy her tea and sugar.

A ride of some thirty miles on this bus takes one over the Dingle Peninsula through some of the loveliest mountain country and over one of the largest sheep pastures in Northwestern Europe. After climbing over the hog-back of a mountain ridge one sees the waters of Dingle Bay a-glistening in the distance. Dingle is a pleasant Elizabethan town with some of the old fortress still intact. A few hotels owned by Irish who made their fortune in the United States line the main street. From here one must contract with a local cabby for a ride out to Dunquin. I was fortunate to have some help at this time. I had noticed even at Westland Row a middle aged man, apparently a civil servant on holiday, having quite a time of it putting his bicycle aboard the baggage car. Again at Tralee he was busy helping a porter strap that vehicle to the top of our bus. By good fortune he was headed for the Dunquin area to practice his Irish for another governmental examination. He told me that he'd handle the cabby, and we would split the fare later. We were soon rolling over the mountain in a coughing ancient Chevrolet, which broke down only once in the thirteen mile trip.

Luckily I'd met Liam McCarty, for he knew the area very well and introduced me to Maurice O'Sullivan's aunt, "Old Kate" Ó'Cathasaigh, with whom I boarded for the next month. Mrs. Casey was the daughter of a former "King" of the Blaskets and was known thereabouts as "The Princess," and she lived in a comfortable house alongside the Dunquin Chapel (R. C.) and across the way from an ancient cemetery no longer in use. She was an excellent teacher in Irish, for she and her late husband had for years opened their house [every summer] to teachers of the Irish language who had come every summer to brush up on the purest form of the Irish language still used. In her front parlor I found a run of *Béaloideas*, the journal of the Irish Folklore Society. She told me many stories of such worthies as Carl Marstrander [7] whom

---

[7] Carl Johan Sverdrup Marstrander taught Old and Middle Irish at the School of Irish Learning in 1910, served as associate editor of *Ériu* V-VI (1911-1912), and began the *Dictionary of the Irish Language,* bringing out the first fascicle *D-degóir* in 1913.

she remembered coming to the Great Blasket when she was a young girl. Later came others such as Professor Kenneth Jackson.[8] Once she came to the mainland she met many others, and in his last years the late Robin Flower [9] used to stay at her house for a few days before going out to the Island.

This may call for some explanation: the Great Blasket Island [10] lies some three miles off the Dingle Peninsula and the intervening waters are very treacherous because of heavy undercurrents due to the tides. It requires the labor of three strong men to row one of the *naomhogs* out to the Island, and the visitor must himself pay them three or four Irish pounds for the round trip ($ 9 to $ 12 in our money). The weather was not always propitious to "go out" and often enough people had to put up at a guest house on the mainland for a few days. Similarly, when one "came off" the Island, sometimes there would be several day's wait for a ride back to Dingle or Tralee.

---

[8] Kenneth Hurlstone Jackson published tales he had taken down in the Blasket: "Dhá scéal ón mBlascaod" (two tales from the Blasket) *Béaloideas: Journal of the Folklore of Ireland Society* IV (1934) 301-311; "Scéalta ón mBlascaod" (tales from the Blasket) *ibid*. VIII (1938) 3-96.

[9] Robin Earnest William Flower (1881-1946) was Deputy Keeper of the Western Manuscripts in the British Museum and served for some time as Hon. Director of the Early English Text Society. He completed O'Grady's *Catalogue of Irish Manuscripts in the British Museum* (London, 1926) and in addition to the translation of O'Crohan's *Islandman* (*cf*. note 1 *supra*) he wrote *The Western Island, or, The Great Blasket* (Oxford, 1944) and *The Irish Tradition* (Oxford, 1947). He was lovingly named *Blaithín* [pron. blawheen] by the Blasket Islanders, meaning 'Little Flower.' He spent every summer holiday on the Blasket until the beginning of World War II and on his death-bed directed that his ashes be broadcast over the island. For an obituary and bibliography cf. *Proceedings of the British Academy* XXXII (1946) 353-379.

[10] The Blaskets (Ir. *na Blascaodaí*) comprise a group of islands off the Dingle Peninsula in West Kerry, Ireland. The Great Blasket is about five miles long, one half mile wide, and soars to almost one thousand feet at the peak. Only fifty people lived on it in 1953, and it was evacuated the following year by government order. Other islands were *Inish-vick-ilaun, Inish-na-Bró*, and the *Tearacht* to the west with the lighthouse. *Inish Túiscirt*, northernmost of the group has an ancient oratory of Saint Brandan, the patron saint of this district. Professor Marstrander derived the term Blasket from the Norse, from an original Blaksey, the older English form on early maps being Blaskey. In the Old Irish Annals the name is *Inse Tarbhna iar nÉirinn*, 'the Island Tarbhna west of Ireland.' Cf. *Tonn Tóime* (Dublin, 1915), p. 160.

Living in a cottage in Dunquin one was so much closer to
the people than one should have been in a hotel. One could
learn much about local customs, and the people were always
glad to explain things. A man in the neighborhood had died the
first week I was there, and on Thursday night they brought his
body to the chapel. Four men carried the coffin on their shoulders, and the next afternoon about one o'clock people came walking from all over the surrounding country for the last rites. A
good many elderly people dropped into my landlady's house for
a "spot of tea." When it was time for the body to be carried from
the church, Mrs. Casey drew all the window shades and told me
not to leave the house until after the funeral procession was well
down the road. This is the local custom: all shades are drawn,
no one dares look out the window, no one enters or leaves a
cottage whilst the funeral is passing by.

The procession proceded on foot for well over a mile to the
"new cemetery," which was on the very edge of the Atlantic. An
old cemetery is "closed" and the last grave is filled only by some
one who has died and has no known living relatives as it is "bad
luck" to be a surviving relative of one who is last to be buried
in a graveyard. Likewise it is very bad luck to be the surviving
relative of one first buried in a new cemetery. So it often happens
that a new graveyard is begun, before the old one is completely
filled, with the body of some old man or woman who has no
living relatives. I do not recall that there were any flowers at this
funeral. After the customary prayers had been said and the *De
Profundis* (Psalm 129) recited by all in Latin, everyone came up
and threw a clod of earth upon the coffin. I found the cemeteries
all in a state of hopeless disorder, long grass and weeds, uncared
for graves, broken down tombstones. (I am not speaking of spick
and span places like Glasnevin now!).

There seems to be great superstition concerning the dead in
these parts. Fine blackberries grew on a vine which drooped
over the stone wall of the cemetery across the lane from Mrs.
Casey's place. A group of us were standing there talking one
day, and I reached unconsciously for a large berry the size of
my thumb. Mrs. Casey pulled my hand away in terror, and they
were all afraid, and none dared even mention what might befall
me were I to eat such a berry. However, a spring flowed from

under that same wall nearby and people drew water there for tea and dishwashing and saw no harm in that. One day I asked her if I could see her father's grave in that same "closed" cemetery. She thought there would be no harm in that for *me*, but warned me against photographing the stone. He had been "King of the Island" and as such had merited a very fine stone, and I copied off the Irish inscription unbeknownst to her.

However, she was very anxious for me to see her husband's grave 6 miles away by Ventry church over the mountain. She packed me two ham-sandwiches for the trip, and I found some large blackberries growing along the road, which I ate with a chocolate bar and refreshed myself with water from various springs which ran down the mountainside. At the bottom of the mountain, I found Ventry church and, a half mile beyond, the little church-yard; and I copied off on a chocolate wrapper the inscription on Mr. Casey's tombstone. His wife had composed it herself in literary Irish. I little realized it at the time, but that afternoon I had passed the very house where Jeremiah Curtin had stayed in 1891 whilst collecting some of his Irish folk-tales. [11]

As I walked about on Ventry Strand that lovely afternoon I was thinking back to a curious Middle Irish text I had read as a graduate student, the famous *Cath Finntrágha* [12] (Battle of Ventry) wich tells the story of a great pre-Christian battle which the local Irish still say was as momentous for Western civilization as the defeat of the Persians at Marathon. Archaeologists from Dublin had found many Stone Age weapons there on the strand, which proves of course that it was an ancient battle field. That evening when I satisfied Mrs. Casey that I'd seen her husband's grave, and read off the inscription I'd copied down, I mentioned the *Cath Finntrágha,* and her face lit up.

[11] Jeremiah Curtin, (1835-1906), *Memoirs edited with notes and introduction by Joseph Schafer* (Madison, 1940) [Wisconsin Biography Series, vol. II] 448-451. Cf. also his *Tales of the Fairies and of the Ghost-World collected from oral tradition in South-West Munster* (London, 1895).

[12] *The Cath Finntrága or Battle of Ventry* edited from MS Rawl. B.487 in the Bodleian Library by Kuno Meyer (Oxford, 1885) [Anecdota Oxoniensia ... Mediaeval and Modern Series, vol. I. pt. IV]. This text is now available in a new edition by Cecile O'Rahilly (Dublin, 1962).

"O yes, the *Cath Finntrágha* we know well. When I was at school on the Island we never heard of it, because they tried to make us use English in the schools in those days. But after the "troubles" in 1916 and 1923 the men in Dublin said that Irish was to be the language of the new Irish Free State and school teachers and scholars from all over Ireland came here to learn Irish and to write text books in Irish.

She went to her bedroom and brought back a little school edition of the *Cath Finntrágha.* [13] I could see at once that it bore little similarity to the tale I'd read ten years earlier. The plot was there to be sure, but the grotesque mock epic style, drawing upon both the Fenian and Ulster epic cycles had been omitted. Some weeks later at the Bodleian Library in Oxford, I asked to see the oldest extant copy of the *Cath Finntrágha.* When the great vellum manuscript was brought to me I noticed that the scribe had signed his name as Finnlaech Ó Chathasaigh (Finley O'Casey). No wonder the Caseys should leave directions that their bodies be buried in historic Ventry near the great white strand!

One did not have to look for folklore; it came to one, often with an explanation voluntarily given. On August fifteenth I went for a walk down to the *cuisheen* to wade. This is a place where a small creek runs into the ocean about a mile from Dunquin. There I met the only two Protestants of the whole area, an old woman and her middle aged daughter, who was bringing ocean water in a pail to her mother who sat nearby soaking her feet in a small tub. The younger woman explained that today being a feast of Our Lady was particularly good for the rheumatic to soak their limbs in the salty ocean brine. So one found the belief in the efficacious value of springs, many of them dedicated to some sainted hermit, either man or woman, who lived there long ago. A pilgrimage is made once a year to the Well of St. Gobnait after whom the local national school is named. Many coins cover the bottom of the spring which is only about eighteen inches deep. An earthworks enclosing about a half an acre of land encompasses the spring. The land is never ploughed up or

---

[13] *Cath Fionntrága*: aith-innsint ar an Seinsgéal as Gaedhilg na haimsire seo an Seabhac (Dublin, n.d.).

worked, but sheep graze there freely and keep the grass well cropped.

But alongside of such piety where the saints of old were concerned, one found the utmost superstition: middle aged men afraid to walk alone in the dark because of the "fairies." I had a feeling at times that I was myself suspect of being in league with the Powers of Darkness, since I sometimes took long walks in the evening after supper and returned long after dark with no apparent concern. On one occasion I was warned that if I must walk by night, I should keep to the middle of the road as it was highly dangerous to walk close to the hedges on either side. There is a great deal here of telling ghost stories and often a man pays dearly for a convivial evening afterwards when it is time to go home. We were discussing ghosts one evening, and someone asked me whether we in America are troubled with ghosts. I was beginning my favorite about the haunted house we once lived in near Leesburg, Virginia, when Mrs. Casey threw up her hands in terror and begged me to desist:

"For," said she, "the winter will soon be here and me alone in my house so close to the cemetery and the great winds out-doors a-howling and then I'll fear the more when I do be remembering the stories we told tonight."

Afterwards I had to accompany a man home because he was afraid of the fairies, and he forty-five years old and the father of four children.

It was a great time I had there in the Gaeltacht, and when I got back to Dublin with its dirt and noise, many was the time I longed for the quiet of West Kerry where only the seals in the coves along the ocean kept one awake at night. So successful was my venture into Modern Irish that I went home and classified my material and wrote a paper entitled "Some Remarks on Blasket Irish," for the Linguistic Society of America at the following Christmas meeting. [14] I was encouraged by the discussion afterwards to go ahead and apply for a grant-in-aid from the American Philosophical Society for a second summer trip. In

---

[14] *Language* XXX (1954) Bull. no. 27, p. 16, report on 1953 Meeting of the Linguistics Society of America in New York City; discussion by Proff. Martinet of Columbia and Whatmough of Harvard.

the meanwhile I read various Irish folktales, and when I went back the following year I had a present of a translation of *Fiche Blian ag Fás* for Mrs. Casey's library.

That second trip was made earlier in the season, and I was not the sole boarder, for people were there preparing for the state examinations in Irish for positions as teachers, the civil service, etc., and they were for the most part not genuinely interested in the language. Many of them considered themselves superior to the poor people of the district and looked down upon them. They wasted a good deal of my own time as they always tried to side-track me into talking about how we lived here in the States. Here again they were avid readers of the British version of *Reader's Digest* and saw many Hollywood films in the cinema. A theologian from Trinity College, Dublin was also there, and he was genuinely interested in Irish, as he was soon to be ordained for the Church of Ireland. His background in Irish was the same as my own, having learned the forms of the older language from the philologists in Dublin. He was more apt to be critical of the West Kerry people in their pronunciation of Irish.

I made the acquaintance of old Marthan, the parish "clark" who at 84 still served the priest at daily Mass. I had heard that he had a great store of *sheanachas*, "old traditions," so I told him one day I'd stop by very soon. I ventured forth, then, one afternoon when the weather did not look very promising for a long walk over the mountains. After picking my way carefully from stone to stone in his manure-spread yard, which served as pig-sty and cow byre as well as a duck and goose run, I reached the one-roomed house with the hearth at one end and the sleeping quarters to the other. Marthan's niece opened the door and shooed away the ducks and goose, and I entered, finding the old man by the fireside smoking his pipe. First of all he told me stories in Irish, some of these of the punning variety which require a good knowledge of the language and a fine taste for distinctions in meanings. I needed help from one of the Dublin folklorists later in getting the meaning of some of these. Finally old Marthan nudged me in the ribs — a "good one" was coming:

ísel úasal agus úasal ísel
['the low (shall be) high and the high (shall be) low']
merely a variant of the *Magnificat* verse:

Deposuit potentes de sede et exaltavit humiles, [Luke I. 52]

which old Marthan's ancestors must have sung at many a Sunday vespers in the Dunquin chapel in the old days.

The afternoon was passing on, and soon the inevitable four o'clock shower drove the harvesters into the house. They had been cutting oats on the mountain field above the house with small hand sickles, nothing as complicated as our own old fashioned grain-cradle. The fields are so small and rock-bound that there would be no place here for the grain binder, let alone a large combine, although I'd seen some of them at work in the large farms in Central Ireland the day I came out by train.

The motley crew of farm hands moved into the cabin and listened to the stories and proverbs. Old Marthan was a skilled teacher and would make me repeat the phrases to him as he recited. In the case of longer sentences, I would read it back to him from my notebook. My audience was a quiet and attentive one, but at last one of the men noticing my phonetic notation spoke up:

"Whatever is that writing you have there that makes the language come out just right? I say, we should have just such a writing to put down our words by." I told him that this was a system of writing devised by the scholars to take down dictation of different languages. No use here to go into the fine points of theoretical phonetics and phonemics. The Irish people out here do speak the language, but when they go to school they have the same difficulty as we do in Modern English. They find out soon enough that the ideal spelling system, a separate symbol for each sound does not exist any more in Irish than in our own language. Somehow the Irish people connect this orthographically difficult system with the disappearance of Irish — nothing, of course, could be farther from the truth.

Marthan's niece was now appoaching the fire-place to give another stir to the supper boiling in the great pot over the fire. She simply took his walking stick out of his hand to stir the mess and replaced the stick afterward. So much for the simplicity of life in the Gaeltacht. Needless to say I did not stay for supper, although I'd been invited. I paid off Marthan with a package of cigarettes and was off to my own lodgings.

Pretty soon the librairies would reopen in Dublin, and I was anxious to meet old Peig Sayers [15] whose son Micheál Ó Gaoithín [16] I had visited in Dunquin. I left on Saturday noon and put up at Benner's Hotel in Dingle for the week end as there would be no bus to Tralee nor train to Dublin until Monday. Then I betook myself to the Sisters' Hospital on the outskirts of Dingle to see old Peig. Bed-ridden and blind, she sat in her cot at the end of a long room, the old women's ward. Here was the great story teller of the Blaskets, back once more in Dingle where she had taken service as a young girl. She had no Irish for me, was more interested in the way I'd come across the Atlantic on the great ship. And she fell into a great description of a storm at sea and the winds blowing, so that one forgot for the moment it was in a charity-ward in a hospital in Dingle that we were. It was an impassioned piece of oratorical description resembling in its intensity and crescendo the *hwyl* I have heard in Welsh sermons. One could see why they had called her *Peir mhór* (great Peig) on the Island, for even sitting in that bed in a charity ward, waiting to die, and well past eighty, one noticed her large frame.

When I left the hospital an hour later I asked the Sister in charge whether I might return the following Sunday afternoon, inquiring whether there were some little gift I might bring Peig. She answered:

"Sure there is and there be nothing she likes so well after night-prayers but a little *tuiscín,* a glass of water and a wee bit of *uisce* and a lump of sugar in it."

---

[15] Some four hundred folk-tales were taken down orally from Peig Sayers (1873-1958) and over forty folk-songs. Her autobiography in Irish, *Peig* (Dublin, 1936) was edited by Mary Kennedy as where her memoirs, *Machtnamh Seana Mhná* (Dublin, 1939), recently translated from the Irish by Séamus Ennis, *An Old Woman's Recollections* (Oxford, 1962).

[16] An account of a visit to the home of Micheál Ó Gaoithín is to be found in R. T. Meyer, "West Kerry Interlude" *Carroll Quarterly* 11 (1958) 31-40.

I went out to the nearest pub and bought for thirty-five bob the largest bottle of Jameson's whiskey in the place and went back with it Sunday afternoon. As I entered the old women's ward one of the old ladies shouted out:

"Oh, Peig, the *Ameiricaneach* is back again, and ooh, he's got a present for ye!"

I gave her the well wrapped bottle and she asked:

"Is it a baby?"

Then feeling of the package, the hands gradually worked their way to the top and recognition came.

"Oh, God in High Heaven bless the good man. Sure and 'tis a bigger bottle than ever Dr. Delargy [17] brought me all the way from Dublin. May God bless you, my good man."

And thus ended my sojourn of three summers in the *fior-Gaelthacht* of West Kerry. Some years later a letter came from Dr. Séamus Delargy, Director of the Irish Folklore Commission that old Peig had died, last of a noble race of story-tellers.

---

[17] For an account of Irish story-telling, cf. J. H. Delargy, "The Gaelic Story-Teller, with some notes on Gaelic Folk-Tales," *Proceedings of the British Academy* XXXI (1945) 177-221.

FREDERICK II'S TRUE NOBLE FALCON

JAN A. NELSON
University of Iowa

Frederick II, author of the classic *De Arte venandi cum avi-bus* [1] logically opens his discussion of falcons with a general statement about their classification. Of the two categories which he recognized, the first and the more highly regarded he terms the noble falcons; these being: the gyrfalcon, the saker, the peregrine, the true noble falcon and the lanner. The second category is comprised of the goshawk and the sparrowhawk which he properly terms accipiters. According to Frederick II these seven types were the ones commonly used by the medieval falconer. He excludes the eagle in keeping with the practique of western falconry on the grounds that it is too heavy for easy transport and that it frightens other falcons with which it might be flown. He also excludes the merlin and the hobby inasmuch as he considered them to be too small and ineffective against desirable quarry. The distinction which Frederick II makes between the noble falcons and the accipiters is still accepted by falconers [2] and is based primarily on the natural differences existing between the two groups and secondarily on the sporting techniques proper to each, the latter being a practical application of the bird's instinctive behavior. For example, the long-winged hawks, Frederick II's

---

[1] Frederick II, *The Art of Falconry being the De Arte venandi cum avibus,* ed. and trans. by Casey A. Wood and F. Margorie Fyfe (Stanford: Stanford University Press, 1961).

[2] E. B. Michel, *The Art and Practice of Hawking* (Boston: Charles T. Branford Co., 1959), 9-11.

noble falcons, take their quarry by stooping at it from above and with great speed so that the kill is made by sheer impact while the short-winged hawks, the accipiters, pursue their quarry which is killed only after having been seized. The fundamental importance of these differences in behavior to both the theory and the practice of falconry should be obvious. The accipiters, for instance, can be used to take a variety of game including some animals and they can be flown in wooded areas as well as in the open. Despite these apparent utilitarian advantages, however, medieval and modern falconers alike concur enthusiastically in their opinion that it is the long-winged hawk, the falcon, which provides the most satisfaction. Coming after long periods of constant vigilance and great patience, the falcon's successful stoop must be one of the most exciting experiences of the field. It is this superior performance to which Frederick II refers in his designation of these birds as noble falcons, but a certain ambiguity is betrayed by the designation of one among the noble falcons as the true noble falcon. The emperor himself admits confusion on this point. He relates that many of his comtemporaries regarded the true noble falcon as a separate species, but comments that he had been unable to distinguish it from the peregrine in such a way as to justify this distinction. [3] Still, he finds it necessary to give separate standing to the enigmatic creature.

The contemporary opinion to which Frederick II refers is attested in the *Letter of Aquila, Symmachus and Theodotia to King Ptolomy of Egypt*. This little treatise must have enjoyed considerable vogue during the 13th century judging by the number of manuscripts, known translations and by its contribution of source material to the *Dels auzels cassadors* of Daude de Pradas [4] and Brunetto Latini's *Livres dou Tresor*. [5] It is regrettable that this valuable document has not had the attention it deserves.The only two published versions in existence, the one a fragmentary Latin text and the other in Catalan, are to be found in the rare

---

[3] Frederick II, 127.

[4] Deude de Pradas, *Dels Auzels Cassadors,* ed. Alexander H. Schutz (Columbus: Ohio University Press, 1945).

[5] Brunetto Latini, *Li Livres dou Tresor,* ed. Francis J. Carmody, Publications in Modern Philology, Vol. 22 (Berkeley and Los Angeles: University of California Press, 1948).

ΙΕΡΑΚΟCΟΘΙΟΝ: *Rei accipitaria scriptores nunc primun editi. (Accessit Lutetia, Sumptibus H Drouart, 4to. 1612)* edited by Nicholas Rigaltius. As indicated, the Latin text is fragmentary and lacks precisely the section treating the noble falcon. Turning, then, to the Catalan version and the chapter entitled "Dels ocels qui son appellatz falcons" it will be noted that seven types are given: *laner del qual son II maneres, pelegrins, montasi, gris la qual es appellada gentil vulgarment, Gathena, VI manera es sobre tots,* and *Breton.* [6] The antique character of this material may very well be indicated by the mythological character of the last two "falcons". [7] Of the others, the *pelegris, montasi* and *gris* are the ones which requiere special attention with respec to the question of the true noble falcon. The Catalan text provides the following information:

> ...La seconda manera es aus pelegrins, lo qual es leus de nudrir. La terza manera es montasi. La IIII manera es gris, la qual es apellada gentil vulgarment, & nobla de noble de nom & d'persona... (189)

Daude de Pradas has preserved a somewhat less abbreviated version:

XVI

Lo segons linhatges

Lo segons es lo pelegris.
Leu si te e leu si noiris;
e per so a nom pelegri
car hom no troba lo sieu ni.
Auzels es valens e cortes,

---

[6] Rigaltius, 189.

[7] Schutz proposed the identification of the Breton with the saker following information provided by Albertus Magnus (See: Daude de Pradas, 208, note 397), however the description of the two creatures justifies their classification as mythological: La Vi. manera es sobre tots, laqual ha semblansa dangilla blancha, exceptat q̄ los peus & los huyls & en loget, & en altres coses sembla falcon. Lo VII. linatge es Breton, loqual pren tots au, & ha principat sobre toz ocels de cassa: si q̄ neguna nogosa pendre d'uant ell, ni volar sobre ell volant. Rigaltius, 189. See also: Daude de Pradas, 80 and Brunetto Latini, 140.

de bon adop en totas res.
Ben fai parer que estranhs sia;
aisi es de bona bailia.

XVII

Lo ters linhatge

Lo ters es lo falcx montaris;
sest es asatz nostre vezis.
Totz proz om lo conois, so cug;
pos es privatz, a tart s'en fug.

XVIII

Lo cart linhatge

Lo cart a nom falco gruër
ho gentil, car de son mester
li don'om nom, per que val mais.
Auzels es de trop gran pantais;
az ome a pe non val re,
car trop asegre lo.ill cove.
D'aquetz tres dic comunalmen
una retgla d'ensenhamen:
que sel que a lo cap menor
deu hom cauzir per lo meillor.

(79)

Finally there is the corresponding text of Brunetto Latini:

>   2.   La seconde ligne est faucon ke l'en apiele pelerins,
> pour çou que nus ne trueve son nit, ains est pris autresi
> comme en pelerinage; et est mout legiers a norrir et mout
> cortois et vaillans et de bone maniere. 3.   La tierce ligne
> est faucon montardis; assés est connus par tous lieus; et
> puis k'est privés, il ne s'enfuira jamés. 4.   La quarte lig-
> nie est faucon gentil ou gruier, que vaut mieus que li
> autre; més il n'a mestier a home sans cheval, car trop
> li covient ensivre. Et tant sachés que de ces iiii lignies vous
> devés eslire celi ki a plus petit chief... (140)

It is clear from the available evidence that the fourth variety is
called not only the noble falcon, but also either *gruër* or *gris*. It

is not unreasonable to explain the isolated Catalan term *gris* as a misreading of *gruër*. The fragmentary condition of the Latin text, however, makes it impossible to support this supposition. It would appear from the Catalan text that the term noble falcon is merely a common name for the bird and the inference can be made on a basis of all three texts that as such the term derives from the general regard for the bird's superior qualities. There is, in addition, no information about its origins as there is for the peregrine and the *montaris,* the former remarkable because its nesting grounds are unknown while the latter is treated as extremely common and well known everywhere. In short, the evidence of the *Letter to Ptolomy* does not provide an accurate definition of the designation noble falcon and when considered alone it might well lead the modern reader to little more than a simpathetic understanding for Frederick II's failure to clarify the problem.

The *Letter to Ptolomy* becomes more pertinent when it is considered in the light of Pero Lopez de Ayala's *Libro de la Caza de las Aves.* [8] Pero Lopez de Ayala proceeds in his treatment of falconry with the same thorough concern for information based on practical experience that characterizes the *De Arte venandi cum avibus.* The number of first hand accounts and personal experiences with which the writer substantiates his material is reassuring after the fabulous nature of certain of the statements passed on by such others as Daude de Pradas and Brunetto Latini. Pero Lopez de Ayala is also as specific in his presentation of information as Frederick II and he provides a full account of each species of interest to the falconer. It is information that serves to elucidate the laconic *Letter to Ptolomy* and its progeny with bearing on the problem posed by Frederick II.

Pero Lopez de Ayala prefaces his remarks on the peregrine with a general comment about those birds which he regards as falcons:

> Falcones entre los cazadores comunmente son llamados seis plumajes, ó seis linajes de ellos, que es á saber:

---

[8] Pero Lopez de Ayala, *Libro de la Caza de las Aves, Biblioteca Venatoria,* Vol. III, *Libros de Cetraria del Principe y el Canciller,* ed. José Gutiérrez de la Vega (Madrid: M. Tello, 1879).

neblís, baharís, girifaltes, sacres, bornís, alfaneques. De
los tagarotes non facen mencion, porque son acordados
por baharís. (158

He then continues and qualifies this generic use of the term
falcon in a manner which is significant:

> Et debedes saber que en todas las tierras de cristianos,
> salvo en España, son llamados estos seis plumajes por sus
> nombres, ca el girifalte, llaman así por su nombre girifalte,
> mas non falcon, et al sacre dicen sacre, et al borní et al
> alfaneque llamanlos laneros. Et á estos todos non los
> llaman falcones, antes dicen que son villanos, así como
> quien dice falcones bastardos, ó fornecinos, et solamente
> al neblí, et al baharí llaman falcones et gentiles, ca hán
> las manos grandes, et los dedos delgados, et en sus talles
> son más gentiles, que hán las cabezas más firmes et más
> pequeñas, et las alas en las puntas mejor sacadas, et las
> colas más cortas, et más derribados en las espaldas, et
> más apercebidos, et más ardidos, et de mayor esfuerzo;
> et en sus gobernamientos son más delicados que los otros
> que dicho habemos. (158)

It would appear from the foregoing that the generic use of the
term was not accepted outside of Spain and that only two of
the six listed, the *neblí* and the *baharí*, were legitimately referred
to as falcons and regarded as noble; the other hawks being referred to by type: gyrfalcon, sacer, lanner, etc., or simply as *villa-
nos*. Nevertheless, the Spanish generic use of the term falcon or
noble falcon which can be inferred from Pero Lopez de Ayala's
statement would correspond to its use by Frederick II. The noble
falcons listed by Frederick II are given in order of size with the
implication that this factor is essential to the worth of the several bird: *girofalco, falco sacer, falco peregrinus, falco absolute
gentiles, falco lanarius.* [9] The list provided by Pero Lopez de
Ayala is likewise organized in terms of individual worth but in
this case the element of size is given no importance: *neblí, ba-
har, girifalte, sacre, borní, alfaneque.* As the following discussion will illustrate, these falcons can be identified by a careful
comparision of medieval texts and by the confrontation of the

---

[9] Frederick II, 111.

medieval material with information provided by modern orni-
thology whenever necessary. The confusing and often contradic-
tory identification of these falcons as offered in existing glos-
saries, dictionaries and encyclopedias makes it clear that a simpathetic comparative study of the medieval documents themselves
has never been undertaken before. [10]

The *nebli* is identified with the peregrine by Pero Lopez de
Ayala himself.

> Et los falcones neblís en todas las tierras son llamados
> gentiles, que quiere decir fijos dalgo, et en Castilla et en
> Portugal son llamados neblís, pero al comienzo fueron
> llamados nebís, et por tiempo corompióse este vocablo,
> et dícenlos neblís, et en Aragon et en Catalueña lláman-
> los pelegrines, por comparación de los peregrinos et rome-
> ros que andan por todas las tierras, et por todo el mundo,
> que así son los falcones gentiles, ó neblís, ó peregri-
> nos, que todo el mundo andan, et traviesan con el su volar,
> partiendo de la tierra donde nacieron. (160)

The same writer lists the *baharí* as a separate species but indicates
a recognized similarity between it and the *nebli* or peregrine.

> ...el falcon baharí es llamado gentil en todas las tie-
> rras salvo en España, segund sus condiciones et faciones
> et manos et dedos et ardideza, en que parece al falcon
> neblí... (168)

The salient fact to be derived from this information is that
the *baharí* is designated as noble by virtue of its similarity to the
peregrine in physical characteristics and behavior. It is apparent
that the two falcons were enough alike to invite confusion if not
outright identification as implied by the classification of both as
noble. This possibility is in fact attested by none other than Don
Juan Manuel in his *Libro de la Caza.*

> ...Et dize Don johan que sinon porque de tiempo aca les
> llaman neblis e baharis e fazen entre ellos este departi-

[10] Don Juan Manuel, *Libro de la Caza,* ed. José María Castro y Calvo
(Barcelona, 1947). The editor of this valuable treatise provides a brief discussion of the falcons in question, but it will be noted that his identification
of these birds is not supported by evidence and does not always agree with
the facts established by the comparative study reported here.

> miento que el por vna natura los judgaria. ca non fallan entre ellos otra defferencia sinon que los neblis son tomados andando bravos, Et los baharis son tomados enlos nidos e son mayores los neblis quelos baharis. (25)

Don Juna Manuel's remarkably lucid observations not only help to clarify Pero Lopez de Ayala's statement, but also recall the information provided by the *Letter to Ptolomy* so specifically as to invite a second comparision. According to the latter source, the peregrine, even as its name suggests, is a stranger to southern Europe. In obvious contradistinction is the *montaris,* a well-known native of the region. A similar remark is made by Pero Lopez de Ayala comparing the *neblí* and the *baharí.*

> Et cuanto en Castilla, los mejores neblís que se toman son los de las rocinas, et en tierra de Sevilla, et otrosí son muy buenos en Portogal los que se toman en el Campo de Santaren, et todos estos falcones salen muy buenos, ca se toman muy lejos de la tierra donde nascen ca segund todos cuidan, ellos vienen de Nuruega et Pruza et Asuega et de cabo de la alta Alemania, dó criaron et nascieron, et vinieron con el paso de las aves, ca en España no fué home que fallase nido de falcon neblí. (163-164)

> Primeramente devedes saber que los falcones baharís crian dellos los más en la Isla de Cerdeña, et son llamados sardos, et otros baharís crian en la Isla de Mallorcas, et son mejores; et otros crian en Romanía, et estos son grandes falcones et muy buenos... (169)

The identification of the *baharí* with the *montaris* suggested by the information given in the sources cited is confirmed by Pero Lopez de Ayala who, in his lengthy discussion of the *baharí,* categorically states that: *en Aragon llaman á todos los baharís monterís.* [11] There remains the identification of the *baharí* in modern terms. Two pertinent facts are known: the *baharí* is strikingly similar to the peregrine and it is a native of southern Europe including the islands of the Mediterranean. The falcon which answers this description is the Elenora Falcon *(Falco elenorae).*

---

[11] Pero de Ayala, 171.

In its light phase this falcon suggests the immature peregrine not only in its coloration and general configuration, but also in its flight characteristics. Furthermore, the Elenora falcon's breeding grounds are restricted to the rocky islands of the Mediterranean and the coastal areas of southern Europe. [12] The latter fact is in perfect accord with the information given by Pero Lopez de Ayala and is in no way contradicted by the less specific indications of the *Letter to Ptolomy*. It will also be noted that Frederick II recognized a more southerly breeding ground for the true noble falcon than for the peregrine.

> The peregrine falcon constructs its nest in the far north, beyond the seventh zone and near the coast, on islands and (like the gerfalcon) in lofty sites. (111)

> True noble falcons breed from the seventh climatic zone southward and choose the same environment as peregrine falcons. (111)

As already stated, the Elenora falcon was associated with the peregrine in as much as it approached a c e r t a i n physical and behavioral standard set by the latter. That standard has been conveniently provided by Pero Lopez de Ayala during the course of the discussion of the falcons as cited above. The noble falcon is distinguished from its less highly esteemed kin by its large feet, slender toes, small and firm head, more elongated wings, shorter tail and lighter shoulders. These traits contribute to produce a keener and more ardent hunter demonstrating greater strength in the chase, but the falconer's price for such superiority is exacted in the more delicate treatment required by his favorite. One detail, the small head, can be regarded as especially significant inasmuch as it provides a link with the information given in *Dels Auzels Cassadors* and *Livres dou Tresor*. [13] To repeat the words of Daude de Pradas:

---

[12] James L. Peters, *Check-List of Birds of the World,* Vol. I (Cambridge: Harvard University Press, 1931), 293. Roger T. Peterson, Guy Mountfor and P. A. D. Hollom, *A Field Guide to the Birds of Britain and Europe* (Cambridge: Houghton Mifflin Co., 1954). 90.

[13] This significant detail is lacking in the Latin versions of the *Letter to Ptolomy*. As mentioned above, the Latin texts examined were all fragmen-

D'aquetz tres dic comunalmen
una retgla d'ensenhaman:
que sel que a lo cap menor
deu hom cauzir per lo meillor.
(79)

The three falcons to which Daude de Pradas is referring are precisely the three in question: *lo pelegris, lo falcx montar*is and the
falco gruër ho gentil. In other words, the peregrine and the Elenora falcon have been singled out once again and associated as a
class apart, the only difference here being their association with
the *falco gruër.* The one trait essential to this special classification
is precisely one of the traits given by Pero Lopez de Ayala as
essential to his designation of the *nebli* and the *bahari* as *falcones
et gentiles.* The fact that Daude de Pradas and Brunetto Latini
qualify the noble falcon as a *gruër* would again reflect a designation established with reference to performance. The former
writer is the more specific:

Lo cart a nom falco gruër
ho gentil, car de son mester
li don'om nom, per que val mais.
(79)

Frederick II, Don Juan Manuel and Pero Lopez de Ayala are in
general accord that the most dangerous and difficult game birds
are the crane and the heron. The first two writers deem it
advisable to dedicate entire chapters to the conditioning of falcons to take such quarry and Pero Lopez does not fail to comment on the potential success of such conditioning during his
discussion of the various falcons. He makes it clear that crane
and the heron, because of their size and ferocity, are not natural

---

tary and lacked the passage devoted to the noble falcon. The Catalan texts
is not so specific as either Daude de Pradas or Brunetto Latini, but the trait
in question may very well be implied by the rather vague *nobla de noble de
nom & d'persona.* It will be noted that Brunetto Latini includes the lanner
when stating that the relative size of the head serves as an indication of
quality, but he had already distinguished the lanner as having a large head
and his final comment can be interpreted in reference to the lanner as
merely a guide to the best of an inferior type.

quarry for any falcon and that the success of such a conditioning process is a tribute to both falcon and falconer.

> ...que asaz es sotileza et maravilla que por arte et sabiduría del home una ave tome á otras de las que por su naturaleza nunca tomara, nin en aquella manera que gela facen tomar; así como un falcon tagarote veemos que por su arte et sabiduría del home toma un grua, que es ave tan grande et tan leida... (145)

> Fermosa maravilha es, et otrosí grand bondat que un ave tan pequeña como es un falcon trabe de une crua, que es ave tan grande et tan brava, que cuando un home la toma en un lazo non osa llegar á ella, temiéndose del golpe que della recela haber, et pues el falcon es loado por tomar una tal ave, mucho mayor loor debe haver el cazador que por su sotil arte pone el falcon en se atrever á ello, et haver tan esforzado el corazon. (293).

The result of this difficult combination of conditioning and superior quality was a higher regard and an increased value. Daude de Pradas states this categorically and Pero Lopez de Ayala goes into some detail on the point.

> Et vale un neblí pollo altanero cuarenta francos de oro, et si fuese garcero, sesenta, et si son mudados, valen mas; que todo el peligro mayor ... es en la muda... (195)

Even Frederick II casts aside all doubt when it becomes a question of the true noble falcon's superior performance.

> There is so little difference, however, between these two varieties (peregrine and true noble falcon) in both plumage and bodily form that it is not easy to draw such a distinct line between them that an inexperienced man can differentiate one from another; and only long practice can prevent a falconer from mistaking the one for the other. On the other hand, the divergences in their accomplishments are so manifold and so apparent when in action that one cannot be mistaken for the other...
>
> (127)

The list of long-winged hawks employed by the medieval falconer can now be established with considerable certainty. The order adopted for this listing will be that of Pero Lopez de Ayala and will, therefore, be set with respect to his appraisal of their value as hunters. In descending order from the most highly respected are: the peregrine, the Elenora falcon, the gyrfalcon, the sacer and the lanner. That the first two hawks were further distinguished as an elite class to which the terms falcon or noble falcon properly applied and that the Elenora falcon was often confused with the peregrine as a single type has been sufficiently stressed. It will also be remembered that the designation of the elite noble falcons was based on a relative conformity to an ideal physical type. The unscientific nature of this designation should be clear enough and there should be no confusion of this classification with the highly scientific identification of the various species by an authority such as Pero Lopez de Ayala or Frederick II, but the two systems tend to conflict inasmuch as the long-winged hawks were and still are commonly known as falcons. The Latin for any one of these hawks is *falco* qualified in some way such as *falco peregrinus, falco sacer,* etc. It is unquestionably evident from such phrases as *falco montaris, falco gruër,* etc. that this Latin usage carried over into the vernacular and explains the generic use of the term. Even the falconer is forced to rely on the generic use of the term falcon as Pero Lopez de Ayala's discussion of the classification of the long-winged hawks amply illustrates.

The reasoning behind the falconer's special usage of the term falcon applies equally in the case of Frederick II and the true noble falcon. It can be seen from his statements as cited above about the true noble falcon that the emperor was able to distinguish it from the peregrine on a basis of only two characteristics, its vastly superior performance and the more southerly breeding grounds which he attributed to it. The recognized similarity of the true noble falcon to the peregrine and Frederick II's indication of its southern breeding grounds would immediately identify the true noble falcon with the Elenora falcon were it not for one objection. No falconer, medieval or modern, states that the Elenora falcon is superior with respect to the peregrine as does the emperor in such emphatic terms when speaking of the true noble falcon. If this elusive falcon is to be identified the facts must be reconsidered. The peregrine and the Elenora falcon are so similar that medieval falconers were prone to regard them as the same. The peregrine breeds in the north of Europe. The Elenora falcon breeds in the south of Europe. The peregrine and the Elenora falcon can be distinguished as a superior class and were alone referred to as falcons or noble falcons in the strict usage of falconry. The bird which Frederick II designates as the true noble falcon is distinguished from the peregrine by its superior performance. In addition, the emperor attributed to the true noble falcon the same breeding grounds recognized later by Pero Lopez de Ayala as those of the Elenora falcon. One identification of the true noble falcon can be suggested which does not violate the facts. Frederick II, like other medieval falconers, must not have distinguished between the peregrine and the Elenora Falcon. Contemporary falconers, in turn, were accustomed to a special designation for the superior hunters and these were in reality merely the superior peregrines or Elenora falcons, but the same contemporary falconers were not always as clearly scientific in their method as was Frederick II and they tended to consider the superior hunter as a separate species. This tendency is attested in the *Letter to Ptolomy* where the *gruër* is treated as the fourth of seven species. Frederick II makes the same mistake when he continues to treat the true noble falcon separately. One fact would support this error, that is, knowledge of the Elenora falcon's breeding grounds together with the failure to distinguish the latter from the peregrine which the emperor knew bred only in the far north. Significantly, this conjecture gains strength with the recollection that the emperor's hesitation with regard to this question reflects the conflict between contemporary opinion and usage and his own scientific acumen.

It is no wonder that it required long experience to unfailingly separate the true noble falcon from the peregrine, for success in this task depended on the recognition of a subtle gradation among individuals of one and the same species. Such success implies first hand experience with a very large cross section of peregrines, certainly more than any one modern falconer would ever handle in a life time.

THE GENESIS OF THE ROMAN DE THÈBES: INDIVIDUAL AND COLLECTIVE LITERARY CREATION *

DANA PHELPS RIPLEY
Duke University

In considering the origins of the *Roman de Thèbes,* the central problem which has not been satisfactorily solved is the date of composition of the primitive version of the poem. In fact, this problem has given to the poem an air of mystery, for while being obviously a source for many of the Romance works of the second half of the twelfth century, the versions which have come down to us in thirteenth and fourteenth century manuscripts have been dated by various scholars all the way from the 1150's to the early years of the following century. [1] Internal evidence supports dating

---

* Parts of this study were originally prepared as sections of the introduction to my Ph. D. thesis, *A Critical Edition of the Roman de Thèbes (lines 1-5394) with an Introduction, Notes, and Glossary* (Dept. of Romance Languages, University of North Carolina, 1960, reproduced photographically by University Microfilms, Ann Arbor, Michigan). In using the terms individual and collective with respect to literary creation, I have in mind the continuing controversy over the genesis of the *Chanson de Roland* and the compromise approach suggested for this problem by P. Le Gentil in his article, "Réflexions sur la création littéraire au Moyen Age," *Cultura Neolatina,* XX (1960), 2/3, 129-140. See also the series of studies concerning the relationships between epic and romance presented with discussions at the Heidelberg Colloquium in 1961, *Chanson de geste und höfischer Roman:* (Heidelberg: Carl Winter, Universitätsverlag, 1963). ("Studia Romanica," 4. Heft).

[1] See R. Harris, "A *terminus a quo* for the *Roman de Thèbes,*" *French Studies,* XI (1957), 201-213; and R. Levy, *Chronologie approximative de la littérature française du Moyen Age,* Tübingen: 1957 (Beihefte zur *Zeitschrift für romanische Philologie 98*). For detailed consideration of the dating, see Ripley, *A Critical Edition,* xxiii.

both at the end and at the beginning of the great flowering period of twelfth century literature which sawthe creation of the masterpieces of Marie de France and Chrétien de Troyes.

It is the purpose of this study to propose a solution to this problem. Study of the manuscripts of the *Thèbes* and the genesis and development of other Romance works of the period seems to support the following conjecture. The poem as we possess it is a work of both individual and collective authorship which in its first form was created near the beginning of the second half of the century; it evolved through the years, gaining new episodes and amplifications of the original poetry. The work changed in style and was corrected with regard to its main source, the *Thebaid* of Statius. The love element was developed, and Arthurian material added. The final version is the result of the work of many individuals, poets and scribes. The continuing creation kept in step with history: at one point the poem reflects events of the Second Crusade, at another the Fourth. And, what is most important, the *Thèbes* appears to have passed through a period of disuse at some time in its history. A gap in time is indicated between the earliest versions and the ten to fourteen thousand line poems at the end of the tradition.

It has, of course, always been understood that the *Thèbes* passed through periods of evolution in which it underwent change in the hands of poets other than the first author. This is the conception on which the Constans edition is based, [2] and scholars have assumed that the primitive version is the earliest one that appears in the extant manuscripts. This new conjecture proposes that the earliest *Thèbes* is lost and that the two distinct versions which appear in the MSS date from the last part of the century and are contemporary with the twelve syllable *Roman d'Alexandre*. [3]

The *Roman de Thèbes* is preserved in five manuscripts and one fragment. [4]

---

[2] L. Constans (ed.) *Le Roman de Thèbes, publié d'après touts les manuscrits* (S. A. T. F.; Paris: Firmin Didot et Cie, 1890), II, xlviii-lxv.

[3] The loss of a primitive version of the poem does not mean, of course, that no portions of the original appear in the extant MSS. See below, p. 7.

[4] For further description of the MSS, see Constans, II, ii-xiv.

—C. Paris, B. N. fs. fr. 784, f. lv-67r. French; late thirteenth century, 10,562 lines. —B. Paris, B. N. fs. fr. 60, f. 1-41. French; late fourteenth century. Closely related to MS C, 10,541 lines. — S. London, British Museum Add. 34,114, f. 164r-226v. Anglo-Norman; last third of the fourteenth century, 11,546 lines. This MS is used by Constans as the base for his edition. —A. Paris, B. N. fs. fr. 375, f. 36r-67v. French; 1288, date supplied by the scribe, 14,627 lines. —P. Cologny-Genève, Switzerland, Bibliothèque Bodmer (formerly Phillipps 8384), 13,296 lines. —D. Bibliothèque d'Angers, No. 26 (Cat. gén., XXXI, 199). French; late twelfth century. Two fragments: one of 110 lines, the second of 112 lines.

The MSS fall clearly into two groups: CBS, the earliest extant versions of the poem; PA, later versions. [5] MSS C and B are closely related. They have the same interpolations and differences of minor importance. MS B was not copied from C, nor C from B, but the two have similar sources; S is related to the group CB, but not closely; there is considerable variation, notably in respect to interpolations. There is some evidence that S represents in some of its parts a slightly older version than that of CB. [6]

The length of MSS P and A in relation to those of the other tradition is at once an indication of a later version, larger through interpolation. Close examination of the variants found in these two MSS bears this out. From the opening lines on throughout the poem, we find large and obvious expansions of the earlier versions, both amplification of earlier material and insertion of new episodes. [7]

---

[5] This grouping is clearly demonstrated by variants; see Constans, I and II, passim. For a detailed analysis of the grouping, see II, xlviii-lxvi, and Ripley, vii ff.

[6] The fact that MS S shows none of the attempts (found in all the other MSS) to correct earlier versions of the poem in respect to its model, the *Thebaid,* is an indication of possible anteriority. And the episode of the second presentation of the riddle of the Sphinx (ed. Constans, II, p. 7) appears in CB (Ripley, 11. 2883-2942) in a form obviously a shorter version of an earlier one found in S. On the other hand, the presence in S or large interpolations in the episode of Daire le Roux (Constans, 1. 7643 ff.) seems to suggest a younger version, for amplifications of this episode occur also in PA. A fourteenth century MS may have been copied from several sources and reflect thereby different parts of the evolutionary creation of the poem.

[7] For a complete listing of these variants, see Constans, II, pp. 106-313.

The origins of the *Thèbes* and the circumstances surrounding its creation are known in part, and what is known is established with certainty.[8] This is an art form growing out of and continuing, with significant innovations, the epic which it apparently replaced in some circles. There is a strong influence from lyric poetry, the Crusade epics, and the works af Ovid and other Latin poets. The *geste* is taken from the *Thebaid,* although many purely medieval episodes are added; the Oedipus legend which serves as a preface comes from an unknown source. The poetry comes from a learned atmosphere, that of the *clerc* and the school, and has a new style derived in part from Latin models.

The following passage from the prologue of the poem indicates clearly the source and tells why the first version was composed. This is an interpolation in the PA *Thèbes* near the beginning of the poem and is an apparent addition to the prologue in its more primitive from. It is in this text that we note an interval in time between this and earlier versions of the work.

> Conter vous voel d'antive estore
> Que li clerc tiennent en memore
> Et conter d'une fiere geste,
> Leu on le list estuet grant feste.
> De batailles et de grans plais,
> Onques plus grans n'oïstes mais,
> De mervilleus confusions,
> De grans dolours, d'ocisions,
> Conte li livres ke on fist,
> Or escoutés ke il en dist.
> Il le fist tout selonc la letre
> Dont lai ne sevent entremetre,
> Et por chou fu li romans fais
> Que nel saroit hon ki fut lais.
> (B. N. fs. fr. 375, f. 36r, a.)

In the earlier composition to which reference is made here, another *geste,* found only in Latin and read only by the *clerc,* was put

---

[8] Two of the more significant studies in this regard are those of Ed. Faral, *Recherches sur les sources latines des contes et romans courtois du moyen âge* (Paris: Champion, 1913), and M. Wilmotte, *Origines du roman en France, l'évolution du sentiment romanesque jusqu'en 1240* (Paris: Boivin et Cie, 1942). See also the essays from the 1961 Heidelberg Colloquium in *Studia Romanica,* 4. Heft (cited above).

into Romance so that the layman might read it. Is it a lost version being used as a source by the later poet, and if so when was the earlier poem composed? In the episode of Daire le Roux (ed. Constans, 1. 7643 ff.) an author is cited who in the mind of the later poet is the writer who composed his Romance source: "Si com dit li liver d'Estace." (7823). This Estace (variants Estaisce, Estase, Estance) is obviously Statius with a prosthesis from *de Stace,* a form which occurs in MS C, 1. 2739; but the Daire le Roux episode is entirely medieval and not in the *Thebaid* at all. This testifies to a long lapse of time between the earliest version drawn from the Latin poet and the second period of literary creation when the Latin source was long forgotten. The later poet (or perhaps scribe) thought Estace to be a writer of Romance, the author of the *Roman de Thèbes* .

It is from this episode that Harris draws his evidence for dating the *Thèbes* after 1180. [9] The text containing the legal custom, *quarantaine le roy,* is found in all the MSS, and this is further indication that we have only a late twelfth century version of the poem. The "livre d'Estace" had the Daire episode, perhaps in an earlier form without the legal concept, and it was probably only a middle stage in the evolution of the *Thèbes* rather than the primitive version. The *terminus ad quem* may be as late as the opening years of the thirteenth century; there are apparent references to the Fourth Crusade in thirteenth century interpolations. [10]

Evidence of the great length of the time gap between late and early versions is found in the position of the poem in regard to influences on other romances, an apparent reference to the poem by Wace in 1160, and mention of the battle of Laliche (Laodicea),

---

[9] *A terminus a quo.* Harris dates the poem by means of a legal concept found in the Daire le Roux episode. The *quarantaine el roy* was established by Philip Augustus.

[10] In a couplet appearing in all the MSS except C, there seems to be a reference to the Venetians and their role in the Fourth Crusade and during the period following: "Tornez vos en arriére en Grece, / Si conquerez ceus de Venece." (Constans, 11. 2865-66). The allusion to Alixandre de Moncenis (MS C, 1. 4812 ff.) may belong to this period; see Constans, II, lxii, and Harris, "A *terminus a quo,*" p. 202.

an event during the Second Crusade. [11] If the primitive version of the *Thèbes* is lost, it will probably be impossible to establish an accurate *terminus a quo*; we shall be obliged to be content with the notion that the poem did exist in some form near mid-century.

Often a problem in medieval literature is created in part by the imposition of modern concepts of literary creation in an environment far different from that in which books are created in our day. In the mid twelfth century individual literary creation had to be a slower process, and one may well ask whether a ten thousand line poem, entirely the work of one poet, was possible. It is more likely that a shorter work set in motion the collective creation which had as its result decades later the composite version. The difficulties of composition are evident in two well known works, the *Roman de Rou* of Wace and the *Vie de Saint Thomas Becket* of Guernes de Pont-Sainte-Maxence; and in the long evolution of the *Roman d'Alexandre* we have a graphic

---

[11] The comparison technique is often successful in determining the relative order of works. See especially G. Otto, *Der Einfluss des Roman de Thèbes auf die altfranzösischen Literatur* (Coburg: Rossteuscher, 1909), a study which establishes the position of the *Thèbes* in relation to later Romance works. This evidence is unreliable because of the nature of the genesis of the poems and the fact that the whole structure rests on uncertain dates.

Wace wrote in the *Roman de Rou* which he himself dates 1160, "De Thebes es grant reparlance." (ed. Andresen, I, 1. 23).

Reference to Laliche occurs in the following lines (Constans, 5277-5281):

> Un cheval ot ferrant oscur,
> Dont il ocist antan un Tur
> De grant tenue, forment riche,
> Al tornei qui fu a Laliche:
> Isneaus esteit a grant merveille.

This is important if it is a question of the battle in which the French under Louis VII suffered a defeat at the hands of the Turks in 1147. The passage is found in all the MSS, but Laliche is not mentioned in PA; the Second Crusade would not have been as well remembered late in the century. The city may be Laodicea ad Mare in Syria, and if so the name came to the *Thèbes* from the *Chanson d'Antioche* (ed. P. Paris, II, 1. 293). There is, however, no battle taking place there; the crusaders merely pass through the town. The scene of the battle in 1147 is Laodicea ad Lycum in Asia Minor (near Denizli, Turkey). For a full account of the battle, see V. G. Berry (ed.), *Odo of Deuil, De profectione Ludovici VII in orientem* (New York: Columbia University Press, 1948), p. 109 ff. The Turks are involved in events both before and after the battle, and emphasis is put on the speed of their horses.

example of collective authorship which developed perhaps as a continuing creation parallel to the *Roman de Thèbes.*

We know that Wace worked on the *Rou* for more than a decade without having a completed version. He made a new start at one point, and wrote thereby both original and a revised version of the poem. [12] Guernes spent four years writing his six thousand line poem in the early 1170's. He relates how the first two years were required to make a first draft which was completely re-written and amplified after his visit to Canterbury. [13] Speaking of this first version, Guernes is careful to point out that it is incomplete, often in error, and imperfect in style; he notes, however, that the first version is being widely used while he is writing the second:

> Mes cel premier romanz m'unt escrivein emble,
> Anceis que je l'oüsse parfet e amendé
> ... ...
> E meint riche umme l'unt cunquis e achaté.
> (ed. Wolberg, 11. 151-58.)

The making of an original poem of thousands of lines was a matter of years rather than months; and it is likely that during such periods unfinished works were frequently put into use, especially when a new kind of poem (and episodic in form) was first attempted. Revision, correction, and amplification of successful episodes were inherent parts of this literary creation. It is of interest to examine here the Alexander legend which in its earlier form, the ten syllable version, was the unfinished work (continued by other poets) of an unknown author.

---

[12] H. Andresen (ed.), *Maistre Wace's Roman de Rou et des ducs de Normandie* (Heilbronn: Henninger, 1877), I, ii ff. Literary production of this sort is found also among the writers of Latin. A series of variant versions of Geoffrey of Monmouth's *Historia Regum Britanniae* were composed either before or after the so-called Vulgate text. The *Historia* passed through various stages of composition, perhaps the work of more than one writer. See J. Parry and R. Caldwell, "Geoffrey of Monmouth," *Arthurian Literature in the Middle Ages, a Collective History,* ed. R. Loomis (Oxford: The Clarendon Press, 1959), pp. 86-87.

[13] E. Walberg (ed.), *Guernes de Pont Sainte-Maxence, La vie de Saint Thomas Becket* (C. F. M. A.; Paris: Champion, 1936), p. v. The first version of the Guernes poem has not survived.

This decasyllabic fragment, the ADéca, may belong to the period during which the first *Thèbes* was written. Notably significant in this regard is its style. P. Meyer points out that this work has the terseness of the earliest Old French poems while going well beyond them in the studied perfection of its poetry, a poetry which is the best made of any found in the medieval period. [14] The composite *Alexandre* (15,000 vss.) is of necessity less carefully made and is characterized by imitation and amplification. As one might expect, it is unequal in quality, having passed through many hands. [15] The same contrast is present in the two extant versions of the *Thèbes*. The first thirty-six lines of the CBS tradition (what might be called the prologue) show a construction and style very carefully studied and executed, and many

[14] *Alexandre le Grand dans la littérature française du moyen âge* (Paris: Vieweg, 1886), II, pp. 109-110.

[15] The following verses assembled from various parts of a late version of the *Roman d'Alexandre* demonstrate the manner in which the legends were expanded in the process of passing from one poet to another through the middle and on to the end of the century. These citations come from a lost MS of Tours, No. 242, fs. Marmoutier, and are found in a work of L. Delisle, *Notice sur les manuscrits disparus de la bibliothèque de Tours la première moité du dix-neuvième siècle* (Paris: Imprimerie Nationale, 1883), p. 130.

Moult par fu grant la presce, si com raconte Ystace
Des morts et des navrés qui gissent en la place.

D'un bon livre latin fis ces translatement,
Qui mun nom demande ai nom Thomas de Kent.

La verté de l'istoir' si com li roys la fist
Un clers de Chastiaudun, Lambert li Cors l'escrit
Qui du latin la trest, et en roman la mist.

Alexandre nous dit que de Bernay fu nez
Et de Paris refu ses sournoms appellez
Qui cy a les siens vers o les Lambert mellez.

We note here the importance of the names of the poets and contrast this emphasis with the anonymity of the ADéca and the *Thèbes*. It would seem that in the environment of the genesis of the romance it became the custom at a certain point to be concerned about publication of authorship; perhaps the earliest works were written — as the prologue of the *Thèbes* indicates (Constans, 13-14 — only by the *clerc* or *chevalier* who did not want their names associated with a vernacular work. The style changed with the changing times.

parts of this version (except some of the interpolations) have a refined and painstaking style. These sections may have been parts of the primitive version; the poetry in them was probably long in the making, and as Ed. Faral demonstrates so convincingly, this is an art coming from the school, carried out by the learned *clerc* who was performing scholarly exercises based on Latin models. [16] In the PA tradition the work is not as fine in style; swelled by many additions and revisions, the poetry seems to have been produced more rapidly.

This evolution in style links the later versions of the *Thèbes* with the general literary blooming about mid-way in the second half of the century, the period which saw the creation of the *Eneas* and the long *Roman de Troie* (30,000 vss.) which is related to the *Thèbes*. The *Alexandre* was passing through the Bernay stage, and all of these poems are close in date to the works of Marie de France and Chrétien de Troyes. [17] A further indication placing the PA *Thèbes* near these works is the presence in that tradition of elements of Ovidian type love intrigue. In MSS CBS we find only a sort of *courtoisie,* the kind of love play seen in lyric poetry themes of the time (ed. Constans, 1. 3887 ff.). In the PA, Ovidian love is strongly present in deeply felt monologues,

---

[16] *Recherches,* passim, especially pp. vii-xi; 3-33; 307 ff.; 391 ff. See also *Les arts poétiques du XIIe et du XIIIe siècle* (Paris: Champion, 1924), Part II, especially chap. ii. Although these treatises appeared late in the century, their content was apparently in existence earlier and was an influence in the composition of the *Thèbes.*

[17] The works of this period in a sense merge and blend into a complex tapestry. Each work has elements of collective literary creation, and the individual author must have true qualities of genius to raise his work above the common denominators of an art which had become tradition. See P. Le Gentil, "Réflexions," p. 16. Under such circumstance dating becomes extremely difficult if not impossible. This is evident in the attempts to place the *Troie* and the *Eneas.* Faral (*Recherches,* pp. 169-187) in deciding that the *Troie* came before the *Eneas* lists the findings in fourteen other studies, only six of which are in accord with him. In fact, these works cannot be set finely in time with a single relationship to each other. In their continuing evolution through a series of versions they touched at a series of points. The author of the *Eneas* used parts of the first *Troie* (see below, pp. 8-9) while the author of the later *Troie* borrowed from the *Eneas.*

fainting spells, and sleepless nights, passages similar to ones in the *Eneas* and in the works of Marie de France.[18]

The evolutionary process in the creation of the romance form appears, then, to have passed through distinct stages in which both individual and collective contributions appear. The Alberich fragment indicates that beginnings were made early in the century. A second period of development seems to be that represented by the ADéca, a period in which well written poems were produced on a small scale in a learned atmosphere, perhaps without widespread success. The learned nature of the movement may have limited its scope at first. At the end of the *Troie,* a passage (ed. Constans, 1. 30305 ff.) suggests that considerable opposition to this type of poetry existed among the *jongleurs.* In the prologue of the *Thèbes,* the same impression is given in lines 13-14 (MS C): "Or s'en tesent de cest mestier / Se ne sont clerc ou chevalier." Later in the century, the earlier works were compiled and expanded into fifteen and thirty thousand line poems.[19]

In conclusion, I should like to point out that in the prologue of the *Roman de Troie* there occurs an interpolation much like the one cited above (p. 4) from the *Thèbes.* A second poet is looking back to the time when the poem was first composed and names the author of the primitive version, Beneois de Sainte-More:[20]

---

[18] See Constans, II, pp. 255; 280-282. The Céfas episodes (276 ff.), which is found only in MS P, is close in style, theme, and spirit to the *Eneas* and to the *Lais* of Marie de France. A typical example of Ovidian love is found in MS A, (Constans, II, 11. 13287-89:

> ... on ja puist trover ne querre
> Si grant dolor ne si grant gerre
> Com est Amors a cex quil servent.

[19] In this connection, it is difficult to evaluate the roles played by poets, scribes, and *remanieurs.* See P. Gallais, "Formules de conteur et interventions d'auteur dans les manuscrits de *la Continuation-Gauvain*," *Romania,* LXXXV (1946), 181-229, who coins a new term (183), *copistes-remanieurs-interpolateurs.* The situation is further complicated, as I note above (n. 6), when a late MS is copied from a number of earlier MSS.

[20] Further evidence for this double authorship is found in at least one other part of the poem (ed. Constans, 11. 2061-2065):

> De sa vie ne de son fait
> Ne sera plus par mei retrait:
> Jo ne le truis pas en cest livre,

Ceste estoire n'est pas usee,
N'en gaires lieus nen est trovee.
Ja retraite no fust encore,
Mais Beneois de Sainte-More
L'a contrové et fait et dit
Et de sa main les mos escrit
Et si tailliés et si curés
Et si assis et si posés
Que plus ne mains n'i a mestier.
Ci voel l'estoire conmenchier.
Le latin saurai et la letre;
Nule autre rien n'i volrai metre
S'ensi non con je truis escrit.
Ne di mie c'aucun bon dit
N'i mete se metre le sai,
Mais le maistrie ensieverai.
(B. N. fs. fr. 375, f. 68r, c.)

At some point in the last quarter of the century, a writer of Romance is assembling the long *Troie* as we have it. His sources are the various Latin versions and an earlier poem in Romance, that of Beneois. The work of this later poet is much like that of Alexandre de Bernay; he will add episodes if he can: "Ne di mie c'aucun bon dit / N'i mete se metre le sai." In similar fashion the PA *Thèbes* received its new episodes. The second author relates that the Beneois *Troie* was carefully and finely made; so well are the words assembled that "plus ne mains n'i a mestier." It seems that this earlier poem had the same style as the ADéca and parts of the CBS *Thèbes*. The *Roman de Troie* was first composed in a primitive version which has disapeared.

Ne Daires plus n'en voust escrire,
Ne Beneeiz pas ne l'alonge.

See also a variant reading, IV, p. 387: "Jo nen sai plus, ne plus nen dist / Beneoiz qui cest romanz fist.

The presence of two authors is pointed out by A. Joly, *Benoit de Sainte-More et le Roman de Troie, ou les métamorphoses d'Homère et de l'épopée gréco-latine au moyen âge* (Paris: Franck, 1870), I, 7 ff. His explanation, that the second author is Jehanes Mados, one of the scribes in 1288 of B. N. fs. fr. 375, is not convincing. It is generally assumed that the *Troie* in its thirty thousand line form is the work of one poet, Beneois.

Tomb of Blanche of Lancaster and John of Gaunt in Old St. Paul's Cathedral, designed and executed by Henry Yevele. The inscription on the engraving erroneously mentions Constance

THE HISTORICAL SETTING OF CHAUCER'S
BOOK OF THE DUCHESS

D. W. ROBERTSON, JR.
Princeton University

Criticism of Chaucer's *Book of the Duchess,* the first major work of a young man who was to become England's most famous poet, has sometimes neglected not only the immediate historical setting of the poem and the most probable circumstances of its first publication, but also the *mores* if its audience. At the beginning of the year 1369 the most notable poet attached to the English court was Jean Froissart, who wrote under the patronage of Queen Philippa. Both Edward III and his Queen spoke French (rather than English) as their natural language, and the Queen in particular was quite evidently an admirer of literary fashions as they had developed in the French language. In this year, which marked a turning point in the fortunes of English chivalry,[1] King Edward's court was still the most brilliant in Europe. The glory of English victories earlier in the century and the prestige of the Order of the Garter were still intact. Chaucer himself went off campaigning in France.

Queen Philippa died of the plague on August 14, the Vigil of the Assumption. Chaucer, who had returned to England, was, on

---

[1] The war with France was resumed in this year, the enemy now being the astute Charles V rather than the chivalrous King John. John of Gaunt's venture into Artois and Picardy met with little success, and the invasion of Robert Knowles in the following year was a failure. Edward fell under the influence of Alice Perrers, a woman hardly of the type to inspire chivalric idealism, leaving the guidance of the realm to others. England faced a period of decline, marked by financial crises, social and political unrest, and general decay.

Sept. 1, granted funds for mourning for himself and his wife. On Sept. 12, Blanche, Duchess of Lancaster, also died of the plague. Her husband, John of Gaunt, was campaigning in Picardy, whence he did not return until Nov. 3. England thus lost two of its noblest ladies within a few weeks. The effect of these losses in a society bound together by close personal relationships must have been profound. Froissart spoke of the Queen as "the most courteous, noble, and liberal queen that ever reigned in her time," [2] and of Blanche he wrote,

> Aussi sa fille de Lancastre —
> Haro! Mettés moi une emplastre
> Sus le coer, car, quant m'en souvient,
> Certes, souspirer me couvient,
> Tant sui plains de melancolie.
> Elle morut jone et jolie,
> Environ de vingt et deux ans;
> Gaie, lie, friche, esbatans,
> Douce, simple, d'umble samblance.
> La bonne dame ot a nom Blanche. [3]

The Duke of Lancaster instituted a memorial service to be held for Blanche each year on Sept. 12 at St. Paul's Cathedral, [4] a ceremonial which he continued to support for the remainder of his life. He arranged for an elaborate alabaster tomb to be erected by Henry Yevele, who was to become England's most distinguished mason. [5] An altar was erected near the tomb, and two chantry priests were engaged to sing masses there throughout the year. [6]

---

[2] *Chronicles*, trans. Johnes, Book I, Ch. 272.

[3] *Le joli buisson de jonece*, lines 241-250.

[4] The services were elaborate. For that held in 1371 the Duke allowed Sir William Burghbrigg of his council £38 18s, a considerable sum. See *John of Gaunt's Register*, ed. S. Armitage-Smith (London, 1911), no. 943. For information about the first service attended by the Duke in person (1374), see N. B. Lewis, "The Anniversary Service for Blanche, Duchess of Lancaster, 12 Sept., 1374," *Bulletin of the John Rylands Library*, XXI (1937), 176-192.

[5] On June 8, 1374 (*Register*, no. 1394), we find the Duke ordering alabaster for "new work" on the tomb. He was especially concerned to find material suitable for the effigies. On Jan. 20, 1375 (*Register*, no. 1659), arrangements were made to pay Yevele for his work.

[6] For all of these arrangements, see S. Armitage-Smith, *John of Gaunt* (Repr., New York, 1964), pp. 75-78.

In accordance with the explicit provision of his will, John was buried by the side of Blanche.

Concerning John of Gaunt's reaction, Armitage-Smith observes, "of the sincerity of the Duke's grief there need be no question," adding that his gratitude to the memory of Blanche "never failed." [7] More recent writers, pointing, with appropriate disdain, to the Duke's relations with Katherine Swynford, who was the guardian of his children, and to his marriage to Constance of Castile, have been more cynical. But the alliance with Katherine indicates nothing except the fact that the two were thrown together by circumstance at a time when the Duke was still relatively young and vigorous in an age that was neither sentimental nor especially squeamish about sex. The marriage to Constance, which was made for political reasons, has no bearing on John's feelings for either Blanche or Katherine. For our purposes the Duke's feelings, for which we have little evidence, are not, in any event, important. What is important is the Duke's public posture. And there is nothing in that posture to cast doubt on Armitage-Smith's conclusion. The tomb, the altar, the chantry-priests, and the annual memorial service were all reminders of the inspiration Blanche had been, not only to John personally, but to all those who had known and loved her. Chaucer's *Book of the Duchess,* a work prepared by a young squire who was to receive very substantial favors from John of Gaunt in the future, should be considered as a kind of literary counterpart of Henry Yevele's alabaster tomb, a memorial to a great lady celebrating neither Chaucer's nor anyone else intimate feelings and "psychological" reveries, but the kind of tribute a great lady, still "jone et jolie," suddenly destroyed by a terrible malady, deserves from all men of good will.

Perhaps it is futile to speculate about the unfulfilled potentialities of history. Nevertheless, it seems reasonable to suppose that if the Queen had not died, depriving Froissart of his position at the English court, we might very well have had a formal elegy for Blanche in French. Blanche's father, Henry of Lancaster, had been the author of a devotional treatise, the *Livre de Seyntz Medicines,* written in French. The fact that Chaucer wrote the elegy is an indication of the "Anglicising" of the English nobility

[7] *Ibid.,* pp. 76, 77.

during the second half of the century. It is also a tribute to the growing prestige of Geoffrey Chaucer. If Speght was right, and the "A. B. C." was actually written for Blanche during her lifetime, that poem may be regarded as further evidence indicating Blanche's preference for literature in English. It would serve at the same time as a foretaste of the serious attitudes to be expected from the young squire. But when Chaucer did begin his poem, he introduced it with an echo of a poem by Froissart, an echo which is at once a clue to the thematic content of the poem and a tribute to the French poet who was in a very real sense Chaucer's predecessor.

In cannot be emphasized too strongly that *The Book of the Duchess* is essentially a funerary poem, a poem designed to be delivered orally before an orthodox audience of noblemen, great men of London, ladies, and clerks, whose literary tastes were traditionally French. It is also true that medieval poems other than those written for private devotion or for evangelical instruction were "occasional" poems, composed for an audience assembled for some specific social occasion. [8] The gathering might be anything from a dinner to a festival of the Pui. We should think of Chaucer's poem as being "public," written neither to express the very private feelings of the author nor to inspire the very private reactions of anyone sitting alone in the silence of a study. The most probable occasion for its presentation would have been one of the memorial celebrations held each year on Sept. 12, perhaps at supper at the Savoy, perhaps in the nave of St. Paul's, which was thought of as "belonging to the people" and used for a variety of lay activities. As we read *The Book of the Duchess,* then, we should try to image ourselves hearing it read as we sit (or stand) in an audience of fourteenth-century ladies and gentlemen assembled especially for the purpose of paying tribute to the memory of Blanche, Duchess of Lancaster, who had been one of the ladies of highest rank in the English court.

The men and women who sit around us as we listen to the poem are chivalric in outlook and orthodox in sentiment, attitudes

---

[8] This point has been well made with reference to the lyric especially by John Stevens, *Music and Poetry in the Early Tudor Court* (Lincoln, 1961). See especially Ch. 10, and the remarks about "applied" or "practical" art on p. 235.

that were by no means thought of as being inconsistent. The Duke of Lancaster was, throughout his life, a generous benefactor of ecclesiastics and of religious institutions. His later patronage of Wyclif had nothing to do with any lack of orthodoxy on his part, [9] and the status of Katherine Swynford as his mistress after 1372 neither made him a "pagan" nor caused him to be thought of by his peers as a "great sinner." The fulminations of politically hostile chroniclers should not be taken too seriously, no matter how much they may appeal to the ingrown Calvinism of certain modern historians. With reference to Chaucer himself, it is significant that some of his closest associates at court were Lollard knights, men who were Lollards not out of any lack of orthodoxy, but by virtue of the fact that the spiritual corruption of their church and society was a matter of grave concern to them. [10] Whatever we may think of either the Duke or the poet, however, *The Book of the Duchess* was a public poem, and since it was a public poem and not an expression of personal feeling, we may expect it to exhibit certain proprieties. There can be little doubt that Blanche of Lancaster was a lady who attracted much genuine affection in courtly circles. Her rank was great enough to inspire a certain devotion to begin with, and her youth and charm must have attracted many persons of importance in addition to Jean Froissart.

Considering the occasion of Chaucer's poem and its probable audience, there are then certain things we might expect of it in advance: a generally chivalric attitude; a tactful restraint with reference to the lady, her family, and her associates; a statement, either direct or indirect, of the conventional ideas associated with funerary consolation; and, finally, a fairly close adherence

---

[9] See *John of Gaunt*, Ch. VIII. The Duke may have been more concerned about ecclesiastical abuses than these pages indicate, although it is probable that he thought of them as being personal rather than institutional. The revolutionary character of Wyclif's thought was not due merely to the fact that he attacked abuses, for the abuses he attacked were deplored also by many persons whose inclinations were essentially conservative. His desire to reform the organization and theology of the Church was revolutionary.

[10] There is a good discussion by Derek Brewer, *Chaucer in His Time* (London, 1963), pp. 226-237. The quotation from Clanvowe on p. 226, however, is not a condemnation of "courtliness" or "chivalry," but of wordly wisdom, which is a different matter entirely.

to the techniques and general attitudes of the popular French poetry of the time. At this point my literary friends will object: "It is unfair to go outside of the poem. One should begin with the text, without any presuppositions whatsoever." Let me reply that it is impossible to read anything "without any presuppositions," and that what has happened is that most critics of the poem have brought to it a great many post-romantic presuppositions concerning both the subject of the poem and its technique, which are entirely inappropriate to its cultural setting. In any event, let us consider the above points in reverse order.

To begin with, scholars have long since pointed out that Chaucer does indeed rely heavily on French sources for the materials of his poem. They have gleaned a number of parallel passages which are quite convincing, as well as some which are not so convincing. [11] What they have not done is to make useful comments on the significance of the borrowings. That is, the passages used have a contextual significance in the works from which they are derived, a significance of which Chaucer was certainly aware and of which many members of his audience were probably aware. As a consequence of this failure literary critics have frequently disregarded the parallel passages as constituting so much dusty and irrelevant information. And, indeed, in their present form, they are just that. The situation is made worse by the fact that there are hardly more neglected European poets anywhere than the poets of fourteenth-century France. When one looks for interpretations of their works, which are frequently allegorical in technique, one finds instead of interpretation a series of statements to the effect that the poems are "conventional." To say that a poem by Machaut or Froissart is merely an agglomeration of "conventions" is simply to say, with a certain professorial profundity, that one does not know what the poem is about. There are thus many details in *The Book of the Duchess* which must remain relatively obscure until serious studies of the French sources have been made. [12]

---

[11] See most recently J. Burke Severs, "The Sources of 'The Book of the Duchess'," *Mediaeval Studies*, XXV (1963), 355-362.

[12] Mr. Richard Detlef is currently preparing a study of the French backgrounds of *The Book of the Duchess* for the light they throw on the poem's meaning.

It is possible to make a general statement about the French poetry Chaucer drew upon that has some bearing on the thematic content of *The Book of the Duchess*. That poetry shows a heavy reliance on themes from *The Consolation of Philosophy* of Boethius, a work that enjoyed increasing popularity during the course of the century and that Chaucer later undertook to translate into English. The *Consolation* has not fared well in modern times, having been victimized by literal-minded comments, by irrelevant analyses on the part of philosophers trained in nineteenth-century German metaphysics, and by a general failure to take its themes seriously or to assume that anyone ever did take them seriously. In the fourteenth century, however, the *Consolation* was a book regarded with genuine love by many, especially by those who had witnessed the devastations of the plague and suffered personal losses in those devastations; its themes appear not only in literary works but also in the visual arts of the time, penetrating even to country parishes. The book was thought of as being thoroughly orthodox, a fact that one modern authority fully appreciated, observating that "there is nothing in this work for which a good case might not have been made by any contemporary Christian theologian, who knew his Augustine." [13]

Since the commentaries of Guillaume de Conches and Nicholas Trivet on the *Consolation* have never been printed, perhaps the best short introduction to the work as it was understood in the later Middle Ages is that provided by Jean de Meun for the translation he presented to Philip the Fair of France.[14] After identifying himself, explaining the reasons for his translation and the techniques he employed in it, Jean goes on to outline the thesis of the work. He points out first of all, with a rather elaborate argument, that all things tend toward the good. In this respect, however, man differs from other things, since his course is not predetermined (i. e., he has free choice). The true good of man lies in the intelligible, but sensible goods (i. e., those goods perceived by the senses rather than by the understanding) impress him first, and he is misled into deserting his proper good in favor

---

[13] E. K. Rand, *Founders of the Middle Ages* (Cambridge, Mass., 1928), p. 178.

[14] Ed. V. L. Dedeck-Hery, *Mediaeval Studies*, XIV (1952), 165-275. Jean's Preface, here briefly summarized, appears on pp. 168-171.

of those things which are sensible. He must therefore be taught to distinguish reasonably between the two kinds of good and to know what kind of good he should enjoy. Most men go astray in this respect, enjoying things of the wrong kind. And this causes their lives to be full of bitterness. For sensible things, which are transitory and mutable, cannot be enjoyed without sorrow. The *Consolation,* Jean says, is most useful in teaching the distinction between true and false good, in showing what things are to be enjoyed, and in demonstrating how other things are to be used. [15] Among all the books ever written, Jean assures his royal patron, this is the best one for teaching us to despise false and deceptive goods (later called "biens forains et fortunieux," or alien goods of Fortune) and to seek instead true and immutable goods that will lead us to happiness. Boethius, we are told, was wrongfully imprisoned, but he endured his misfortune well and wisely as a strong man of good heart. In his book, he is presented as a man divided into two parts: first, as a man cast down by "passions sensibles," and second, as a man divinely raised up to intelligible goods. That is, the figure "Boethius" in the book is the man cast down, while the other reasonable part of him is represented by Philosophy. [16] The actual Boethius, we assume, always endured his trouble patiently.

What relevance has all this to a funerary poem? An inkling of the answer to this question may be found in the pages of Dante, who tells us in the *Convivio* (2. 12) that he was inconsolable after the death of Beatrice until he had read the *Consolation* of Boethius and the *De amicitia* of Cicero. In the *De amicitia* he would have found that true friendship, or true love of one human being for another, is based on virtue; and in the *Consolation,* that such friendship, or love, is not subject to Fortune. That is, the virtues of another humane being are intelligible rather than sensible goods which, in a Christian context, are derived from Good and do not perish. Moreover, the memory of the virtues of one who has died can act as an inspiration, just as the memory of a loved

---

[15] Jean is here reflecting the Augustinian distinction between use and enjoyment. See Peter Lombard, *Sententiae,* 1. 1. 3.

[16] This idea may also be found in Trivet's commentary. See D. W. Robertson, Jr., *A Preface to Chaucer* (Princeton, 1962), p. 359.

one as a physical being that has perished can bring a sense of acute loss.

If we turn our attention to *The Book of the Duchess,* it is apparent at once that one character in it, the Black Knight, regards the loss of Blanche as the loss of a gift of Fortune. He is introduced, much like the *persona* "Boethius" in the Consolation, in a condition of despair arising from the loss of Blanche as a sensible object, and this loss is attibuted specifically to the operations of Fortune. In Boethian terms, this kind of sorrow, although it occurs spontaneously in all of us, is actually a kind of foolishness. Chaucer is careful to make his Knight a beardless adolescent who gave himself up to "love" in "idleness" before he ever saw Blanche. [17] He is obviously in need of the kind of instruction that, as Jean de Meun assures us, may be found best expressed in the *Consolation.* It must be emphasized that themes from this work were common in French poetry—perhaps the most obvious example being Machaut's *Remede de Fortune,* which Chaucer drew upon heavily— that they appeared in the visual arts, and even found a prominent place in highly "secular" works like Geoffrey de Charny's treatise on chivalry. That is, Chaucer's audience would have been in a position to realize fully the implications of losing a chess game to Fortune. Of the two principal "characters" in Chaucer's poem, one, the Knight, despairingly recounts his experience with reference to Blanche— his first sight of her, his conception of her person and character, his first unsuccessful approach, his acquisition of the lady's grace, and finally, the fact of her death. The other "character," the dreamer, acts as a confessor, pressing the Knight to reveal the whole course of his experience and offering a certain amount of wise advice, like that, for example, on the folly of suicide. The parallel between this general situation and that in the *Consolation* is obvious and would hardly have escaped Chaucer's audience. The plight of the Black

---

[17] Lines 759-804. In effect, the Black Knight tells us that he entered the Garden of Deduit as it is described in the *Roman de la rose.* Although we may expect this to have been a fairly common procedure, it was nevertheless a foolish one, leading to what Chaucer calls in the Prologue to *The Legend of Good Women* (F 472, G 462) "falsnesse" and "vice." The early reputation of the *Roman,* which was not attacked on moral grounds "in its own century," is discussed in a forthcoming article by John Fleming.

Knight expressed in terms of Fortune would have suggested a more "proper" attitude, even if such an attitude were not otherwise indicated in the poem. As we shall see presently, however, the "proper" attitude is very definitely suggested.

As we have suggested earlier, a funerary poem, to avoid boorishness, might be expected to show considerable restraint in its implications concerning actual persons. The young poet would have been particularly careful not to offend John of Gaunt, no matter what his "private" feelings, if indeed he had any as distinct from his "public" feelings; about the Duke, we should in all likelihood have no evidence of its existence today. However, in June, 1374, the Duke, as he put it, "by our special grace and for the good, and so on, that our good friend Geoffrey Chaucer has done for us" granted to Chaucer and to his wife "for the good service... performed for our very honored dame and mother the Queen, whom God pardon, and for our very dear friend and companion the Queen [of Castile]," a pension of ten pounds a year for life. [18] The sum is exactly half that granted Chaucer many years later by Richard II as a recognition for his services in the very distinguished office of Clerk of the King's works. It is not unlikely that the phrase "for the good, and so on" referred in part to *The Book of the Duchess* itself. The Duke was in England for the first time on Sept. 12 in this year to attend the memorial service for Blanche in person. It is significant that he referred to this grant specifically on January 20 of the following year. [19] Under the circumstances, the traditional view that the beardless adolescent who appears in the poem as the Black Knight overcome by the loss of Blanche as a gift of Fortune was intended to represent John of Gaunt is absurd. Whatever we may think of the Duke, there is little doubt that he felt grief for the loss of Blanche, but there is also little doubt that any public representation of the Duke's grief contrived by a good friend would have shown him, like Jean de Meun's Boethius, suffering "tout sagement sa douleur comme homme fort et de grant cuer." The Black Knight shows a consistent blindness to the intelligible, even when it is suggested by his own words. There is no probability what-

---

[18] *Register,* no. 608.
[19] *Register,* no. 1667.

soever that he was meant to represent literally anyone in Chaucer's audience, least of all John of Gaunt. He may well have represented, however, a certain aspect of almost everyone in the audience.

Much of the confusion concerning the poem has arisen from our inclination to see the grief of the Black Knight in a "psychological" context rather than in the moral and philosophical context familiar to the society of which Chaucer was a part. Efforts to demonstrate this distinction have met with rejoinders like "We are back again in an idealized Middle Ages peopled only with righteous Christians."[20] The fact that people thought of human conduct in "moral" terms during the Middle Ages does not mean that their behavior was "moral," especially from our point of view. We tend to think of human beings in "psychological" terms, but this fact does not imply that people in our own society are generally sane and well-adjusted. On the contrary, our literature shows a strong preoccupation with themes of isolation, *anomie*, and alienation. We seek as best we can to regard persons suffering from social maladjustment and psychological weakness with sympathy and understanding. Although this sympathy may sometimes imply criticism of society, it does not ordinarily imply any criticism of the "terms" of the psychology used to depict the suffering of the individual. For example, O'Neill's *Mourning Becomes Electra* reflects certain principles of Freudian psychology, but this fact does not imply any criticism of Freud.

Medieval men were also urged, as they are in the *Consolation*, to take pity on sinners, since a malady of the spirit is more serious than a malady of the flesh.[21] But this pity does not imply either that sinners are not sinners or that there is anything wrong with the conceptual system upon which the pity itself is based. If we look at the Black Knight (rather vaguely and without paying any attention to the connotations of the terms used to describe him) from a "psychological" point of view, his grief seems quite understandable and not reprehensible at all. If we look at him in the context of the moral philosophy of the fourteenth century,

---

[20] Donald R. Howard, *Speculum,* XXXIX (1964), 541.
[21] 4 pr. 4 and met. 4. For the manner in which these passages were understood in the fourteenth century, see Chaucer's translation.

he appears, not as a "psychological entity," an individual like ourselves alienated in an absurd world, but as an exemplification of an understandable but errant attitude toward the lady that is not very complimentary to the lady. Had she, after all, no intelligible virtues? Was she mere flesh? Most frequently, the Black Knight has been seen romantically, with an attitude that has its roots in the cult of melancholy that grew up in the eighteenth century and that has been reinforced by various outgrowths like *ennui,* existential absurdity, ambiguity, and so on. Our "psychology" as it appears in literary criticism is, as a matter of fact, little more than an amorphous reflection of these attitudes. It is a product of a society in which the tightly-knit communities of the past have broken down so that the individual is left with a somewhat diminished and fragmented identity as a member of large and loosely organized groups in which the ties of organization do not form channels of personal satisfaction. Chaucer lived in no such society. He and his contemporaries would not have understood what we mean by "psychology," and, what is more important, would have felt no need for it. In any event, *The Book of the Duchess* is a public funerary poem that may be expected to reflect the most elevated public philosophy available for its conceptual framework.

The "anguish of a troubled heart" is something that we are inclined to regard with a certain reverence. The phrase brings to mind lingering fancies decked with wisps of autumnal melancholy we have heard echoing in the finest sonatas of Mozart, in the grand symphonies of Beethoven, in the graceful strains of Chopin's nocturnes, in the nostalgic memories inspired by Brahms, or even, if our tastes are more advanced, in those brief moments of tenderness in Weber, where the anguish is intensified by poignant feelings of alienation and despair. We know that Chaucer had not heard these things and was not familiar, indeed, in spite of his elegy, with the theory that the most beautiful and appropriate subject for poetry is the death of a beautiful woman. But, we assure ourselves, he was human, and so must have felt as we feel, but without the richness of association that we are able to bring to his poetry. [22] We are in a position to find much in it, quite legitimately, of which he had only a rudimentary apprehension. This line of argument has a certain appeal, but it is, nevertheless, sheer nonsense.

In 1853 Delacroix wrote in his journal,

> Exquisite music at the house of charming Princess Marcelline. I especially remember Mozart's *Fantasia* [K. 475], a serious work, verging on the terrible, and with a title too light for its character; also a sonata by Beethoven which I already knew — but admirable. I really like it exceedingly, especially the mournful imaginative passages. Beethoven is always melancholy. Mozart is modern too; I mean by this that like other men of his time he is not afraid of touching on the sad side of things. [23]

Although Delacroix was not an historian of music, his observation that "modern" music is distinguished by melancholy and sadness touches on a profound truth: the glorification of "the anguish of a troubled heart" as an aesthetically appealing theme to be revered in itself is relatively modern. Chaucer uses the phrase once, in his Parson's Tale, where it is a definition of the sin of "accidie": "Thanne is Accidie the angwissh of troubled herte; and Seint Augustyn seith, 'It is anoy of goodnesse and

---

[22] Cf. H. S. Bennett's discussion of the word *alone* in connection with the "pathos" of Arcite's farewell to the world (KT I (A) 2779), *Chaucer and the Fifteenth Century* (Oxford, 1947), p. 83. It has, he says, "little of the evocative effect that it has for us with centuries of association behind the word 'alone' — associations magnificently called on by Coleridge in

> Alone, alone, all, all alone,
> Alone on a wide wide sea..."

Chaucer, it is said, had to rely on "cumulative effect" rather than association. It may be objected in the first place that the word *alone* had, in the fourteenth century, associations which had been gathering for some centuries since the text of Ecclesiastes 4. 10 became available in the West. Moreover, at the risk of being accused of "literary insensitivity" once more, let me add that the passage in question is not "pathetic" at all. We shall do better to forget Coleridge, except for purposes of contrast, when we read Chaucer.

[23] Trans. Lucy Norton (London, 1951), p. 192. The great painter was troubled by feelings of multiple personality and loneliness. E.g., see pp. 15, 40, 214. He speaks, p. 97 (1849), of an "unbearable sense of emptiness" to his friend Chopin, who was suffering acutely from "boredom."

Ioye of harm.' Certes, this is a dampnable synne." [24] The branches of this sin include sloth, despair, lassitude, and *tristitia,* "the
synne of wordly sorwe." Its remedies are fortitude, magnanimity,
sureness or perseverance, magnificence, and constancy, virtues
which are distinctly chivalric. [25] Perhaps some will reply that Chaucer's humble and devout Parson, who taught "Cristes lore and
his apostles twelve" after he had" folwed it hymselve" was an old
Puritan, to whose strictures Chaucer, who was, after all, a great
poet and hence "advanced," could have given small credence. [26]
But this is to misunderstand both the Parson and his creator.
With reference to the "Puritanism," we should recall that the
Parson, although he was a learned man and a clerk, was also "to
synful men nat despitous." This does not mean that he relaxed
his principles. What it does mean is that the Parson employed
"fairnesse" and "good ensample." He was, that is, no Pharisee who
said one thing and did another. No one in the Middle Ages except
for a few pious hypocrites who were condemmed with equal se-
verity by Jean de Meun, Petrarch, Boccaccio, and Chaucer,
thought that "sinners" were "those others." Every man since the
Fall was by nature a child of wrath, to paraphrase St. Paul; and
no one expected any individual to refrain from sin altogether.
Everyone was required to confess his "deadly" sins at least once
a year. If society had been made up of the righteous, the ecclesiastical hierarchy might just as well have closed its doors and
gone out of business. With reference to the *"accidie"* of the Black
Knight specifically, it is obvious that it deprives him of virtues
like magnanimity and magnificence and that we should consider
his conduct to be unreasonable. His virtues have been turned
to vices (lines 598 ff.), he seriously contemplates suicide (lines
689-690), and he desires to do nothing worthwhile. This attitude

---

[25] *Works,* ed. Robinson, 2 ed. (Boston, 1957), p. 249.

[25] Magnanimity, for example, is defined as "greet corage," which "maketh
folk to undertake harde thynges and grevouse thynges, by hir owene wil,
wisely and resonably." The virtue of magnificence appears "whan a man
dooth and perfourneth grete werkes of goodnesse." It is not difficult to
think of these virtues in connection with the Knight as he is described in
the General Prologue.

[26] The more "advanced" figures in the General Prologue to *The Canterbury Tales,* like the Monk and the Pardoner, are not treated with much
sympathy.

is hardly, in fourteenth-century terms, a fitting tribute to a great
lady in a chivalric society. In other societies it might have a certain appeal. Thus, if we accept for a moment Rousseau's account
of the affair (whose verisimilitude is all that is important here), [27]
when F. M. Grimm deliberately adopted a posture very similar
to that of the Black Knight because he had been rejected by Mlle
Fel, he won for himself an enormous reputation as a prodigy of
love and devotion and was warmly received by the best society
of Paris. But Chaucer did not live in eighteenth-century Paris.
The age of *sentiment* had not yet arrived. If we glance back at
Froissart's remarks quoted earlier, we shall notice that the old
poet shows no inclination to cultivate the melancholy he feels
when he remembers Blanche, and that his sighs follow an excla-
mation that is vigorous and positive.

The Black Knight, like F. M. Grimm, is a lover; and this fact
also should lead us to read Chaucer's poem with a certain caution.
Some critics of the poem have written about it as though they
were themselves spiritual descendants of Emma Bovary and
expected everyone else, including Chaucer, to share the same general outlook. Perhaps nothing has been more characteristic of
the past two hundred years than the violence and rapidity with
which attitudes toward sexual relations and love between the
sexes have changed. [28] There is no need to go into the history of
these matters in detail here; it is obvious that the place of sexual
relations and love in a society where feelings of loneliness, boredom, namelessness, and alienation are common, and environ-
ments created by an industrial society seem inhumane, should be
very different from their place in a predominantely rural society
where everyone had a more or less natural position in a small
community. It is true that war and pestilence created dislocation
in the fourteenth century. But the dislocated, in general, tended
to become outlaws, not authors, especially in England. The Middle Ages had experienced none of the glorification of sentiment

---

[27] *Confessions* 2. 8 (1750-1752). It is possible that this story is colored
by Rousseau's later hostility to Grimm.

[28] For some hints of this change, see J. H. Van den Berg, *The Changing
Nature of Man* (New York, 1961), Ch. III. For the nineteenth century in
particular, see the brilliant study by Werner Hofmann, *The Earthly Paradise*
(New York, 1961), especially Ch. X.

(the beginnings of which are apparent in Rousseau), the strong urge toward the brotherhood of all mankind (which led Baudelaire to think that prostitutes are holy, and has produced many golden-hearted whores since), the squeamishness of the Victorians, nor the crisis marked by the revolt of D. H. Lawrence and the observations of Freud, all of which, together with some more recent "revolutions," lie in our immediate background. Although in the Middle Ages contemplatives and, perhaps, apprentices, took vows of chastity, and priests were not encouraged to have concubines, and medieval manors supported many unmarried serfs, it is unlikely that many persons, especially among those of gentle birth, suffered long from sexual frustration. What we call "the facts of life" were not concealed from children; [29] they were not mysteries for adolescent fumbling; and no one felt any compulsion to be either "sincere" or sentimental about his miscellaneous sexual activities.

It is true, as churchmen disturbed by Albigensian errors insist throughout the later Middle Ages, that fornication was considered to be a "deadly sin." But so were getting drunk, eating too much or too delicately, envying your neighbor's goods, dressing yourself up proudly beyond your station, and, indeed, a great many other kinds of fairly common behavior "deadly sins" also. These were things that everyone was expected to fall into occasionally and which everyone was supposed to reveal to his confessor. No one was encouraged to do any of these things, but no one was especially surprised when anyone did. A vicious inclination to pursue sins of any given type, sexual or otherwise, was heartily discouraged, but the medieval ecclesiastical hierarchy did not pursue the subject in such a way as to encourage what we might call "Ruskin's Problem". Nor was there much need for "Rousseau's Solution." Sinning did not make anyone a "pagan," and no one thought that pagans enjoyed life more than Christians. Adultery was, naturally enough, another "deadly sin." In this matter the feudal Middle Ages maintained a "double standard" for social reasons. Feudal holdings were hereditary, and feudal

---

[29] Medieval houses, even among the wealthy, afforded little bedroom privacy. In this connection, see also Philippe Ariès, *Centuries of Childhood* (New York, 1962), pp. 100ff., and p. 128.

tenants wished their holdings to descend to their own children, not to the children of intruders. But the ladies, although a few may have been misled by "the book of Launcelot de Lake," did not have their "psychological needs" stimulated by the kind of romantic picture books that fascinated little Emma Bovary, did not immerse themselves vicariously in novels, and did not, finally, live in a dull, postrevolutionary middle-class society. In the fourteenth century, in short, sex was neither a mystery nor a mystique. Although it was quite profitable for summoners, archdeacons, and rural deans, it did not constitute a profound personal problem, especially among noblemen, who in general found "venison" plentiful. To use an example pertinent to our present discussion, the first child of John of Gaunt of whom we have any record was born when John was about eighteen, and the lady in question, one Marie de Saint Hilaire, was probably by no means his first love. [30]

If fornication was simply one among many "deadly sins," and adultery occasioned little surprise among the male nobility, [31] there was something else that was severely condemned by the ecclesiastical authorities and ridiculed by laymen because it led to impenitence spiritually and to a foolish neglect of social obligations. And that was a single-minded and impenitent fixation on a single member of the opposite sex as a means of enjoyment to be venerated above all other things. As this sort of passion is usually described, it has pleasure, not marriage, as its end; and

---

[30] See *John of Gaunt,* pp. 460-462.

[31] In 1396 the Duke and Katherine petitioned the Pope to sanction their marriage, stating as one of the impediments the fact that they had lived in adultery during the lifetime of Constance. In connection with "sin" itself, we should be aware of the fact that the connotations of the word have changed enormously since the Middle Ages. The intense introspective concern for the subject exhibited by Bunyan in *Grace Abounding* would have then seemed unnatural, and Arnold's feeling that sin is "a positive, active entity hostile to man, a mysterious power" would have seemed Manichean, smacking a little of devil-worship. Arnold's further view that "the true greatness of Christianity" lies in "righteousness," a view that seems to be taken for granted by many modern writers, would have been regarded as Pelagian. Perhaps it would be better to translate "sin" in most medieval contexts as "unwise conduct." Christ was conventionally regarded as the "Wisdom of God," and His message was love, not righteousness, which was the message of the Old Law.

it deprives the victim of the solaces of all other women except the one fixed upon. This kind of "idolatrous" love is not, in substance, of medieval origin. It is described by Lucretius. [32] In the Middle Ages it is illustrated in Abelard's *Historia calamitatum,* in the Tristan romances of Béroul and Thomas, in Chrétien's romances of Cligés and Lancelot, in the *Roman de la Rose,* in Chaucer's *Troilus,* in *Celestina,* and, in the Renaissance, in Shakespeare's *Antony and Cleopatra.* Medical authorities described it as "heroic" love, an appellation in which the word *heroic* is pejorative. It is the same sort of thing that in Rousseau's account M. Grimm pretended to feel for his opera singer. We are naturally inclined in reading medieval texts of the kind just mentioned to react in much the same way that fashionable Paris reacted to Grimm's predicament, and to add to our sentiment a further veneer of Biedermeier sentimentality glossed with a dash of existential loneliness. From a medieval point of view, the great difficulty with a passion of this kinds is that it leads almost inevitably to frustration, or even death, and it deprives its victim of the mercy of the New Law.

It would be foolish to accuse John of Gaunt of any such impenitent passion. But the Black Knight in *The Book of the Duchess* seems to have been thrown by his grief into a condition very much resembling it. Without Blanche, he can do nothing constructive, and life itself seems worthless. When his interrogator suggests to him that he has, in view of his description of Blanche, had "such a chaunce as shryfte wythoute repentaunce," he can reply only that it would be treasonable for him to repent of his love. He has no notion of what his description of the lady has implied: the virtues of Blanche belong to the realm of the intelligible and are not subject to Fortune. The quest of the idolatrous lover is not a quest for virtue, but for his own "bliss." And it is this, the Knight assures us, that he has lost. Without it, death seems the only solution. His "shrift," in other words, has not led him to see the essential selfishness of his passion.

Turning now from the Black Knight to the description of Blanche, we find that scholars and critics have insisted, in spite of the fact that Chaucer's materials are clearly derivative, on seeing it as at least in part an actual description of the lady. In one

---

[32] *De rerum natura* 4. 1058-1072.

sense it may be, but it is hardly a visual portrait. We know more, in so far as details of feature are concerned, about some of the characters in *The Canterbury Tales*. What does Chaucer, in fact, tell us? Blanche outshone the other ladies as the sun does the stars. She was of good stature, she maintained a steadfast countenance, and her demeanor was noble and friendly (lines 817-847). She danced, sang, laughed, and played in an attractive way; she had golden hair, a steady glance, and an eye that seemed merciful (lines 848-877). She was temperate in mood, neither too solemn nor too gay, and she loved charitably (lines 878-894). She had a beautiful face, red and white, that was "sad, symple, and benygne" (lines 895-918). She spoke softly, reasonably, and truthfully, without malice, flattery, or chiding (lines 919-938). Her neck was round, fair, and straight. Her throat was like a round tower of ivory and of moderate size (lines 939-947). She had fair shoulders, a long trunk, well-proportioned arms, white hands with red nails, round breasts, broads hips, and a straight, flat back (lines 948-960). She outshone the other ladies in comeliness of manner, and was, like the Arabian Phoenix, unique (lines 961-984). The description goes on to considerer intangibles: Blanche's goodness, truth, and well-ordered love (lines 985-1.034). He who looks for an individualized "portrait" in these lines will look in vain. Did the lady have long lashes? What color were her eyes? Was her nose long or short, her chin slightly jutting or round and dimpled? Was her lip full?

We are told that Blanche was a beautiful, attractive, and well-mannered blonde, exceptionally well shaped and with the coloration to be expected. In other words, the description is highly stylized and is not, in the modern sense, a "portrait" at all. If we look carefully at the description in the original we shall find it to contain much more emphasis on *invisibilia* than on *visibilia*. Moreover, it contains features like the ivory tower which are clearly iconographic, or, in other words, features that point to ideas rather than to things. The *invisibilia*, both stated and implied, moreover, all point to Blanche's virtues, so that lines 895-1032 form a logical conclusion to the description. The emphasis on virtue in the description, which may be detected even without reference to conventional iconography (a subject which seems to irritate most of my fellow-Chaucerians about as much as virtue itself does), is hardly surprising in a funerary poem. What is surprising is that the Black Knight fails to see the wider implications of what he has said. He has been lamenting the loss of Blanche as a physical being, a gift of Fortune. But the virtues he has described have nothing to do with Fortune and cannot be destroyed by anything Fortune may do. This fact could hardly have escaped Chaucer's audience, and did not escape the Black Knight's interrogator, who remarked,

> Hardely, your love was well beset;
> I not how ye myghte have do bet.

A lady of such virtue is truly lovable.

Two "characters" in the poem remain to be discussed: the Emperor Octovyen, and the speaker. The usual notion that the Emperor or king (line 1314) is meant to represent Edward III is hardly very convincing. What, exactly, would have been the point of the dreamer's undertaking a hunt under the auspices of King Edward in which the king himself did nothing but ride toward the manor of Richmond after an unsuccessful day in the field? If Octovyen was meant to be Edward, we can conclude only that Chaucer must have succeeded very well in puzzling his royal master.

There remains the speaker, who acts also as interrogator in the questioning of the Black Knight. It is usually assumed that the dream in the poem is, in spite of the warnings in lines 270-290, a literal dream experienced, or feigned to have been experienced, by Geoffrey Chaucer, our young squire. Let us picture the situation. Chaucer, a member of the court of comparatively low rank, rises at a memorial gathering for Blanche, and says, in effect, "I am in very low spirits, having suffered for the past eight years, and cannot sleep. But I read a tale about Ceys and Alcione and went to sleep. Then I dreamed about waking in an elaborately decorated chamber and taking part in a hunt, led by the Emperor Octovyen, where I met a Black Knight lamenting the death of a lady under a tree. He told me how much he loved Blanche, whom he described; but he refused to be consoled. As I woke up, I saw Octovyen riding to Richmond." If we are to believe the most recent critics of the poem, he added somewhere in this account a remark like the following: "Oh, I say. Life, love, and all that. Frightfully ambiguous, what?" The only reasonable reaction to all this would have been to send the poor squire to St. Bartholomew's. Nobody in the audience, unless Philippa Chaucer were there, could possibly have had any interest in the squire's personal feelings, or in whether he had been ill for eight years or twenty, or in what he might have dreamed. What is the Emperor Octovyen, or, if you prefer, Augustus Caesar, doing in the English countryside? It is small wonder that a distinguished literary historian finds the poem "crude," with a "story" that "drags," full of "hackneyed" conventions, and without "profound emotion" or "serious thought." [33] As it is usually read today it is worse than this. It is a piece of foolishness which would have been an affront to the court and a disgrace to its author. Those who insist on clinging to "what the poem says literally" are only offering some justification for the usual connotations of the word *academic*. Do they also engage in disputes about the number of petals growing on the girl whom Burns describes as being "like a red, red rose"?

It is much more probable that the "I" at the beginning of the poem represents not Chaucer individually and specifically but the initial reaction of the mourners for Blanche generally, somewhat exaggerated for poetic purposes. The story of Ceys and Alcione is not something he chanced to have read, but something of significance for all the mourners, who have set before them an example of someone who endure a temporal loss "comme homme fort et de grant cuer," and cannot understand the consolatory implications of the message,

> Awake! let be your sorwful lyf!
> For in your sorwe there lyth no red,
> For, certes, swete, I nam but ded.

There is only one sense in which the statement "I nam but ded" can be taken as a reason for not sorrowing, and, considering both the occasion for the poem and the nature of the audience, that sense would have been obvious. It can be found explained fully in the Epistle of the Mass for the Burial of the Dead, which begins, "Brethren: We will not have you ignorant concerning them

---

[33] *Chaucer and the Fifteenth Century*, p. 36.

that are asleep, that you be not sorrowful, even as others who have no hope; for if we believe that Jesus died and rose again, even so them who have slept through Jesus, will God bring with Him." Alcione, who looked up and "saw noght," is among those "who have no hope."

In the dream, as we have seen, there is an obvious parallel between the interrogator and Lady Philosophy in the *Consolation,* and between the Black Knight and the mournful "Boethius" of the same work. Every man, including every man in Chaucer's audience, has, as it were, two parts, one involved in the senses and the other capable of comprehending the intelligible. What is revealed in the Black Knight's long confession is the significance of an Alcione-like attitude, an attitude typical of that part of any man that is involved in temporal things. It is for this reason that Spenser names his "man in black" in the *Daphnaida,* who is certainly not John of Gaunt, "Alcyon." The attitude depends on our being overcome by idleness (or neglect of virtuous activity) in the first place, and by love for those things that may be apprehended by the senses. Then the object finally settled upon becomes, through desire, a gift of Fortune, the loss of which leads to "accidie" and despair. But at the promptings of the interrogator, the Black Knight, together with the audience, is led to dwell upon Blanche's virtues. If Blanche was as virtuous as the description implies, as noble, temperate, truthful, and charitable as the Black Knight indicates, then a despairing attitude like that of Alcione is neither necessary nor, in fact, complimentary to her. Aside from a few hints, like the observations on suicide, and a generally reasonable tone (sometimes described as "realistic" or inappropriately humorous), the interrogator leaves the positive side of his message unstated. It was stated openly in the Burial Service and in Commemorative Masses, but *The Book of the Duchess* is a poem, or, in other words, a work in which indirect statement may lead the audience to certain conclusions that are only suggested. Meanwhile, the Black Knight and the dreamer represent two aspects, not only of Geoffrey Chaucer, but of everyone who loved Blanche.

Whether the poem conveys "profound emotion" depends entirely on the reader's experience and training. The Burial Service can in itself be very moving, and the ideas in the *Consolation* of Boe-

thius can be moving also. Whether the doctrines of St. Paul and of
Boethius actually constitute "serious thought" I leave to the gentlemen who, a moment ago, were discussing the number of petals
growing on the girl. In the past, some of them have complained
loudly about the inadequacy of Pauline and Boethian doctrines,
which fail somehow to cope with the rich ambiguity of life. However, there is no reason to imagine that there was much sniveling
about "ambiguity" in the court of Edward III. Had there been
peaches there, men would have dared eat them.

The chivalric character of the poet and of his audience remains
for our consideration. It is manifested, first of all, in the pervasive
shimmer of good humor that glances from the surface of the
poem, a tone that we can detect, without too much difficulty, in
the little lament from Froissart quoted at the beginning of this
essay. In a famous letter to his brother Toby, Mr. Walter Shandy
strongly urged him to have his beloved Widow Wadman read
"devotional tracts" and to keep from her such authors as Rabe-
lais, Scarron, or Cervantes. Their books "excite laughter," thus
making them inappropriate, for "there is no passion so serious
as lust." Mr. Shandy here hit upon a great truth. If he had lived
in our age, he might have added that certain forms of aesthetics
and psychology share the same seriousness, since they are not
unrelated to the passion mentioned. Morality, except in its nineteenth-century guises, is not nearly so serious, a fact that has
resulted in the destruction of much of Chaucer's humor at the
hands of the aesthetically or psychologically inclined. In the fourteenth century specifically, young noblemen were discouraged
from maintaining a solemm attitude in public, for "papelardie," or
false holiness, was considered foolish and in bad taste. [34] The light
tone of much of Chaucer's poem is not difficult to point out. For
example, when the speaker introduces his book of "fables," he
says that it spoke.

> Of quenes lives, and of kinges,
> And many other thinges smale.

The bantering tone continues in the story itself. Alcione's grief is
not always treated with great solemnity:

---

[34] See *A Preface to Chaucer*, p. 461.

Ful ofte she swouned, and sayd "Alas!"
For sorwe ful nygh wood she was...

Again, the scene between Juno's messenger and Morpheus is openly humorous:

This messager com fleynge faste
And cried, "O, ho! awake anoon!"
Hit was for noght; there herde hym non.
"Awake!" quod he, "whoo ys lyth there?"
And blew his horn ryght in here eere,
And cried "Awaketh!" wonder hye.
The god of slep with hys oon ye
Cast up, axed, "Who clepeth ther?"
"Hyt am I," quod this messager.

The light tone is marked in the dreamer's reaction to the story — in his elaborate promise to Morpheus "in game," and in his introduction to the dream that "nat skarsly Macrobeus" could understand. Although the speeches of the Black Knight are serious in intent, his behavior as he describes it not infrequently borders upon the ridiculous, and, in any event, the reactions of the interrogator maintain a courteous but good-natured tone. His response to the final revelation of Blanche's death, for example, is one of detached but good-natured sympathy:

"Is that your los? Be god hyt ys routhe!"

Most critics of the poem have been disappointed by the fact that this response is not more lugubrious. Its tone is not very different from Froissart's

Haro! Mettés moi une emplastre
Sus le coer...

In neither instance should the light tone be taken as an indication of lack of feeling. Chaucer was not attempting to encourage the serious, basically lustful attitude of the Black Knight. He had no desire to encourage grief. On the contrary, the serious, melancholy, slothful mood was exactly what he wished to discourage. He is saying, in effect, to all the mourners for Blanche, "let be your sorwful lyf!" When the light of reason is allowed to play on the scene, grief departs from those who have hope. Meanwhile, the general tone of the poem is aristocratic and good-humored, consistent with the predominantly chivalric nature of the audience.

In addition to presenting a contrast to a reasonable attitude toward Fortune, the Black Knight's behavior contrasts sharply with the current conception of Chivalric love. In the little poem that Edward III is said to have written for the Black Prince, the poet says,

> Des femes venent les proesces
> Et les honours et les hautesces.

He refers to the fact that great ladies were frequently regarded as sources of chivalric inspiration to men who loved them for their nobility and virtue. Such love had little to do with lust or sentiment and did not have sexual satisfaction, readily available elsewhere, as its aim. It was basically similar to the kind of love any vassal owed to his overlord or any subject owed to his queen. In short, it was exactly the kind of love that Chaucer himself and the noblemen in his audience owed to Blanche, Duchess of Lancaster. In an age like ours when a long period of adolescent frustration, or semi-frustration is common, and when love of any kind involving generosity of spirit is reported to be difficult,[35] we may find this convention hard to understand. But the attitude had been popularized in the fourteenth-century poems of Machaut, and it is illustrated in Chaucer's poem itself.

When the Black Knight first approaches Blanche, he feels that he will die if he does not speak to her (line 1188). He is so fearful that he can only grow pale and blush by turns (line 1215), and when he does finally speak, he can say nothing but "mercy!" The lady, who, as we have been told, "loved as man may do his brother" (line 892), and "loved so wel ryght, she wrong do wolde to no wyght" (lines 1015-1016), quite properly refuses to have anything to do with the Knight. His approach shows no virility, and, certainly, no chivalry. On the contrary, it reveals a merely selfish "sensible passion" without any virtue to commend it. The

---

[35] E.g., by such diverse witnesses as T. S. Eliot in *The Cocktail Party* and Camus in *The Stranger*.

fact that the lady shows no resemblance to the Parisian ladies who, years later, were to be so overwhelmingly impressed by the antics of M. Grimm should surprise no one. "Another yere," when the Knight is able to desire nothing but the lady's "good," he receives a ring, and his inclinations become harmonious with hers. If the description of Blanche means anything at all, this harmony implies a virtuous and noble demeanor on the part of the Knight. In other words, Blanche was an inspiration to truly chivalric conduct to those who loved her reasonably. This, after all, is exactly the idea Chaucer wished to get across. If the virtues of the Duchess were an inspiration to reasonable and noble conduct in life, her memory should continue to inspire such conduct. Once this point has been made, or strongly suggested, the "characters" in the poem — the Black Knight and the dreamer — have served their usefulness and may be quickly dismissed. They are, of course, not "characters" at all in the modern sense, and what happens to them is not a "story." Their dismissal is a logical consequence of the poem's thematic development. The poem itself ends "abruptly" only if we read it in the same spirit that we read, let us say, "The Little Red Hen."

In conclusion, let us consider very briefly the poem "as a poem." At the time it was delivered, the memory of the young duchess was still fresh in everyone's mind. England was still free of the disillusionment that was to result from failures abroad and social unrest at home, justly confident of its place as a great European power. In the minds of the nobility, the inspiration afforded by noble ladies like the Duchess of Lancaster, gracious and beautiful in demeanor and steadfast in heart, was at least in part responsible for their success. What does Chaucer's poem, then, mean to us? It means nothing at all in so far as "emotional profundity" or "serious thought" are concerned unless we can place ourselves by an act of the historical imagination in Chaucer's audience, allowing ourselves, as best we can, to think as they thought and to feel as they felt. If we cannot take the themes of the *Consolation* of Boethius seriously, if the text of the Burial Mass leaves us unmoved, and, above all, if we insist on demanding romantic and post-romantic emotionalism in everything we read, there is small likelihood that Chaucer's poem will move us in any way. The poet was not seeking to create "purely literary" effects; and there is no virtue in poetry itself, in spite of certain recent notions of Frazerian-Jungian archetypes, operating by sympathetic magic in the enchanted mists of the collective unconscious, that will bring Chaucer's tribute to life for us in any other way. It would be better, indeed, not to read the poem at all unless we can, in imagination, picture Blanche, young, gay, and of humble cheer, suddenly lost to the family of the Duke and the court of the King, and exclaim with Froissart, "Haro!"

SOME DOCUMENTS ON ENGLISH PARDONERS, 1350 - 1400

ARNOLD WILLIAMS
Michigan State University

In general, Chaucer's Pardoner has received the attention due the most thorough and shameless scoundrel among the Canterbury pilgrims. Among many analyses of his character and studies of his tale, however, one misses any addition to or correction of the collection of documentary material concerning pardoners made by the great French scholar and long-time ambassador to the United States, Jean Jules Jusserand. His *English Wayfaring Life in the Middle Ages,* originally published in French as *Les Anglais au moyen âge* in 1884, was translated into English by Lucy Toulmin Smith in 1890, with added material. The documents there presented as illustrative of the frauds practiced by those who were called "sometimes *quaestors,* on account of what they asked, and sometimes *pardoners,* on account of what they gave" [1] were based principally on materials in print when Jusserand wrote.

In the course of investigations concerning the mendicant friars of Chaucer's time I have come across several additional documents in episcopal registers, both in print and in manuscript. It is remarkable, considering the short life of most scholarship, that I have found nothing which contradicts or seriously modifies the picture Jusserand builds up from his documents. In only one minor detail, whether friars also served as pardoners, is any modification indicated. However, the new documents add some rather interesting material to what is now available and are published here for that reason.

---

[1] *English Wayfaring Life,* p. 312.

The following passages I have arranged in chronological order. Where the original Latin is available in print I have given only the English translation, with a reference to the source in the footnote; where the text exists only in manuscript, the footnotes carry also the Latin. If the translation sometimes seems involved and turgid, it is because the Latin of episcopal registers customarily has all the complexity of classical syntax without any of the grace.

i.   Conflicts between Friars and Questors

The grave and rejected complaint of many has come to our attention that when friars of the mendicant orders admitted by us to preaching and hearing the confessions of our subjects according to the form of the constitution [2] issued in that case arrive in the same day as questors or messengers of whatever kind similarly delegated to seek the alms of the faithful to carry on the business commited to them, the question arises between these friars and questors arriving together in this manner which of them is to be allowed first to do what pertains to his office. So arises a matter of dissension by which occasion grave [3] scandals may often arise and public commotion and thence complaints are brought to our ears.

Wishing to make an end to such dissensions insofar as with God we may in this case, we therefore knowing how great is the need of the faithful for the word of God command you and yours firmly enjoining that, insofar as and however often friars and questors shall happen to coincide in their arrival in this fashion at your churches, chapels, or other ecclesiastical places to carry on their business, first freely allow those friars so wishing to preach the word of God to the clergy and the people wishing to hear it and let them receive the alms of the faithful freely given by the urging of divine charity; and then later, after this preach-

---

[2] I. e. the bull *Super Cathedram* first issued by Boniface VIII in 1300, virtually nullified by his succesor Benedict XI, and finally reinstated by the Council of Vienne as its second canon (1312). For the text see S. J. Hefele, *Histoire des Conciles,* 2nd ed., and tr. H. Leclercq (Paris, 1915), VI, 674-78.

[3] Reading *gravia* for *gravis*.

ing is finished, similarly allow the said questors to carry out the business committed to them according to the form prescribed by sacred canons and discharge the other things which pertain to their office... according to the privileges given by the same authority of the Apostolic See and the canonical sanctions as well. Farewell. Given at Ripon the eighth day of the month of December A. D. 1350 and the ninth of our episcopate.[4]

ii. Diocesan Officials not to Help Questors

John etc. to our beloved brothers in Christ, our principal official and the Archdeacons constituted in our church of Exeter and their own officials and commissioners, greetings etc. Because of the damnable abuses of impious questors, abhorrent to the ears of Catholics, we have hitherto by our letters to that effect to you and by the statutes of canon law and the constitutions of the holy fathers caused to be prohibited publicly and solemnly that you should admit (or they should admit) to the practice of

---

[4] "Quod nostrum deduxit auditum gravis & antiquata conquestio plurimorum quod cum fratres ordinum mendicantium per nos ad praedicandum & confessiones subditorum nostrorum audiendum admissi iuxta forman constitutionis editae in hoc casu ac etiam quaestores seu nuntii quicumque pro fidelium elemosinis quarende similiter deputati pro negotiis commissis sibi exponendis concurrunt [or concurrerunt?] uno die inter eosdem fratres & quaestores sic concurrentes quis eorum videlicet praeferatur ad faciendum ea quae suo noscuntur officio pertinere dissentionis materia oritur per quam gravis cuius occasione scandala saepe provenerunt & commotiones in populo ac frequentes inde clamores nostris auribus proferuntur. Nos igitur cupientes dissentionibus huiusmodi finem imponere quatenus cum Deo poterimus in hoc casu attendentes quod [quam?] necessitatem sit Christi fidelibus palulum verbum Dei vobis & vestrum cuilibet mandamus firmiter iniungentes quotienscumque fratres & quaestores huiusmodi ad vestras ecclesias, capellas, seu loca alia ecclesiastica pro negotiis suis huiusmodi exponendis simul contigerit convenire ipsos fratres praedicare volentes primo proponere verbum Dei clero & populo illud audire volentibus libere permittatis & fidelium elemosinas eidem gratis oblatas recipere divinae intuitu caritatis ac subsequenter praedicatione huiusmodi facta dictos quaestores negotia eisdem commissa secundum traditam sacris canonibus formam exponere similiter permittatis & cetera facere adimplere quae ad ipsorum officium pertinere...iuxta indulta eodem auctoritate sedis apostolicae privilegia etiam canonicas sanctiones. Valete. Datur apud Ripon octava die mensis Decembris Anno Domini millesimo CCCmo quinquagesimo et pontificatus nostri nono," Manuscript Register of William de la Zouche, archbishop of York, Borthwich Institute, York, fol. 262[v].

preaching or the office of exhortation by themselves any questors whatsoever or of any of them at all under any color, who busy themselves solely with the collection of alms and care not for the welfare of souls, nor should you commit to your parochial curates the dissemination of documents, brevets, and feigned privileges and indulgences other than those contained in our letters testimonial in this matter or having the meaning of the same strictly word by word. Nor should you curates yourselves so presume (nor should they so presume) under the pains and censures enjoined.

We, therefore, not without disquietude of heart, learn from the quarrels, denunciations, and clamors of many, and in part we are convinced from the inspection of such documents, that you, the officials of archdeacons or your commissioners and registrars, damnably blinded by greed of the money so collected, or more truly reserving to yourselves for the iniquitous labor under color of an infidel fee, not only permit, but even most wickedly assist, advise, and protect such questors both of the Hospitals of the Holy Spirit and St. John but also of other privileged places (who are, as they say, neither friars nor clergy but often laymen or married men) in plying their business in the office of preaching on solemn days within the solemnities of masses, an office which is not permitted to lesser deacons. Who preach and expound to our subject people, to the grave deception of their souls, these detestable and pernicious abuses, undoubtedly knowing them to be heretical error, and [promulgate] privileges prudently abrogated in the last council of Vienne and suspected [or] revoked as well. [5] They indifferently absolve and free from usury and robbery without due satisfaction, even in cases reserved to the bishop or his superiors, and many times from pain and guilt, to use their own words, or at least say, lying, to curates and parish priests that they have the power granted to them from the Holy See for the time of their frantic collection, to the scandal and infamy of the Holy See. You, then, officials of archdeacons, commissioners, and registrars aforesaid, deliver to curates of that sort, fraudulently and mendaciously for the extortion of money, false and fabricated documents or brevets, the aforesaid abuses and other

---

[5] The reference is probably to Canon VII, Hefele-Leclercq, VI, 684-85.

enormities contrary to the Catholic faith and not without liability of heresy, perjury, and contempt of the keys of the Chuch (concerning which we intend to proceed against you insofar as may be just at the appropiate place and time) commonly offering [these indulgences] in offence against canon law and the holy fathers, constitutions of the apostles as well as provincial [councils] and synods and against our prohibitions and to our manifest contempt. And so the aforesaid questors, wandering about our diocese, supported by your underserved work and help and favor, seduce the simple and unlearned folk and, as much as they can, spiritually trick and deceive them.

Wherefore we command you, enjoining you in virtue of obedience, that you, our principal official of our consistory of Exeter, you, indeed, archdeacons and your officials or commisioners aforesaid, in separate chapters to be held by you after solemn publication of the present command, to prohibit or cause to be prohibited, that any rectors, vicars, or other curates within the constituted limits of their own jurisdictions, admit, as we forbid you and them to admit, any questors of alms of the Hospital of the Holy Spirit and that of Sts. John and Anthony, or any other whatsoever, to the performance of the office of exhortation or to the collection of alms or to preaching or offering of privileges or indulgences, except insofar as they can show our letters to that effect. Nor should you, archdeacons and your officials or commissioners and registrars aforesaid, presume to deliver documents of brevets, other than those having our letters annexed, as said earlier, or a copy of the same, with nothing changed, to the aforesaid curates and their parishioners, nor should the same persons presume in any fashion to receive them or set them forth, under the penalty of a major excommunication, which you and they, if you do not comply with anything in the foregoing, ought to fear. Indeed, from the day of the reception of these presents you will certify to us before Passion Sunday [22 March] how you will execute the present command by your or by their letters patent, clearly containing their series and the manner of execution. Provided that whichever of you first receives the present command will, after making a copy for himself, quickly transmit it to the others for execution.

Given at our manor of Chudleigh, the fourth day of the month of March in the year of our Lord 1355 [i. e. 1356] and of our consecration the twenty ninth. [6]

iii. False Questors Not To Be Received

Thomas, etc., to the archdeacons of Exeter, Totnes, Barnstaple, and Cornwall or their officials, greetings, etc. After hearing public rumor and receiving experience of its truth, we have learned that some questors, equipped with false and forged letters bearing seals, both from the Apostolic See and from us (as the liars assert), in public places falsely preach the writs and abuses contained in these letters before the clergy and the people of our city and diocese, to the deception of souls and for the purpose of extorting money and other goods from our subjects, so that, like false prophets, they deceive the simple. And they offer, not without much boldness and deception of souls, and in fact grant indulgences to the people on their own authority. They dispense from vows, absolve those confessing to them from perjuries, murders, and other sins; for an amount of money they remit things stolen or doubtfully obtained; they relax the third or fourth part of penances enjoined [on those having to do with them]; lying, they assert that they can extract from purgatory the parents or friends of those who give alms to them; to the benefactors of the places where these questors are they grant plenary remission of sins, and many they absolve from all penalty and guilt (as we use these words), contrary to the decrees of the Holy Fathers wholesomely issued in this matter.

Hearing of these dangers, by which the keys of the Church are held in more than usual contempt, and the authority of the Church is debased [7] and the souls of many of our subjects are in many ways [8] deceived by the foregoing and other abuses, for whose health we are forced by our pastoral office to care, we therefore, by virtue of obedience and under penalty of a major excommunication more strictly prohibit each and every one of you, and

---

[6] *Episcopal Register of John de Grandisson,* Bishop of Exeter, ed. F. C. Hingeston-Randolph (London, 1897), Pt. II, pp. 1178-79.

[7] Reading *vilescitur* for *vilescit* .

[8] Reading *multipliciter* for *multiplicitur.*

through you we wish and command that each and every one of
our subjects, inasmuch as they are subject to you, be prohibited,
lest any of these questors [be received] unless [he shows] our letters written after the present date with our seal containing the
impression of our ring... [9]

iv. Against False Friars and Questors

Thomas, etc. to our principal official or in his absence to the
presiding officer of our consistory of Exeter and to our archdeacons of Exeter, Totnes, Barnstaple, and Cornwall or their officials, greetings. Certainly informed by public rumor and by experience of the fact, we understand that some friars of the mendicant orders and other with lies assert that they have the power
of hearing confessions of our subjects and absolving them of
their sins, even in cases reserved to the Apostolic See and to us;
and that others, pretending to be questors of alms and falsely
fabricating and counterfeiting our seal, pretending to have letters from us about indulgences which they pretend to be conceded to them, presume to set them forth in order to extort money
more quickly from our subjects by such means to the deception
of many souls of our subjects. Therefore, we commit and command you collectively and individually to prohibit all and each
of our subjects openly and expressly, under the penalty of a major
excommunication to be hurled justly against those who violate
this prohibition, from presuming to confess their sins to any such
friars or admitting any such questors of alms, unless their power
be evidently known by true apostolic letters, not revoked, or by
our own letters signed with our seal and with the impression of our
ring on the back.

Whichever of you indeed shall receive the present command
first, let him transmit it to another not having it to be carried
out quickly. And what you do about the foregoing, insofar as it
concerns you individually, certify it to us by your letters patent

---

[9] *Register of Thomas de Brantingham, Bishop of Exeter*; ed. F. C. Hingeston-Randolph (London, 1901-06), p. 380. Incomplete and undated, probably 1377. After it a space is left for its completion, but the space was never
filled in. Was the document ever officially issued?

containing the list of these things, signed by your authentic seal. [10]
[Dated London 13 March 1384-5]

v. A Pardoner's License

On the twentieth day of the month of June in the year of Our
Lord aforesaid, viz. [M] CCCC at Thorp near York the lord by
his letters conceded a license to run two years from the present
date to the proctors or messengers of the hospital or chapel of
the most blessed Virgin Mary of Roncesvalles near Charing
Cross in the city of London to publish indulgences and privileges conceded to the benefactors of the same hospital or chapel
and to collect and receive alms given or to be given by any of
the faithful of Christ to the said hospital or chapel throughout the
archdeaconries of York, Cleveland, and Nottingham. [11]

vi. Why Chaucer's Pardoner Will Not Make Baskets

I wol nat do no labour with myne handes,
Ne make baskettes, and lyve therby. (VI (C) 444-45)

Let us not therefore wonder that men who are shown up and
reproved by your studies, whose attack, which they make against
you, is parried by the impenetrable shield of the scriptures, so
that it does not strike home, should murmur against your spiritual laziness. Wherefore they would have you be farmers, tent-
makers, cobblers, ditch diggers, carters, and such like, and thus
you would be distracted from study and in the end lack clerks
to defend your cause. Let us not therefore wonder at that mur-

---

[10] Brantingham's Register, p. 567-68.

[11] "Die vicesima mensis Junii anno domini supradicto viz. [M] CCCCmo
apud Thorp iuxta Ebor. dominus concessit per suas litteras licentiam ad bien-
nium a dato praesente tantummodo duratur procuratoribus sive nuntiis hos-
pitalis seu capellae beatissime virginis Mariae de Roncesvalles iuxta Charyng-
cross civitatis London ad exponendum indulgentias & privilegia benefactori-
bus ipsius hospital. su capellae concessus [sic] atque ad colligendum & reci-
piendum errogata data erroganda seu dandi [sic] a quibuscumque fidelibus
Christi dicto hospitali seu capellae per Archdiocanatus Ebor. Cliueland &
Nottyngham" MS Register of Richard le Scrope, Archbishop of York, in
Borthwick Institute, York, p. 221.

mur, for it is neither new nor against you only. Indeed it was raised against St. Jerome for a similar reason, as he reminds us in his preface to the Book of Job, saying, "If I wove a basket of rushes, or plaited screens of palm leaves, so that I ate my bread in the sweat of my brow and carried out the work of the belly with anxious mind, none would be vexed, none would blame. Now that, however, following the saying of the Savior, I wish to devote myself to the food which does not perish but remains to eternal life, and to clear of briars and bushes the ancient road of the divine books, a twin error is charged against me: I am called a false corrector of vices, and I am said not to chop away errors but to sow them." [12]

These passages illustrate many details in the confession which Chaucer writes for his Pardoner. Though there is no mention of faked relics, Bishop Brantingham's questors have both papal bulls and letters with the "lige lordes seel," but they are counterfeit, as indeed those of the Pardoner may well be. Archbishop Scrope provides us with an authentic episcopal license. The boast of the Pardoner that he can "assoille" is paralleled by the complaints of Grandisson and Brantingham that questors absolve the ignorant from perjuries, murders, and other sins. The general implication of fraud which permeates the Pardoner's confession receives confirmation from the specific charges in the letters of Grandisson and Brantingham.

This does not, of course, mean that we must take Chaucer's picture as historically verified, but only that the attitude Chaucer implies was shared by some members of the hierarchy. That the abuses existed hardly admits of doubt; how representative or wide-spread they were we cannot know. The number of complaints in the episcopal registers is rather small and all come from two of the seventeen dioceses of England. The picture of the friar which Chaucer gives us is certainly biased; that of the pardoners may also be.

---

[12] Arnold Williams, ed., "*Protectorium Pauperis*: A Defense of the Begging Friars by Richard of Maidstone, O. Carm. (d. 1396)," *Carmelus*, V (1958), 178. The *Protectorium* was written in 1380. The quotation from St. Jerome appears in *Praefatio in Iob, Patrologia Latina*, XXIX, 63, and also in *Glossa Ordinaria, Patrologia Latina*, CXIII, 747.

Chaucer does not suggest what is patent to any careful and informed reader of the records, that if the pardoners were notorious fakers, the hierarchy must bear some of the responsibility for not supervising them more closely. The fact that Scrope's license has no name, that it is not issued to any particular person, may be explained by supposing that it was copied into the book only as a sample to be followed in making out future licenses. [13] But in that case there ought to be a list of recipients of such licenses, like the list of friars licensed to confess and preach which are found in many episcopal registers, Brantingham's and Scrope's among them. It does little good to complain that pardoners are forging letters and fabricating seals and then to command the faithful not to listen to any pardoner unless he has an authentic letter properly sealed. Alone among the critics of the pardoners, Grandisson places the blame where at least part of it belongs, on the archdeacons and their officials who recommended the pardoners and their forged documents to the ignorant parish clergy and the still more ignorant laity. According to Grandisson, the lesser ecclesiastical authorities and the pardoners were playing a neat game of collusion, the pardoners getting a chance at the laity and the officials getting a cut of the pardoners' take—and such a mode of expression seems especially appropriate.

Friars and pardoners are frequently lumped together as though they were the same thing. Jusserand's continental sources suggest that often religious and secular priests peddled indulgences. [14] Our documents clearly distinguish between the two groups, at the same time associating them together in knavery. Since they shared an itinerant life and the function of bringing religion of a sort to the folk, it is natural that the outsider would sometimes confuse them. Chaucer apparently did this in the cancelled lines (252 a-b) of the *General Prologue* which represent the Friar as paying "a certeyn ferme" for exclusive rights to a district. This,

---

[13] See Rev. J. S. Purvis, *An Introduction to Ecclesiastical Records* (London, 1953), p. 11.

[14] See esp. pp. 320-21.

as Daw Topias tells us, was a practice of the pardoners [15]; the friars had other methods of preventing unwanted competition. [16] What more natural then than Chaucer's transference to the Pardoner of St. Jerome's metaphor adduced by Richard of Maidstone as a defense of the mendicant friars?

---

[15] See the reply of the friar, Daw Topias, to the attack of "Jack Upland" in *Political Poems,* ed. Thomas Wright (Rerum Britanniardum Medii Aevi Scriptores), II, 78.

[16] Arnold Williams, "The 'Limitour' of Chaucer's Time and His 'Limitacioun'," *Studies in Philology,* LVII (1960), 463-78.

THE *AUBE* IN *AUCASSIN ET NICOLETTE*

WILLIAM S. WOODS
Tulane University

In the introduction to his edition of the *Aucassin et Nicolette* Mario Roques mentions several elements of the story which were furnished to the author by the literature of his time. In addition to other contemporary features Roques finds that "le gracieux épisode de la 'gaite' apparaît comme une transposition dramatique d'un chant d'*aube*."[1] This passage occurs in sections XII, XIII, XIV, XV, XVI of the *chantefable,* where Nicolette escapes from her prison and comes to take leave of the still incarcerated Aucassin. During the ensuing scene they are aided by the watchman on the tower.

Anyone who is familiar with the *aube* type of poem can see that Roques is correct in his statement that the scene is a dramatized *aube.* However, on reading the description of the *aube* as it occurs in Jeanroy's *Les Origines de la Poésie Lyrique en France,*[2] it becomes obvious that there are certain details of the passage in *Aucassin et Nicolette* which are at variance with the usual *aube* pattern and that these differences are due to reasons other than the exigencies of dramatization. Jeanroy's description of the genre reads as follows: "Il s'agit, dans l'aube, de la séparation au point du jour, de deux amants qui ont passé la

---

[1] Mario Roques, *Aucassin et Nicolette,* CFMA (Paris, Champion, 1963), p. x.
[2] Alfred Jeanroy, *Les Origines de la Poésie Lyrique en France* (Paris, Champion, 1904), pp. 61-62.

nuit ensemble, et que le lever du soleil, annoncé ordinairement par le cri d'un veilleur de nuit, avertit de se quitter. Ces trois personnages sont comme stéréotypés: leur présence est le trait caractéristique du genre. La pièce est remplie, soit par les avertissements du second, soit par les plaintes, les regrets, les promesses qu'échangent les premiers..."

We shall return later in this study to the discrepancies between the *aube* type as thus described and the so-called *aube* passage in *Aucassin et Nicolette*. Before discussing them a rapid review of the *aube* poems might help us to fix the type in mind, for we shall attempt in this study to determine their common characteristics and to contrast the passage in the *chantefable* with them, and finally to reach some conclusions as to why the author of the *Aucassin* felt it necessary to change his passage from the traditional mould.

Jeanroy finds that there are only four *aubes* surviving in Northern France [3] and that the French *aube* remained closer to its popular origin than the Provençal *alba,* for the character of the watchman, who must be a reflection of the more sophisticated court life of the South, appears in only one of the four French *aubes.* The survivals of the pure *alba* in Provence are also few, numbering only seven, for the other poems which are commonly called *albas* are simply love songs or religious poems with the word *alba* introduced into them. In spite of the few survivals this poetic type must have been popular for we find widespread evidence of it; in Germany (with Dietmar von Aist, Wolfram von Eschenbach, Walter von der Vogelweide, and Otto von Botenlauben), in Italy, and in England, where the best known survival is found in Shakespeare's *Romeo and Juliet,* Act III, Scene V, when Juliet refuses to believe that dawn has come. The earliest example of the *aube* is probably the bilingual Latin and Provençal *alba* of the 10th century. Jeanroy reckons that the constitution of the genre as a love poem probably dates from the eleventh century and that it probably ceased being cultivated in France by the end of the 12th. Because of the relatively short duration of its popularity he concludes that the form of the *aube* did not become fixed as happens to genres which become "classic." How-

---

[3] Ibid., pp. 61-77.

ever the content of the poems makes them easily identifiable, and he wisely prefers to make distinctions between genres according to the situations which they develop, for the situations tend to fuse, overlap, and become confused.

We should like to examine briefly the four French *aubes* and an equal number of Provençal *albas* in order to fix the genre in mind before preceeding to the examination of the passage in *Aucassin et Nicolette.*

In *Entre moi et mon ami* it is the lady who speaks and tells of the lovers' delight until the lark warned them that dawn had come. The man refuses to leave her for dawn could not have come so soon.

In *Quant voi l'aube du jor venir* it is again the lady who curses dawn for it drives away her lover, whom she commends to God.

In *Un petit devant le jor* there is a short narrative introduction wherein the poet tells of arising just before dawn and going to an orchard. There he witnessed the separation of the lovers, who, this time, had not passed the night together. The man was at the foot of the tower in which the lady was imprisoned by her jealous husband. It is an *aube* for the heroine sends the man away when she sees the day dawning. He leaves his heart with her and takes away her love.

The fourth French *aube* is more like the Provençal type for in it we find the character of the watchman. In *Gaite de la tor* we hear the conversation of two watchmen who tell us of the love tryst which they witness. At the end the man comes out and thanks them for their kindness and protection and laments the arrival of dawn.

In the anonymous Provençal *alba, En un vergier,* which takes place in the open, the lovers are disturbed by the cry of the watchman. The poem consists of the lady's laments for dawn will cause her lover to depart.

The anonymous Provençal *Quan lo rossinhols escria* consists of one stanza spoken by the male lover. He remains with her until the watchman calls to him to get up and depart for dawn has come. It also occurs in the open, "ios la flor."

4 Alfred Jeanroy, *La Poésie Lyrique des Troubadours,* vol. II (Paris, Didier, 1934), p. 292.

Bertran d'Alamano's *Us cavaliers si iazia* consists of a monologue by the man. He hears the watchman cry "via" and must depart, no matter how cruel the separation might be, for dawn has come. He cannot live if he doesn't see her and he leaves his heart with her.

The famous *Reis glorios* of Guiraut de Bornelh presents a dialogue between the watchman and the man. The watchman, who is a friend of the man, calls him for dawn is approaching and they must be off. The lover hesitates to leave since he is happy where he is.

Certain of the common features of the *aube,* as we have seen it, should be stressed in order to show just at what points the passage in *Aucassin* is at variance, and from those divergencies to advance a theory as to why its author did not follow the usual pattern. They have the following common characteristics:

(a) The lovers have spent the night together (with one exception).

(b) They are awakened at dawn either by the cry of the watchman or by the song of the lark. Usually the watchman is thanked for his services.

(c) They speak of the delights of the preceding night and of the cruelty of the separation caused by the approaching day.

(d) No doubt is expressed about their mutual love.

(e) No idea is expressed of the lack of permanence of their love.

(f) Invariably the man is forced to leave the woman.

(g) They refuse to believe that dawn could have come so soon.

(h) The departing lover shows great reluctance to leave.

(i) No rival love is mentioned.

(j) The dangerous element — i.e., the husband, parents, or the jealous, etc. — never materializes.

In the passage from *Aucassin et Nicolette* we can see the following characteristics which it has in common with the aube type: (1) The three essential persons are there — the man, the woman, the watchman. (2) The man and woman are in love with each other. (3) The action must take place very near dawn for the watchman was able to *see* "a ton sanblant" that Nicolette had talked with her lover; further, after leaving Aucassin she goes into the forest, sleeps for a while, and awakens at "haute prime" when the shepherds come nearby. (4) One of the lovers is forced to abandon the other. (5) The abandoned lover expresses great sorrow over and tries to prevent the separation and sheds many tears. (6) The watchman warns her of the danger from the guards. (7) She thanks him for his good services and departs These elements constitute an outline which would apply to almost any of the extant *aubes* and they furnish enough evidence to verify the statement that the passage is a dramatized *aube.*

There are, however, a number of peculiar deviations in detail from the type which need to be pointed out for some of them are rather startling.

1.   The usual roles are reversed here and it is the woman who is leaving the man.

2.   Contrary to the usual aube the lovers have not spent the previous night together. This is reminiscent of the situation in *Un petit devant le jor.*

3.   Since the lovers have not passed the night together, there is of necessity, no discourse on the delights which they have experienced. There is, rather, a grave doubt on Nicolette's part that they will ever experience those delights.

4.   They are in serious doubt about their mutual love. She suggests that he doesn't love her as much as she does him. He assumes that she will become the concubine of the first man who comes along. He assures her that a woman's love is transitory and cannot be as stable as the love of a man. These statements can hardly be described as typical of a love-poem.

5.   There is no idea of a future meeting between them. Nicolette states that he will never enjoy her and that his tears are futile.

6.   No promises or vows are exchanged between them except perhaps the threat of Aucassin to kill himself.

7.   Nicolette shows a surprising lack of reluctance to leave him.

8.   It is Aucassin who expresses regrets and sheds futile tears. Nicolette seems to have adopted a practical and stoical, almost masculine, resignation to the need for separation. Certainly the usual psychological roles are reversed here. The man is passive, helpless, tearful, devoid of practical solution to the problem, and

full of idle threats. It is the woman, on the other hand, who is practical, sensible, active, stoical, and she doesn't shed a tear.

In other words, while the author has retained enough of the stock material for the identification of the passage with the usual *aube* themes, he has nonetheless altered them to such an extent that it becomes obvious to anyone familiar with the genre that the author's deviation was intentional. To the present writer his intention must have been to parody the themes of the *aube* for the deviations which he introduces certainly produce a comic effect.

(Parenthetically, there is one deviation used — the introduction on the scene of the danger element, or the guards — which must have been for dramatic effect.)

Other details can be pointed out to substantiate the theory that the author was striving for comic effect in his parody of this popular verse pattern. Instead of giving Aucassin her love or her heart, Nicolette offers him a lock of her hair, which he accepts, kisses and embraces, and places in his *sein*. Aucassin says that she will cause his death by going away for he will kill himself. The exaggeration of his statement is comic as well as the method which he says he will use to destroy himself. He will rush against a stone with such force that he will cause his eyes and brains to fall out. The description of love in a woman is certainly a parody. Aucassin places love of woman in the eye, the ninpple of the breast, and on top of the toe. But the word which he uses for the nipple of the breast (cateron) is a term which applies to animals.

It has long been recognized that the author of the *Aucassin et Nicolette* was making gently ironic fun of his hero and heroine. Yet the extent of the irony and satire was first expressed, insofar as the present writer is aware, in an article by Professor U. T. Holmes Jr. In the introduction to a modern English translation of the *Aucassin et Nicolette*, [5] Professor Holmes wrote: "We are firmly convinced that the *Aucassin et Nicolette* was a mocking satire of certain stock themes, already hackneyed, which the minstrels were exploiting everywhere." Among other themes

---

[5] E. F. Moyer and C. D. Eldridge, *Aucassin and Nicolette* (Chapel Hill, 1937), pp. vi-viii.

parodied Professor Holmes pointed out the following: the saints' life in Aucassin's preference of Hell to Heaven, and in the curative powers of Nicolette's legs; the divided lover motif in the separation of Aucassin and Nicolette by the storm and the Saracens; the motif of the captive Saracen girl who is beloved of her master's son; the giant herdsman motif; the knightly quest for war.

The examples of parody of stock literary themes could be multiplied but that lies outside the scope of this study. Once the theory has been heard then the whole work appears as the product of a highly skilled author who was thoroughly familiar with the literary themes and forms of his day. And it suited his purpose to ridicule and parody them in his work.

It is this that we have attempted to prove in this paper in reference to the *aube* passage. The author used enough of the stock elements to make the passage identifiable to his audience as an *aube*. Once they had made this identification and recalled the invariable pattern of the genre, then it must have been highly amusing to them that the love had not been consummated, that Aucassin can do nothing but weep and threaten to kill himself, that Nicolette assumes a masculine decisiveness of mind and action, that the lovers indulge in bickering as to who loves whom the most, that instead of an impassioned love speech Aucassin delivers a comical discourse on love, that the roles are reversed and she abandons him, that Nicolette suggests outright that he will never enjoy her and even chides him for his tears, and that she can abandon him with no great show of reluctance. This part of the *Aucassin et Nicolette,* then, joins the other themes which Holmes has pointed out so cleverly as being parodies of already existing literary themes and whose full flavor can be appreciated only if those themes are kept in mind.

TABULA GRATULATORIA

U. T. HOLMES

N. B. Adams
Jules C. Alciatore
Douglas Alexander
Fred J. Allred
Paul Amash
Walter W. Arndt
Pierre Aubéry
S. W. Baldwin, Jr.
Hal L. Ballew
William H. Baskin
James Rush Beeler
Sarah Fore Bell
Leon Bernard
Martin Biddle
Arthur Bieler
Morris Bishop
Walter H. Bishop
R. B. Bisson
Alexander K. Boada
Richmond P. Bond
Karl G. Bottke
Gerard J. Brault
Germaine Brée
Frank C. Brennan, Jr.
Mrs. Robert E. Brickhouse
Monique H. Brockmann
Diana Brontë
Paul W. Brosman, Jr.
Jean Rider Brummell
Shasta M. Bryant
Eleanor Webster Bulatkin
Kenneth Bunting
James F. Burke
Vicente Cantarino
Robert Cargo
Alex Carriere

Sam Carrington, Jr.
John E. Carroll, Jr.
James A. Castañeda
Jean D. Charron
Beatrice S. Clark
Calvin A. Claudel
Dorothy Craighill
Thomas H. Crais
Ted R. Creech
Alesandro S. Crisafulli
Larry S. Crist
Mary Jane Culverhouse
Elizabeth R. Daniel
George B. Daniel
Helen Pugh Daniell
David M. Daugherty
James Herbert Davis, Jr.
Dale Dawly
Russell D. DeMent
William J. DeSua
F. M. Duffey
Robert E. Duke
Samuel D. Duncan, Jr.
Edwin H. Dunlap
Sergio D. Elizondo
Jacqueline C. Elliott
Patricia A. Elliott
Mary Claire Randolph Engstrom
Alfred Garvin Engstrom
F. S. Escribano
Virginia C. Farinholt
John Fisher
Richard L. Frautschi
Werner P. Friederich
Astrik L. Gabriel
Barbara Gaddy

Patricia M. Gathercole
Warren E. Gates
John M. Grier
John J. Guilbeau
Oscar A. Haac
Ernest F. Haden
Edward B. Hamer
Ruth N. Hanson
Jacques Hardré
Julian Harris
J. W. Hassell
Anna Granville Hatcher
Helmut A. Hatzfeld
Donald W. Haupe
George R. Havens
Elliott D. Healy
William M. Holler
Capt. & Mrs. Hampton Hubbard
Charles Javens
Hiram V. Jenkins
Joseph R. Jones
Philip H. Kennedy
Arthur S. Kimmel
Harry Lee King, Jr.
William Lupo King
Marjorie T. Kirby
Sister M. Amelia Klenke
Charles A. Knudson
Myron L. Kocher
Gisele Lamarque
George S. Lane
William L. Langer
John H. LaPrade
Sturgis E. Leavitt
Philip A. Lee
Albert E. Lindsay
Charles H. Livingston
C. E. Lloyd
A. G. LoRé
Leon F. Lyday
William MacBain
Dougald MacMillan
Catherine R. Macksey
Mrs. Samuel H. Magill
Alfonse Maissen
Augustine Maissen
Warren F. Manning
William R. Manson
Quino Martínez
Robert J. Mayberry
James Waring McCrady
William C. McCrary

Florence McCulloch
Raven I. McDavid, Jr.
Virginia McDavid
William A. McKnight
Mary S. Melvin
Albert Douglas Menut
John V. Meyers
Emanuel J. Mickel
Elsie Minter
Rafael J. Miranda
William J. Monahan
Edouard Morot-Sir
Ruth Mulhauser
Edward W. Najam
Lucy Ann Neblett
Charles L. Nelson
Jan A. Nelson
E. J. Neugaard
Margaret Newhard
Catherine E. Neylans
Carl J. Odenkirchen
Richard F. O'Gorman
Mary Pascal
James A. Patty
John Hunter Peak
Mario A. Pei
Rupert T. Pickens
Dorothy Pitts
R. L. Politzer
Karl S. Pond
Oreste F. Pucciani
C. E. Pupo-Walker
William R. Tuynn
Manuel D. Ramírez
Elizabeth Raney
Harry Redmon
Daniel R. Reedy
Russell Reynolds
Caroline G. Richardson
John Ripley
W. W. Ritter
Gino L. Rizzo
William Roach
Mildred C. Roebuck
Robert S. Rogers
Arthur Drexler Rogoff
Josiah C. Russell
William E. Rutherford
Molly Ryland
Kenneth R. Scholberg
Robert L. Schurfranz
Hugh N. & Ann L. Seay, Jr.

Karl-Ludwig Selig
Lawrence A. Sharpe
R. N. Shervill
Isidore Silver
Dalton L. Smith
James M. Smith
Mary Jean Smith
Maxwell A. Smith
Jackson G. Sparks
Julia Britt Steanson
Bob R. Stinson
H. Reynolds Stone
William E. Strickland
Stoudemire, Sterling A.
Albert Suskin
Lewis F. Sutton
Cecil G. Taylor
Edward D. Terry
John A. Thompson
Stanley R. Townsend
Alison M. Turner

B. L. Ullman
Francis G. Very
Frederick W. and Mary Frances
   Vogler
Ronald N. Walpole
Elizabeth West
Shirley B. Whitaker
Julian Eugene White, Jr.
Joseph W. Whitted
W. L. Wiley
Joseph P. and Evelyn B. Williman
William Burton Wilson
Edward E. Wilson
Kenneth Wilson-Jones
Louis J. Zahn
Bryn Mawr College
Cyprus Hall McCormick Library
Middlebury College Library
University of Oregon Library
Queens College Library